CLIMB
암벽등반

CLIMB 암벽등반
ROCK CLIMBING IN SOUTH KOREA

2012년 11월 10일 초판 1쇄 인쇄
2012년 11월 15일 초판 1쇄 발행

지은이 | 류동일

발행처 | (주)아웃도어글로벌
발행인 | 박요한
주　소 | 경기도 고양시 일산동구 백석동 1323 동문굿모닝타워1차 815·816호
전　화 | 031-921-8850~1
팩　스 | 031-920-8853
홈페이지 | www.outdoornews.co.kr

출판등록 | 2005년 1월 20일(제2005-1호)
가　격 | ₩ 25,000 ($ 25)

ⓒ류동일, 2012
ISBN 978-89-958437-2-7

※도움주신곳 : (주)몬츄라코리아(MONTURA) 02-352-3107　www.montura.co.kr
※이 책의 내용은 저자의 허락 없이 무단 전재 및 무단 복제를 금합니다.

CLIMB 암벽등반
ROCK CLIMBING IN SOUTH KOREA

© Dong-il Ryou, Jonn Jeanneret 2012. All rights reserved.

First edition printed November 2012

This document is copyrighted and may not be reproduced without the written permission of the authors.

© Jonn Jeanneret 2012. All rights reserved.
All Photographs, unless otherwise noted, by Jonn Jeanneret.
All Maps by Jonn Jeanneret.
www.jjeanneret.com
Represented in Korea by Dong-il Ryou.

© Hazel Cruzado 2012. All rights reserved.
All Artwork by Hazel Cruzado.
http://www.hazelcruzado.com/

ISBN 978-89-958437-2-7　$ 25

WARNING: Climb at your own risk and take personal responsibility for your actions. Rock climbing is an inherently dangerous activity and the users of this book are presumed to have undertaken the recommended instruction to climb safely. The authors are not responsible for your actions and take no liability for any consequences of the reader's use of this book.

Dedicated to

Words are inadequate to express my heartfelt thanks to my wife, Jeong Yong-suk, and to my son, Woo-Cheol, for their support and patience. Also, I thank Jonn Jeanneret, who spent much time shooting all the amazing photos, for designing and formatting this book; and keeping me company as I searched for crags many days and nights and whose passion and enthusiasm for this book matched my own. Although there are no tall tales or photos of renowned climbers, we did our very best. I want to thank Lea Gang 강레아, the famous climbing photographer, for sharing her great photos with us. Thanks to all of my Busan crew for their support: Robin, Feliz, Grant, Jake, Rob, Mack, Heeran and also to KOTRers. Special thanks go to Brenna and Vicky, who tediously proofread the text and checked the grammar. Big thanks to Lee Yong-In 이용인, the president of Montura Korea Co, for his generous supports. This guide book would not have become a reality without the help of the publisher, Park Yo-Han 박요한, at Outdoor Global Co. – Ryou Dong-Il, November 2012.

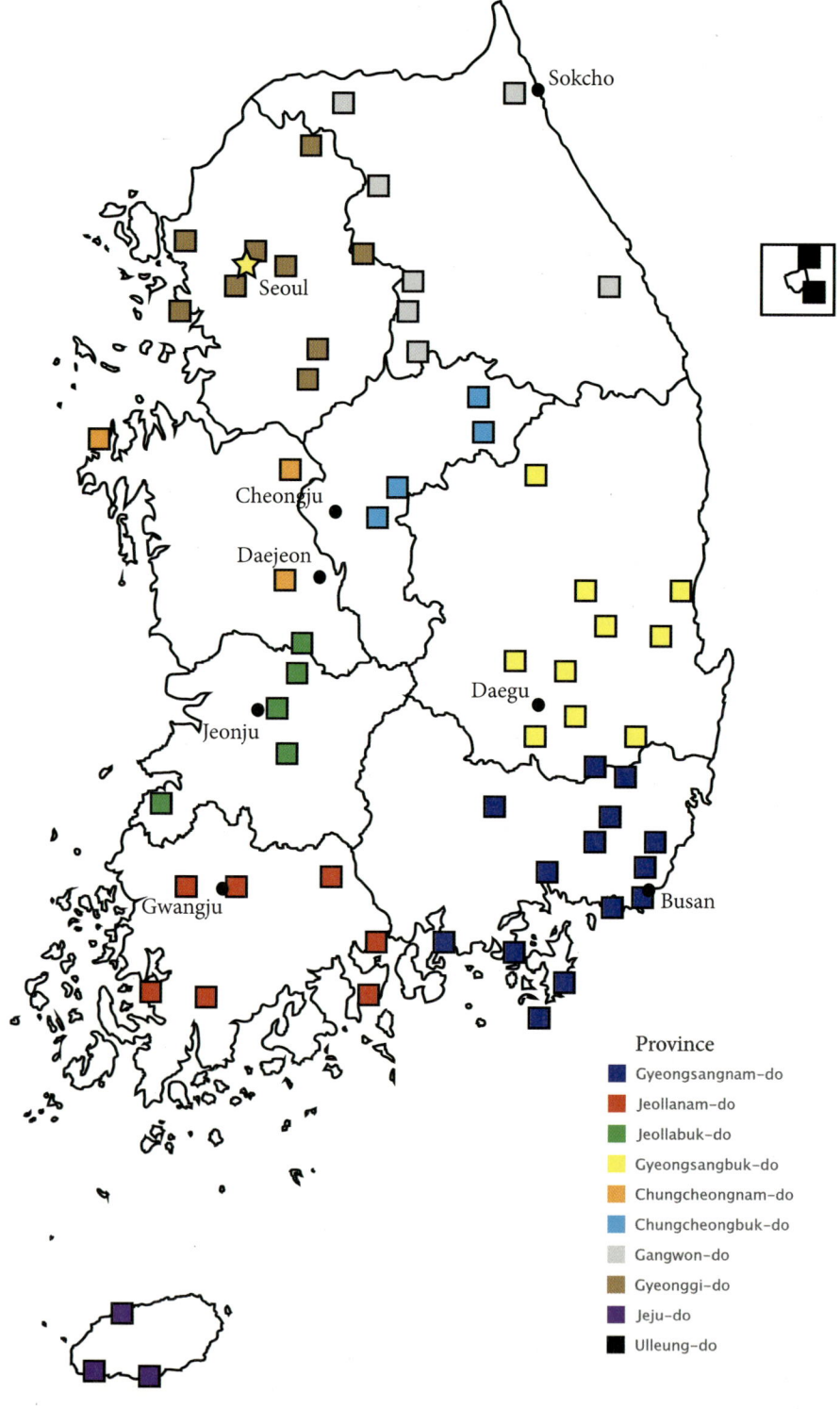

Master Crag List

There are 156 crags included in this book. GPS coordinates and maps have been provided for each one. Common map symbols and their meanings are shown below. Route heights are measured in meters. Crag charts are listed with the routes starting from left to right, unless otherwise noted. For information that is unavailable, or if a general consensus was not reached, an asterik "*" is placed. It is also becoming more common for developers to mark their routes at the crag with the name and grade. There are incredible places to climb in Korea. Explore. Discover a line that inspires you. Climb on.

🚌 Bus	⚓ Harbor	卍 Temple	▲ Peak
🚆 Train/Metro	🅿 Parking	🍴 Restaurant	◆ Identifier

Crag		Routes	Grade	Page
Ami-san, Seoksan-am	아미산 석산암	12	5.9 - 5.12b | A0	157
Amnam Sea Cliff, Geobuk-am	암남 해벽 거북암	14	5.7 - 5.11b	12
Amnam Sea Cliff, Gorae-am	암남 해벽 고래암	6	5.10a - 5.10b	12
Amnam Sea Cliff, Sangeo-am	암남 해벽 상어암	11	5.10a - 5.11b	12
Baealdo	배알도	6	5.10* - 5.12a	85
Baeksuk-amjang	백석암장	11	5.8 - 5.12b	180
Baekun-san, Hanbaek-am	백운산 한백암	18	5.9 - 5.12*	38
Baekun-san, Jowa-byeok	백운산 좌벽	6	*	38
Baekun-san, Wu-byeok	백운산 위벽	6	*	38
Baekwoon-san, Sang-bawi	백운산 상바위	7	5.9 - 5.11c	218
Biseul-san, Surideum-bawi	비슬산 수리듬바위	4	5.10*	138
Bokgyeo-san, Deokgu-bawi	복계산 덕구바위	14	5.7 - 5.12b | A2	224
Bokgyeo-san, Maewoldae-amjang	복계산 매월대암장	10	5.9 - 5.12b	224
Buan, Janggun-bawi	부안 장군바위	27	5.10a - 5.13c	114
Bukhan-san, Insu-bong	북한산 인수봉	51	5.6 - 5.12a | A2	230
Byeongcheon-am	은석산병천암	10	5.8 - 5.12*	168
Byeongpung-Bawi BAC	병풍바위 BAC	19	5.8 - 5.14a	266
Cheongsukkol-amjang	청석골 암장	8	5.10b - 5.12a	178
Cheontae-san, Sumeun-byeok	천태산 숨은벽	5	5.10a - 5.11b	29
Daedap-bawi	대답바위	28	5.8 - 5.12c	216
Daedun-san, Chag-bawi	대둔산 책바위	11	5.8 - 5.13a	118
Daedun-san, Dwaeji-bawi	대둔산 돼지바위	10	5.9 - 5.11d	118
Daedun-san, Sinseon-bawi	대둔산 신선바위	11	5.8 - 5.11a	118
Daedun-san, Wimungongyeon-bawi	대둔산 위문공연바위	8	5.10b - 5.12c	118
Dansan-amjang	단산암장	8	5.8 - 5.11b	286
Do-dong, Yong-bawi	도동 용바위	22	5.8 - 5.12d	134
Dobong-san, Seonin-bong	도봉산 선인봉	37	5.7 - 5.12c	238
Doderum-san, Dwaejigul-amjang	도드람산 돼지굴 암장	13	5.8 - 512a	256
Doyak-dae	도약대	51	5.7 - 5.13a	130
Duta-san, Byeongpung-am	두타산 병풍암	18	5.8 - 5.13*	193
Euiam-amjang	의암암장	25	5.9 - 5.12b	220
Gadeok-do Sea Cliff	가덕도 해벽	45	5.9 - 5.13b	19
Gamak-san, Seolgwi-am	감악산 설귀암	12	5.10* - 5.13*	276
Ganhyeon-am	간현암	57	5.9 - 5.13a/b	212
Gaya-san Amjang	가야산 암장	72	5.6 - 5.12b	82
Gaya-san, Bueungi-bawi	가야산 부엉이바위	5	5.11a - 5.12c	82
Geumjeong-san, Buchae-bawi	금정산 부채바위	29	5.8 - 5.13a	6
Geumjeong-san, Daeryuk-bong	금정산 대륙봉	25	5.10a - 5.13a	11
Geumjeong-san, Eun-byeok	금정산 은벽	11	5.8 - 5.12c	6
Geumjeong-san, Mumyeong-bawi	금정산 무명바위	10	5.8 - 5.12c/d	6

Crag		Routes	Grade	Page
■ Gimhae, Bird's Chorus-amjang	김해 새들의합창암장	11	5.9 - 5.11b	31
■ Gochang, Halmae-bawi	고창 할매바위	25	5.9 - 5.12c	112
■ Goeje, Ae-bawi	거제 애바위	11	5.9 - 5.12a	60
■ Guemseong-san, Mujigae-bawi	금성산 무지개바위	16	5.9 - 5.13b	142
■ Guman-san Amjang	구만산암장	*	*	40
■ Gwanack-amjang	관악암장	17	5.6 - 5.12*	272
■ Gyeong-san, Uksugol-amjang	경산 옥수골암장	9	5.10a - 5.12b	137
■ Gyeoryong-san, Bagaji-bawi	계룡산 바가지바위	15	5.8 - 5.12a	164
■ Gyeoryong-san, Hwangjeok OB Slab	계룡산 황적OB슬랩	8	5.9 - 5.10*	164
■ Gyeoryong-san, Seonbul-am	계룡산 선불암	12	5.8 - 5.12*	164
■ Hagampo-amjang	학암포암장	12	5.8 - 5.12c	170
■ Hakam-ri, Siru-bawi	학암리 시루바위	16	5.10b - 5.12c/d	101
■ Hakga-san, Sangsa-bawi	학가산 상사바위	5	5.10c - 5.11a	158
■ Hamheudongcheon-amjang	함허동천암장	16	5.9 - 5.11c	252
■ Hanagae-amjang	하나개암장	39	5.6 - 5.12b	250
■ Horang-san, Horang-am	호랑산 호랑암	12	5.7 - 5.10b	86
■ Hwayang Gugok, Sol-bawi	화양동 구곡 솔바위	*	*	182
■ Hwayang Gugok, Haksodae	화양동 구곡 학소대	4	5.9 - 5.10a	182
■ Hwayang Gugok, Ul-bawi	화양동 구곡 울바위	20	5.8 - 5.12a	182
■ Jakseong-san, Bae-bawi	작성산 배바위	13	5.6 - 5.11a | A0	184
■ Jakseong-san, Sol-bawi	작성산 솔바위	7	5.8 - 5.11a	184
■ Janggun-bawi	장군바위	8	5.10a - 5.11b	295
■ Jangwhoe-amjang	장회나루 암장	14	5.9 - 5.12a	186
■ Jobi-san, Jobi-am	조비산 조비암	25	5.9 - 5.14a	254
■ Jowan-byeok	좌벽	3	5.9 - 5.10a	294
■ Jukjang, Hakdam-am	죽장 학담암	45	5.7 - 5.13a	150
■ Miryang, Bueongsae-bawi	밀양 부엉새바위	20	5.7 - 5.13b	42
■ Morak-san, Mirae-am	모락산 미래암	29	5.9 - 5.13b/c	262
■ Muakjae Ansan-amjang	무악재 안산암장	31	5.7 - 5.13a	274
■ Mucheok-san, Beom-bawi	무척산 범바위	9	5.8 - 5.12a	22
■ Mucheok-san, Gaya-byeok	무척산 가야벽	7	5.9 - 5.10d	22
■ Mucheok-san, Haneul-byeok	무척산 하늘벽	7	5.8 - 5.10a	22
■ Mucheok-san, Jangun-byeok	무척산 장군벽	38	5.8 - 5.12c	22
■ Mucheok-san, Jeok-byeok	무척산 적벽	3	5.10c - 5.11b	22
■ Mucheok-san, Seong-byeok	무척산 성벽	16	5.10a - 5.13c	22
■ Mucheok-san, Sumeun-byeok	무척산 숨은벽	16	5.8 - 5.12b	22
■ Mucheok-san, Tanggeon-bawi	무척산 탕건바위	26	5.10a - 5.13a	22
■ Mudeung-san, Saein-bong	무등산 새인봉	15	5.9 - 5.13*	71
■ Mudeung-san, Seonbi-bawi	무등산 선비봉	31	5.10b - 5.13*	72
■ Munbok-san, Duerin-bawi	문복산 드린 바위	5	5.9 - 5.11d	141
■ Munsu-san, 91 Boulder	문수산 91 볼더	3	5.12a - 5.13*	33
■ Munsu-san, Cheonseo High-am	문수산 천서 하이암	1	5.9	33
■ Munsu-san, Chosdae Boulder	문수산 촛대 볼더	2	5.10a - 5.11a	33
■ Munsu-san, Eunhasu-amjang	문수산 은하수암장	11	5.9 - 5.11a	33
■ Munsu-san, Family Boulder	문수산 페밀리볼더	7	5.7 - 5.10c	33
■ Munsu-san, Geobyuk-am	문수산 거북암	4	5.9 - 5.10c	33
■ Munsu-san, Gijyeon-amjang	문수산 기존암장	6	5.9 - 5.10c	33
■ Munsu-san, Hyeong Boulder	문수산 형제 볼더	7	5.7 - 5.12a	33
■ Munsu-san, Hyeonggong OB-am	문수산 현공 OB 암	13	5.9 - 5.12a	33
■ Munsu-san, Hyeonjung Boulder	문수산 현중 볼더	4	5.10b - 5.12a	33
■ Munsu-san, Hyeonsan-am	문수산 현산암	11	5.8 - 5.11c	33
■ Munsu-san, Oedolgae	문수산 외돌개암	1	5.9	33
■ Munsu-san, Ottugi Boulder	문수산 오뚜기볼더	6	5.9 - 5.11b/c	33
■ Munsu-san, Rabbit Boulder	문수산 토끼 볼더	13	5.7 - 5.11a	33
■ Munsu-san, Union Boulder	문수산 연합볼더	10	5.10b - 5.12b	33
■ Musucheon Gyeogok-amjang	무수천 계곡암장	34	5.8 - 5.12b	282
■ Myeongsung-san, Chak-bawi	명성산 책바위	*	5.9 - 5.11*	246
■ Naeyeon-san, Arirang Boulder	내연산암장 아리랑볼더	9	5.9 - 5.12a	154

Crag		Routes	Grade	Page
Naeyeon-san, Guimyeon-am	내연산암장 귀면암	4	5.10a - 5.11a	154
Naeyeon-san, Gwaneum-am	내연산암장 관음암	12	5.9 - 5.12c	154
Naeyeon-san, Naeyeon-am	내연산암장 내연암	4	5.10a/b - 5.10b	154
Naeyeon-san, Seoun-am	내연산암장 서운암	5	5.10a - 5.10d	154
Naeyeon-san, Sinseondae	내연산암장 신선대암	2	5.9	154
Namhansanseong, Beomgul-am	남한산성 범굴암	18	5.8 - 5.13c	258
Nocles-amjang	노클스암장	16	5.9 - 5.12a	270
Obong-san, Byeongpung-am	오봉산 병풍암	12	5.7 - 5.11b	260
Oedolgae-amjang	외돌개암장	10	5.7 - 5.11b	288
Palgong-san, Bawitgol	팔공산 바윗골암장	11	5.6 - 5.12b	A0	128
Palgong-san, Byeongpung-am	팔공산 병풍암	8	5.7 - 5.11*	A*	128
Palryong-san, Haebyeongdae-bawi	팔용산 해병대바위	13	5.9 - 5.12a	51
Palryong-san, Sangsa-bawi	팔용산 상사바위	5	5.8 - 5.11c	51
Phochung-sa, Jeok-byeok	표충사 적벽	8	5.9 - 5.12a	A2	44
Phochung-sa, Mae-bawi	표충사 매바위	9	5.9 - 5.11a	A0	47
Samcheon-bawi	삼천바위	23	5.9 - 5.14a	117
Samseon-am	삼선암	3	5.10b	297
Seokmun-san Amjang	석문산 암장	14	5.7 - 5.11a/b	75
Seonun-san, Dosol-am	선운산 도솔암	100	5.9 - 5.13c	102
Seonun-san, Mun-bawi	선운산 문바위	15	5.7 - 5.11b	102
Seonun-san, Soksal-bawi	선운산 속살바위	48	5.9 - 5.13b	102
Seonun-san, Tugu-bawi	선운산 투구바위	56	5.7 - 5.14b/c	102
Seorak-san, Agal-bawi	설악산 아갈바위	11	5.9 - 5.12b	208
Seorak-san, Janggun-bong	설악산 장군봉	12	5.4 - 5.12a	196
Seorak-san, Jeok-byeok	설악산	6	5.9 - 5.12b	A4	196
Seorak-san, Mireukjanggun-bong	설악산 미륵장군봉	5	5.6 - 5.11b	208
Seorak-san, Sinseondae-amjang	설악산 신선대암장	6	5.9 - 5.12a	208
Seorak-san, Sotowanggol-amjang	설악산	12	5.6 - 5.11b	A4	196
Seorak-san, Ulsan-bawi	설악산	26	5.8 - 5.11b	A0	196
Seorak-san, Youseon-dae	설악산	9	5.9 - 5.11a	196
Seunghak-am	승학암	8	5.9 - 5.11a	16
Sin-ri Amjang	신리 암장	10	5.9 - 5.12a	100
Sinban, Byeongpung-am	신반 병풍암	38	5.8 - 5.12c	52
Sinban, Jakeundeom-bawi	신반 작은덤바위	15	5.10b - 5.12c	52
Sinban, Keundeom-bawi	신반 큰덤바위	23	5.9 - 5.12a	52
Siru-bong, Bukseo-byeok	시루봉 북서벽	9	5.9 - 5.11c	29
Siru-bong, Dongnam-byeok	시루봉 동남벽	16	5.10a - 5.13*	29
Somaemul-do, Chotdae-bawi	소매물도 촛대바위	7	5.10a - 5.12b	64
Somaemul-do, Goragae	소매물도 고래개	4	5.9 - 5.10a/b	64
Sori-san, Samhyeongjae-bawi	소리산 삼형제바위	35	5.9 - 5.13*	248
Sumeun-am	숨은암	17	5.9 - 5.12a	A2	268
Surak-san, Daeju-amjang	수락산 대주암장	13	5.8 - 5.13*	242
Surak-san, Naewon-am	수락산 내원암	11	5.8 - 5.11a	244
Suri-san, Mae-bawi	수리산 매바위	14	5.10a - 5.13*	264
Tongyeong, Buchae-bawi	통영 부채바위	2	5.10a	62
Tongyeong, Mumyeong-am	통영 무명암	5	5.10d - 5.12b	62
Tongyeong, Ssangsa-bawi	통영 쌍사바위	38	5.9 - 5.13c	62
Waryong-san, Sangsa-bawi	와룡산 상사바위	21	5.7 - 5.11b	58
Wolchul-san, Mae-bong	월출산 매봉	9	*	88
Wolchul-san, Siru-bong	월출산 시루봉	10	*	88
Wolchul-san, Yeonsil-bong	월출산 연실봉	4	*	88
Yang-san, Byeongpung-am	양산 병풍암	11	5.9 - 5.12c/d	48
Yonghwa-san, Saenam-bawi	용화산 새남바위	11	5.8 - 5.12a	222
Yongseo Pokpo	용서 폭포	76	5.8 - 5.13*	76
Youdal-san, Iron Palms Wall	유달산 아이언팜스월	29	5.8 - 5.14a/b	94
Youdal-san, Koggiri-bawi	유달산 코끼리바위	16	5.9 - 5.11a	93
Youhak-san, Dungji-bawi	유학산 둥지바위	24	5.7 - 5.11d	145
Youhak-san, Hak-bawi	학바위 유학산	48	5.8 - 5.13a	145

TABLE OF CONTENTS 차례

I.	Introduction	1
II.	Gyeongsangnam-do	2
III.	Jeollanam-do	66
IV.	Jeollabuk-do	96
V.	Gyeongsangbuk-do	124
VI.	Chungcheongnam-do	160
VII.	Chungcheongbuk-do	174
VIII.	Gangwon-do	188
IX.	Gyeonggi-do	226
X.	Jeju-do	278
XI.	Ulleung-do	290
XII.	Appendix	298
	Korean Romanization	300
	Korean Phrases	303

Introduction

South Korea is roughly seventy percent mountainous, making it one of the most rugged rock climbing regions. The protruding and folding of Korea's stunning granite slabs, the limestone bluffs, mass of sturdy basalt, and the porous volcanic rocks will lead you to climb in every nook and cranny of the country. The interest in rock climbing in South Korea has exploded in the past decade, as the people of the country explore outdoor sports and seek adventure more than ever before. Already there are more than two hundred established crags to climb throughout the country, roughly one hundred indoor gyms, nearly eighty outdoor walls and a dozen artificial ice walls. South Korea is also home to a female sport climbing world champion. With this amazing growth has come a rapid increase in the number of climbers and competition to develop new routes among climbing clubs. South Korea, hence, offers something for every climber. The scope of this book includes; ease of access to crags by public transportation, quality of the rock, and the quantity and variety of routes with grades throughout every province based on general consent. My hope is to introduce Korea to foreign climbers, and to provide local climbers with a new climbing perspective. For nine months I have traveled all across the nation to gather information from each crag. However, because I work full time, I wasn't able to include every climbing area. The information assembled in this guide is not intended to be an accurate route guide. Neither is it meant to be a book on how to climb. Rather, it is to provide general information and tips on where to find the crags and the type of climbing that is available. The primary focus is on how to get there without the trouble that navigating to a new place sometimes brings. Regardless of how good or how much information I have included on accessing the crags, it can still sometimes be difficult to get to the crag because things will inevitably change even between the time of this book's publication and the moment you read it. If you have discovered an error, a gem crag you want to add, or anything that needs to be in the guide I would be pleased to hear from you.

The real spirit of climbing should be based on climbing the rock. In the climbing world, it is not about hard climbing or about chasing the grades, but climbing lines that inspire us! Be well, stay safe, and just enjoy climbing.

Transportation
Domestic flights and ferry boats are easily accessible for travel around South Korea. Passenger trains operated by Korail are fast and punctual, with many connecting and feeder lines. Be aware that trains are usually full on weekends. Buses like express, intercity, and city buses are comfortable and affordable. Overall, South Korea has an amazing public transportation system.

Accomodation
For budget travelers, there are jjimjilbangs 찜질방. They are basically saunas that include shower facilities, TVs, computers, sometimes amusement arcades, and sleeping rooms. These will be the cheapest places to stay. Minbaks 민박 are another option where a few people or a group can squeeze into one room. Campsites are also available at many of the crags.
For more about Korea, please go to Korea Tourism Organization www.knto.or.kr

Gyeongsangnam-do

경상남도

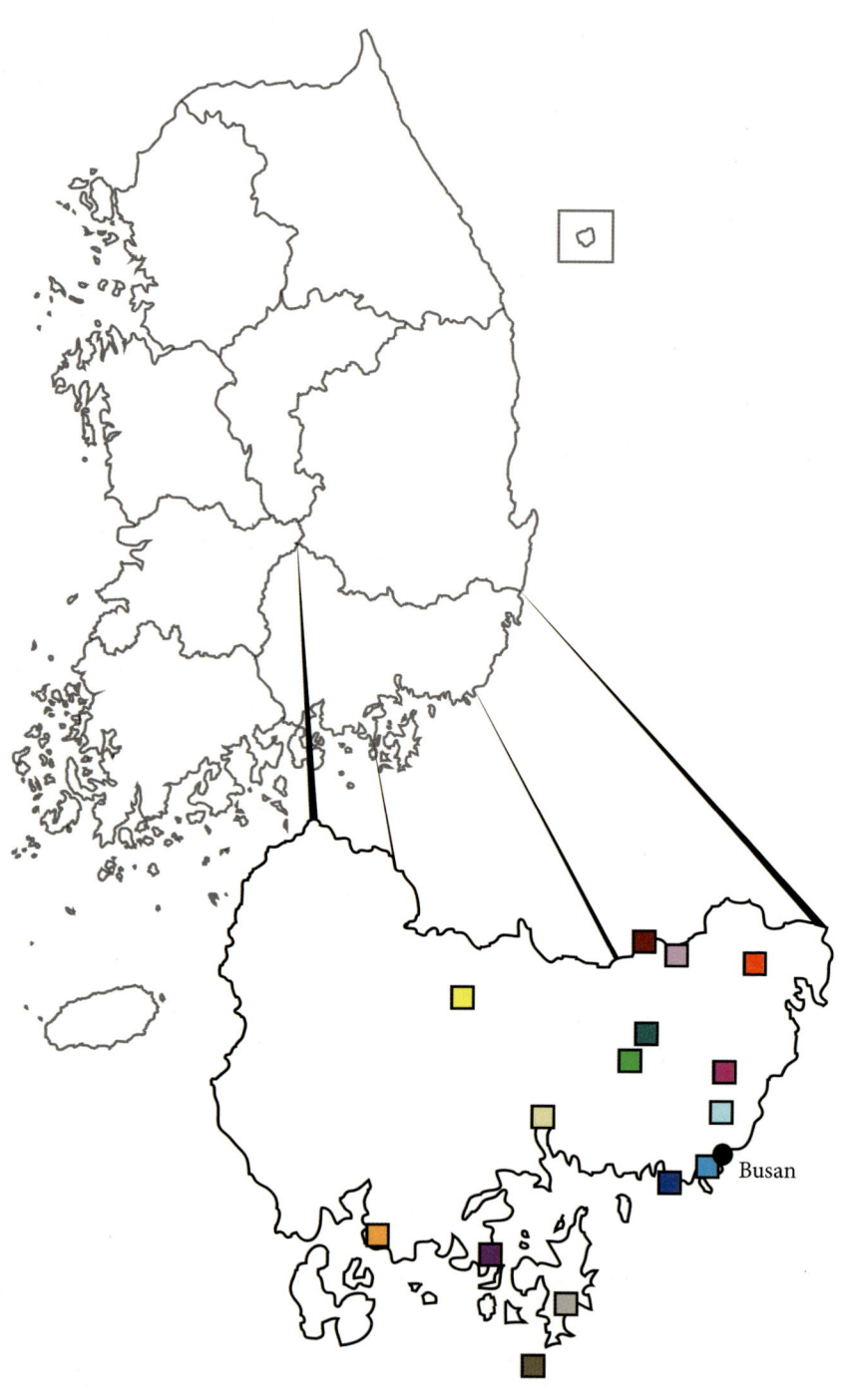

Gyeongsangnam-do Province 경상남도

- Buchae-bawi
- Daeryuk-bong
- Mumyeong-bawi/Seil Gelande
- Eun-byeok
- Geokbuk-am
- Sangeo-am
- Gorae-am
- Samagui-bawi
- Gadeok-do
- Beom-bawi
- Tanggeon-bawi
- Janggun-byeok
- Jeok-byeok
- Gaya-byeok
- Sumeun-byeok
- Haneul-byeok
- Seong-byeok
- Bukseo-byeok, Siru-bong
- Dongnam-byeok, Siru-bong
- Sumeun-byeok, Siru-bong
- Bird's Chorus – Amjang
- Munsu-san
- Guman-san Amjang
- Bueongsae-bawi
- Hanbaek-am
- Jowa-byeok
- Wu-byeok
- Jeok-byeok
- Mae-bawi
- Byeongpung-am, Yangsan
- Haebyeongdae-bawi
- Sangsa-bawi, Palryong-san
- Byeongpung-am, Sinban
- Keundeom-bawi, Sinban
- Jakeundeom-bawi, Sinban
- Sangsa-bawi, Waryong-san
- Ae-bawi
- Ssangsa-bawi, Tongyeong
- Buchae-bawi, Tongyeong
- Mumyeong-am, Tongyeong
- Gorogae
- Chotdae-bawi

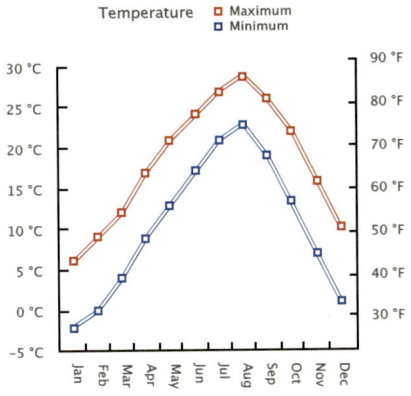

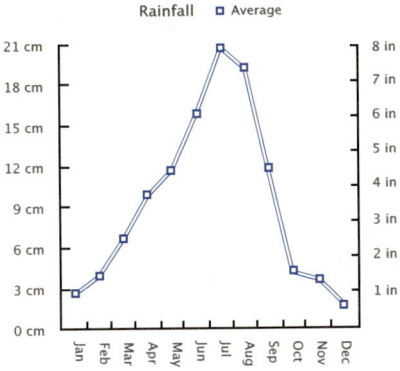

GUEMJEONG-SAN 금정산

Description
(***Buchae-bawi, South***) - As one of the first crags developed in Busan, Buchae-bawi has been beloved by climbers for decades. This wall is mainly sport climbing with one trad climb on an overhanging face. It offers cracks, overhangs, roofs, and a crimpy face for climbing. It is in the sun all day.
(***Buchae-bawi, North***) - The north face is primarily a trad wall. There are great crack climbs to practice leading. It is in the shade all morning.
(***Mumyeong-bawi & Seil Gelande***) - This crag faces south which makes it good for the cold weather season. Ridge climbing is also available here.
(***Eun-byeok***) - Eun-byeok faces northeast and offers granite sport climbing.

Directions
(***Buchae-bawi***) - 35.259541N 129.066149E
(***Mumyeong-bawi & Seil Gelande***) - 35.264657N 129.064046E
(***Eun-byeok***) - 35.265331N 129.062791E
Oncheon-dong, Dongrae-gu, Busan 부산 동래구 온천동

(***Buchae-bawi***) - In Busan, take the subway to Oncheonjang Station 온천장, on the orange line (Line #1). Cross the pedestrian bridge from the subway station, towards Home-plus, and take Bus 203 from the bus stop under the bridge. Get off at East Gate 동문입구 near the top of the mountain. The bus will take twenty minutes to get to the stop from Home-plus. Walk up and pass through the East Gate. Continue on the main trail heading north for twenty minutes until you see some rock array and boulders. Before the trail heads down to a large open area, look for any path that follows the stone wall. Buchae-bawi is just to the right of the stone wall and you will see the butterfly-shaped boulder that is easily recognizable from 500m.
(***Mumyeong-bawi & Seil Gelande***) - From Buchae-bawi, you can see the long ridge of Mumyeong-bawi to the north. There are two different ways to get to this crag. One is to jump over the stone wall at the big open area between Buchae-bawi and Mumyeong-bawi. Walk down the main trail heading to the left for ten minutes until you reach the beginning of the ridge climb. Another is to hike up, following the stone wall to the end of the ridgeline and then walk down, searching for an off-beaten trail by the crag. Follow it for ten minutes to the front wall.
(***Eun-byeok***) - From the end of Mumyeong-bawi ridgeline, pass the fourth watchtower and continue on the northbound trail of the stone wall for 50m. You will see the top of this crag on your right. You can either walk down to the top of the crag or top-rope from the anchor to get to the start.

Gear
(***Buchae-bawi South***) - 7 draws, a 50m rope, and a couple of small cams.
(***Buchae-bawi North***) - 10 draws, a 50m rope, and a full set of cams.
(***Mumyeong-bawi & Seil Gelande***) - 8 draws, a 60m rope, and a full set of cams.
(***Eun-byeok***) - 10 draws and a 50m rope.

Safety
A helmet is recommended for the climbs here as some of the bolts and anchors are old and rusty.

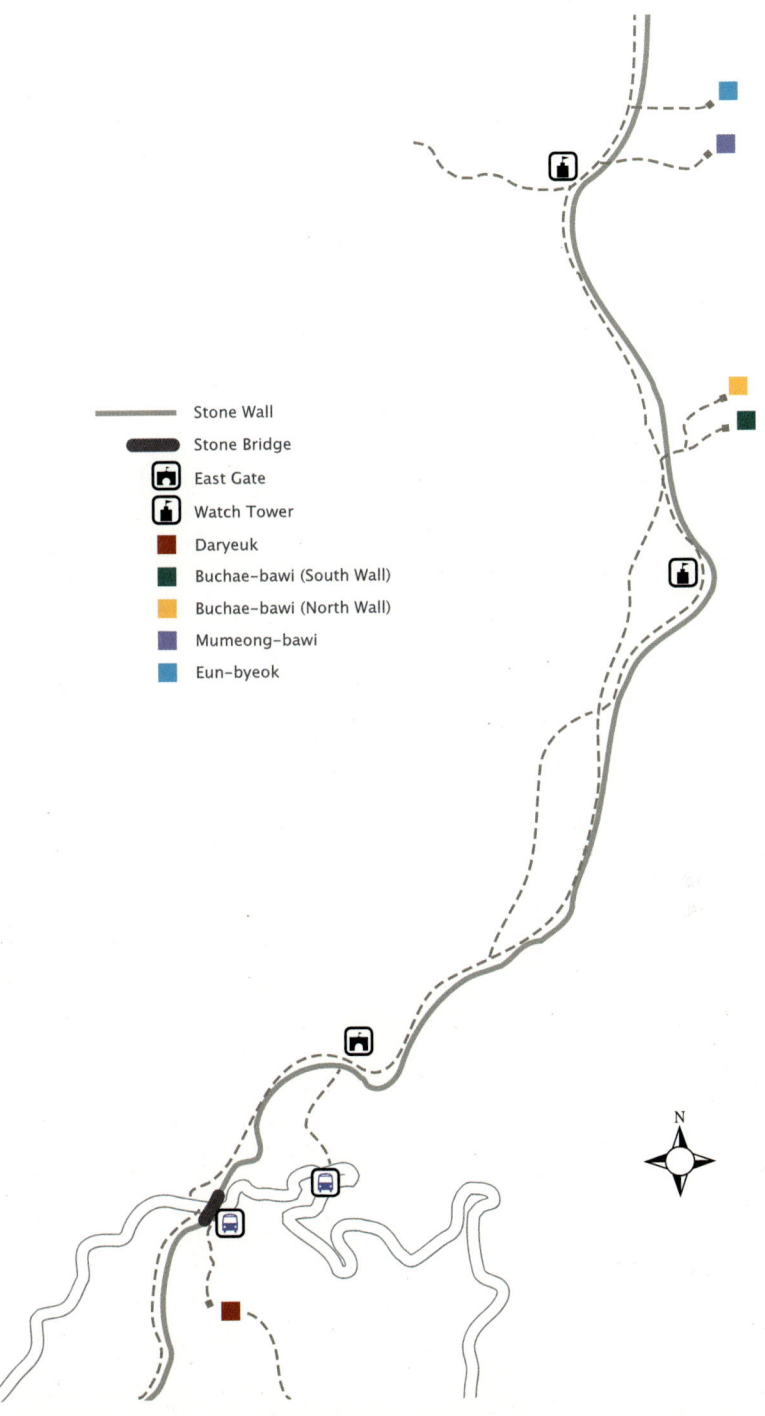

BUCHAE-BAWI (SOUTH WALL)
부채바위 남벽

Route Name	Grade	Height
Road To Door Of Hell 지옥문길	5.9	8
Overture To Fear 공포의 전주곡	5.10a	8
Grim Reaper 저승사자	5.11a	10
Heart of PC PC 의 마음	5.11a	15
Youth 젊음	5.11b	18
Sky Wall 스카이월 2	5.13*	20
Love Of Brothers 형님들의사랑	5.13a	20
Excellent Move 액설런트무브	5.12a	20
Pumping Special 펌핑스페셜	5.11c	20
Christmas Boy 크리스마스보이	5.11a/b	20

BUCHAE-BAWI (NORTH WALL)
부채바위 북벽

Route Name	Grade	Height
Road Of Light 광길	5.10d	25
Road Of Tiger 범길	5.11c	25
Little Prince 어린왕자	5.11a	20
High Road 높은길	5.8	20
Half-Sitting 엉거주춤 1p (5.10a|27m) 2p (5.8|18m)	5.10a	45 (2p)
Obstinate Road 억지길 1p (5.10d|27m) 2p (5.8|18m)	5.10a	45 (2p)
Lightning Road 번개길 1p (5.9|27m) 2p (5.8|18m)	5.9	45 (2p)
PC5	5.10d	25
Existing 기존 A	5.9	20
Existing 기존 B 1p (5.10d|22m) 2p (5.10a|16m)	5.10d	38 (2p)
Existing 기존 C	5.11d	20
Friendship 우정 A 1p (5.11a|22m) 2p (5.10a|16m)	5.11a	38 (2p)
Eyes 시선	5.10b	18
Friendship 우정 B 1p (5.10b|22m) 2p (5.10a|16m)	5.10b	35 (2p)
Mountain Party 뫼무리	5.11b	20
PC4	5.9	20
Violet Line 보라빛선	5.10a	17
Road Of Friend 친구길	5.9	25
112	5.12	30

Mumyeong-bawi & Seil Gelande 무명바위 자일겔렌더

Route Name	Grade	Height
Salty Road 소금길	5.10a	24
Sisyphos 시지프스	5.12a	24
Road Of Baby Octopus 꼴뚜기길	5.10c	27
Road Of Fine Tree 소나무길	5.9	27
Seil Friendship 자일의정	5.8	15
Gangling Uncle 키다리아저씨	5.10d	13
Yellow Sling 노랑슬링	5.12a/b	15
Covered With Blood 피칠갑	5.9	15
Fantasy Substance 환상의물질	5.12c/d	15
Warm-Up 몸풀이	5.8	15

Eun-byeok 은벽

Route Name	Grade	Height
Hanging Out 노니 1	5.9	20
Scent Of An Orchid 난향	5.11d	20
Mist 안개	5.11b	20
Spirit Of Daeryuk 대륙의혼	5.12c	20
Judy 쥬디	5.11c	20
Wild White Chrysanthemum 하얀들국화	5.11a	25
Hanging Out 노니 2	5.11a	20
Existing 기존 C	5.10c	20
To The Nitch 틈새로	5.10c	20
Existing 기존 A	5.8	12
Festival 축제 4	*	*

Geumjeong-san, Daeryuk-bong 금정산 대륙봉

Description
Daeryuk-bong has two walls that face southeast. The lower wall is on the left and the climbs are relatively shorter than the upper wall. It features granite sport climbing.

Directions
35.240073N 129.062861E
Oncheon-dong, Dongrae-gu, Busan 부산 동래구 온천동

In Busan, take the subway to Oncheonjang Station 온천장, on the orange line (Line #1). Cross the pedestrian bridge from the subway station, towards Home-plus, and take Bus 203 from the bus stop under the bridge. Get off at Sanseong Bus Stop 산성, one stop after East Gate 동문입구. There is a stone arch bridge by the bus stop. The trail, heading south, begins on the east side of the bridge. From the first fork in the trail, take the upper path that branches off to the right. Continue south for five minutes. There will be another fork in the trail. If you continue left, it will lead you to the lower wall and the path to the right will take you to the upper wall.

Gear
10 draws and a 50m rope.

Additional Comments
There are a few campsites available and there is a spring on the trail 10m before the crag. Campfires are not allowed in this area.

Daeryuk-bong (Lower Wall) 대륙봉 하단벽

Route Name	Grade	Height
Stella 스텔라	5.10c	10
To Make Love 사랑만들기	5.10a	10
To You 투유	5.13a	10
Trash 쓰레기	5.10a	12
Cash Box 캐쉬박스	5.10b	12
Festival 축제 1	5.11a	12
Threshold Of Autumn 가을문턱	5.12a	12
Stair Case 계단길	5.10b	15
Open Space In The Woods 숲속의빈터	5.11b	15
PC 9	5.12a	15
Brother's Mountain 형의산	5.11b	15
Incompletion 미완성	5.11b	15

Daeryuk-bong (Upper Wall) 대륙봉 상단

Route Name	Grade	Height
Rock Dance 록댄스	5.10c	10
Double Road 이단길	5.10a	10
Blue Mist 푸른안개	5.10c	15
Festival 축제 2	5.12a	18
Route of 66 길	5.10b	18
Yeti 예티	5.10b/c	20
Festival 축제 3	5.10b	18
Existing 기존 C	5.10a	20
Niche Route 틈새길	5.10c	20
Hey Jude 헤이쥬드	5.11b	14
Wall Love Society 벽사모 1	5.10b	12
Wall Love Society 벽사모 2	5.10a	12
Wall Love Society 벽사모 3	5.10a	10

AMNAM 암남

Description
(**Geobuk-am**) - This is the closest crag from the park entrance. It faces northeast and offers easy vertical climbing on sedimentary rock.
(**Sangeo-am**) - This crag offers steep and challenging climbs. The main wall faces east with one route on the right side facing south. It begins to get shade in the afternoon. Climbing here, with the sounds and sights of the waves, is a simple pleasure that washes all the worries of life away.
(**Gorae-am**) - Gorae-am hasn't been climbed for many years. It faces southeast. It offers multi-pitch climbing with one aid route.

Directions
(**Geobuk-am**) - 35.059918N 129.019173E
(**Sangeo-am**) - 35.057955N 129.018164E
(**Gorae-am**) - 35.057538N 129.017617E
Amnam-dong, Seo-gu, Busan 부산 서구 암남동

(**Geobuk-am**) - In Busan, take the bus or subway, orange line (Line #1), to Nampo-dong 남포동. From there, take Bus 7 or 71 to Amnam Park 암남 공원. At the park entrance, follow the main trail that follows the sea side for ten minutes until you see a small wooden suspension bridge. Don't cross the bridge. Look for a trail, on your left and over the fence, 5m before the bridge. Jump over the fence and walk down the trail that heads toward the sea. Geobuk-am is located under the bridge. When the tide is low, it will be easier to get to the crag by walking down the steel staircase after the wooden suspension bridge. Walk down the steel staircase and turn left. Continue down the coast until you reach to the crag. It will take twenty minutes from the park entrance.
(**Sangeo-am**) - From Geobuk-am 거북암, walk south along the coast. You'll see a steep trail past the iron staircase. Continue on this trail to the top of the hill, which is actually the top of the overhanging climb at Sangeo-am 상어암. It will take ten minutes from Geobuk-am 거북암. If you are coming from the main trail, there is a fork after the wooden suspension bridge. Go left at the fork and walk down the iron staircase. At the end of the stairs, turn right and continue on the trail that leads to the top of the short, steep hill and to the top of the crag.
(**Gorae-am**) - You can see the gigantic Gorae-am 고래 wall from the far west side of Sangeo-am 상어암. However, it is almost impossible to traverse the cliff from Sangeo-am 상어암 to Gorae-am 고래암. To get to this crag, take the main trail from the park entrance. After crossing the wooden suspension bridge, take the path that leads to the right. Continue on this trail for five minutes until you reach a pavilion to your left at the top of a cliff. Take the trail on your right from the pavilion. This path has a long fence that heads to the sea. Follow the trail for ten minutes until you reach the crag.

Gear
(**Geobuk-am**) - 8 draws and a 50m rope.
(**Sangeo-am**) - 11 draws and a 60m rope.
(**Gorae-am**) - 12 draws and a 60m rope. If abseiling from the top of the second pitch, two 50m ropes are needed.

Safety
As theses crags are sea cliffs, the ledges and edges are easily eroded so be cautious of falling rocks. Some of the bolts may not be secure because of marine erosion. A helmet is recommended.

Additional Comments
Camping is NOT allowed. Soldiers patrol the area regularly at night and are authorized to fire their weapons.
(**Geobuk-am**) - The ground is sandy. A rope mat is recommended.

Geobuk-am 거북암 (1 of 2)

Route Name	Grade	Height
Green Light 푸른신호등	5.9	17
Sailboat 돛단배	5.9	18
Climbing Up 오르시소	5.9	18
Women & Men In Their 50's 오십대여와남	5.10a	16
Dding Ho Chinese Restaurant 땡호반점	5.10b	17
Swirl 쉬리	5.10b	18
Stay In One Lane 차선엄수	5.10c	16

Geobuk-am 거북암 (2 of 2)

Route Name	Grade	Height
Whale On A Shrimp's Back 새우등의 고래	5.11b	16
Dr. K.B	5.10d	17
Only One Track 오직한길	5.10d	16
Amnam-dong Hurricane 암남동허리케인	5.11a	16
Submarine 잠수함	5.10c	16
First Step 첫걸음	5.7	5
Rock Party 바위잔치	5.8	5

Sangeo-am 상어암

Route Name	Grade	Height
Hate High Tide 만조는싫어	5.10a	23
Seashore Rocks 갯바위	5.10b	23
Seagull Of Busan 부산갈매기	5.11b	23
Calm Before The Storm 폭풍전야	5.11d	22
Viking 바이킹	5.12a	12
Wave 파도	5.11a	20
Starfish 불가사리	5.10d	20
Marine Center 수산센터	5.10c	20
Jagalchi Aunt 자갈치아지매	5.10b	16
Woman At Beach 해변의여인	5.10a	7
Jaws 죠스	5.10d	7

Gorae-am 암남 고래암

Route Name	Grade	Height
Road For Byeokwoo 벽우길	5.10a	50 (2p)
1p (5.10a|28m) **2p** (5.9|22m)		
Y2K	5.10b	35
Road For One's Love 연인의길	5.10a	35
Vertical World 버티컬월드	5.10a	50 (2p)
1p (5.10a|30m) **2p** (5.10a|20m)		
Be Rock 바위그라	5.10a	35
Hillary Step 힐러리스텝	5.10b	50 (2p)
1p (5.10b|30m) **2p** (5.10a|20m)		

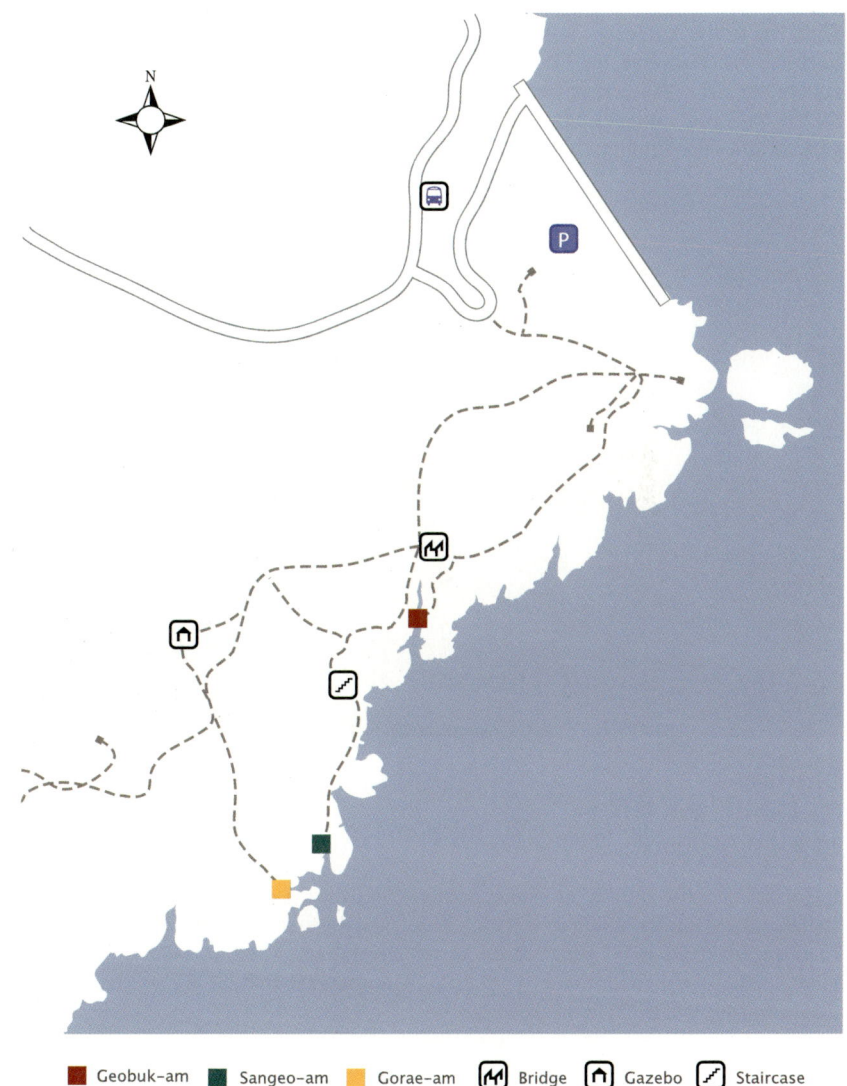

SEUNGHAK-AM 승학암

Description
This crag is also known as Samagui-bawi 사마귀바위. It hadn't maintained for years until KOTR (Korea on the Rocks) members, from Busan, re-bolted and fixed all the anchors in 2011. When they were fixing the bolts and anchors, there were many warts on the wall and Samagui-bawi was named after that. This crag faces south. There is vertical and slab climbing. It's very crimpy and the rock is solid.

Directions
35.110869N 128.97225E
Dangri-dong, Saha-gu, Busan 부산 사하구 당리동

In Busan, take the subway to Hadan Station 하단 on the orange line (Line #1). Take Exit 9 and continue walking straight for 30m. Take the first right, and walk up the steep road until you reach a T-junction on a back street. From there you will see this crag. Hike up the steep trail for twenty minutes. A few KOTR ribbons are still hanging on trees and they will lead you to the crag.

Gear
7 draws and a 50m rope.

Safety
It has been re-bolted and all the anchors are shiny with stainless steel hooks.

Additional Comments
It gets sun all day long and is great for winter climbing.

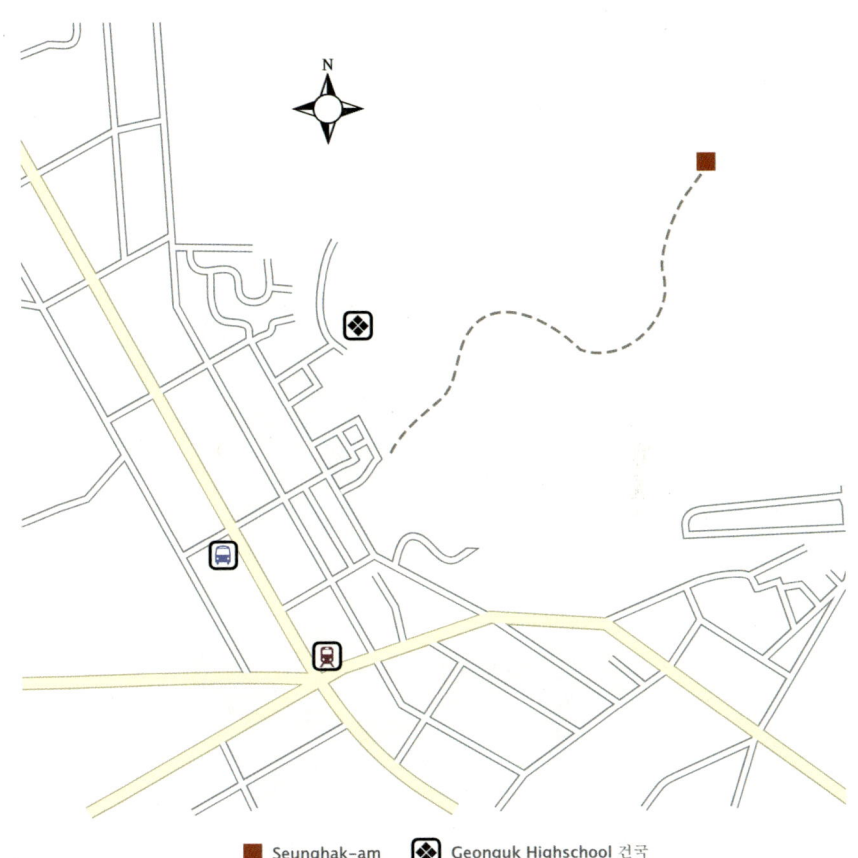

■ Seunghak-am   ◈ Geonguk Highschool 건국

Seunghak-am 승학암

Route Name	Grade	Height
Mozart 모짜르트	5.9	20
DA-93	5.10c	23
Younger Men's Party 후배들의 잔치	5.9	20
The Order Of Rank 위계질서	5.10b	12
Last Leaf 마지막 잎새	5.10b	10
A Feeling Of Waiting 기다리는 마음	5.10a	16
Our Dream 우리들의 꿈	5.10c	6

GADEOK-DO 가덕도

Description
This is the largest sea cliff crag in Korea. Gadeok-do was developed in 2010 and it offers a great view with climbs of various grades and loads of features. The gneiss cliffs are fairly solid even though it sits by the sea. On the harder routes, there are many exotic yoga moves that many will find exciting. It faces south and offers two multi-pitches. The crag is in the sun all morning, but is in the shade after 2 p.m.

Directions
35.019424N 128.8138E
Cheonseong-dong, Gangseo-gu, Busan 부산 강서구 천성동

In Busan, take the subway to Hadan 하단 on the orange line (Line #1). Take Exit 3 and you will see the bus station once you exit. At the bus station, take the bus (58-1 is the best) bound for Yongwon 용원. From Yongwon 용원, which is the last bus stop, transfer to the village bus #1. Get off at the last stop, Cheonseong 천성. From there, take the curvy road that goes underneath the overpass. When you reach a sharp switchback, look for the two concrete drainage ditches that will be on your right. Walk across the small ditch and take the trail that heads to the top of the hill. Then continue down the steep trail that heads down to the sea. There are many guide ropes leading you to the crag. From Cheonseong 천성, it takes forty minutes to get to the sea cliffs.

Gear
12 draws and a 60m rope.

Safety
All the bolts and anchors are solid. However, beware of rockfall, especially the belayer. A helmet for the belayer is recommended.

Additional Comments
When trying to climb on the left side of the crag, look for a reel of string that can be found around the belay spots. As you retrieve your rope after a climb, tie this string on to the end of your rope so you can pull in your rope without it falling into the ocean. On the left side of the cliff, there are a few fun deep water solos available and good cliff jumping spots as well.

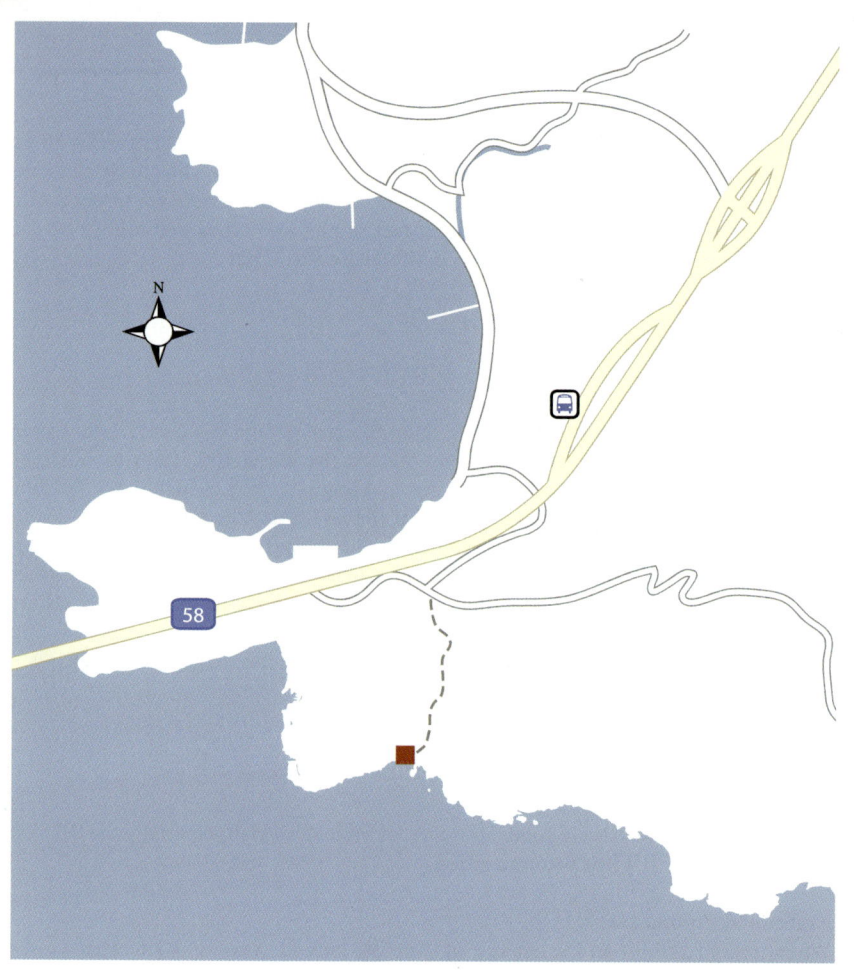

Gadeok

GADEOK-DO 가덕도 (1 OF 4)

Route Name	Grade	Height
(Routes start from right to left on the wall)		
Valley Of Fine Tree 송계	5.11a	17
Land Of Water 물의나라	5.10d	16
Yacht 요트	5.10b	16
Poseidon 포세이돈	5.13a	30
Nephirim 네피림	5.12c	23
Fishing Net 어망대	5.12b	22
Lighter 거루	5.12d	20
Jaws 조스 2	5.12c	22

GADEOK-DO 가덕도 (2 OF 4)

Route Name	Grade	Height
(Routes start from right to left on the wall)		
Swimming 수영	5.12d	20
Snorkeling 스노클링	5.12b	21
Ha Long Bay 하롱베이	5.11d	21
Ark 방주	5.12c	21
Rainbow 무지개	5.12a	21
Noah 노아	5.11b	20
Moses 모세	5.11d	18
Jonah 요나	5.12a	18

Gadeok-Do 가덕도 (3 of 4)

(Routes start from right to left on the wall)

Route Name	Grade	Height
Plankton 플랑크톤	5.12b	18
H2O	5.11a	20
Reef 암초	5.13a	25
Life Jacket 구명동의	5.10d	23
Utopia 유토피아	5.10b	15
Geoga Bridge 거가대교	5.12c	34
Synchronized Swimming 수중발레	5.13b	27
Mermaid 인어	5.13b	27
Pearl 진주	5.12d	28
Webbed-Foot Octopus Dance 주꾸미춤	5.13*	28
Terrifying Ocean 공포의바다 1p (5.12a|28m) 2p (5.11b|16m)	5.12*	44 (2p)
Cheonsudae 천수대	5.10d	12
Village Under The Sea 해저마을	5.10a	12
Sea Cucumber Mutiny 해삼반란	5.11b	12

Gadeok-Do 가덕도 (4 of 4)

(Routes start from right to left on the wall)

Route Name	Grade	Height
Seafood Land 해물나라	5.11a	25
Pirate 해적	5.10d	10
Fishbowl 어항	5.10c	10
Sea Squirt Mutiny 멍게반란	5.11c	20
Shimcheong 심청	5.11b	22
Palace Under The Sea 용궁	5.10b	12
Love Of Sea 바다사랑	5.10d	17
Ocean Palace 해궁	5.10c	19
Ictus 익투스	5.10b	11
Sailor 마도로스	5.10b	12
Landing 상륙	5.10b	11
Dream Of Conch 소라의꿈	5.9	11
Jellyfish's Dancing 해파리춤	5.11b	20
Gadeok Seagull 가덕갈매기	5.11a	27
Water Game 물놀이	5.10a	20

MUCHEOK-SAN 무척산

Description
(*Beom-bawi*) - Beom-bawi is relatively small, but offers pleasant climbing on vertical and overhanging granite walls. It faces southeast.
(*Tanggeon-bawi*) - The granite climbs here are intense with lots of jugs and pumpy holds. It faces south and is in the sun all day. The upper wall is on the right side of the crag.
(*Janggun-byeok*) - As the main crag of Mucheok-san, this crag has various climbs from a crimpy face to an easy, short slab and a hard overhanging wall. It faces south.
(*Jeok-byeok*) - This crag is right by the trail and the climbs are mostly short slabs and vertical climbing on granite rock. It faces southwest.
(*Gaya-byeok*) - The crag is also right by the trail. The climbs are mostly short slabs and vertical climbing on granite rock. It faces southwest.
(*Sumeun-byeok*) - This is a short and small crag with mostly vertical, easy climbs on granite rock.
(*Haneul-byeok*) - Although the crag offers easy and short climbs, a vast view awaits at the top and is a great place for beginners. It faces southeast and opens to the sky.
(*Seong-byeok*) - The hard, overhanging climbing here compares to Seonun-san.

Directions
(*Beom-bawi*) - 35.345744N 128.856208E
(*Tanggeon-bawi*) - 35.348342N 128.861711E
(*Janggun-byeok*) - 35.35041N 128.861488E
(*Jeok-byeok*) - 35.35012N 128.861728E
(*Gaya-byeok*) - 35.350343N 128.861782E
(*Sumeun-byeok*) - 35.350838N 128.861478E
(*Haneul-byeok*) - 35.349935N 128.863229E
(*Seong-byeok*) - 35.351389N 128.864346E
Sangcheol-ri, Sangrim-myeon, Gimhae 김해시 생림면 생철리

(*Beom-bawi*) - From the parking lot at the foot of the mountain, there is a small temple called Seokgol-sa 석골사 to your right. Walk towards the temple and head to the Buddha statue. Then walk 5m towards the temple's main building. Look for a drainage ditch to your right. Follow the trail that follows along the drainage ditch and a steel line for five minutes.
(*Tanggeon-bawi*) - 200m before Moeun-am Temple 모은암, look for a trail on your right at the sharp switchback (and warning sign) on the concrete-paved road. Follow this trail for twenty minutes.
(*Janggun-byeok*) - From the end of the concrete-paved road, right below Moeun-am Temple 모은암, take the path to your left. Continue for 300m, past the Rescue Mark 3-2, and search for a faint trial on your left 30m before the small rock tunnel. Follow the trail for 50m.
(*Jeok-byeok*) - Right after passing the trail to Janggun-byeok, continue up the main trail for 50m. The crag will be on your right next to the rock tunnel.
(*Gaya-byeok*) - Gaya-byeok is located above the rock tunnel on your right, on the main trail past Jeok-byeok.
(*Sumeun-byeok*) - Continue down the trail past Jeok-byeok. Walk through the rock tunnel on your left and follow the path for 100m.

Photo by Ryou, Dong-il

Kim Cheol-Gui 김철규 *on "Delight"* 환희*/5.12b, Janggun-bawi, Mucheok-san. He has been one of the main developers in Busan and is among Korea's most humblest climbers. Unlike many other climbers in Korea, who do not allow other people to fix or replace anchors at their crag, Kim Cheol-Gui announced that his routes can be fixed, rebolted, or even altered if it makes the climb better. This is unprecedented in Korean climbing culture.*

(**Haneul-byeok**) - Continue hiking on the main trail past Gaya-byeok for 300m. Haneul-byeok is located on the highest point of the main trail, above all the crags except Seong-byeok 성벽. Hanuel-byeok can be easily seen from the trail.

(**Seong-byeok**) - From Haneul-byeok 하늘벽, hike towards the prayer retreat 무척산기도원 until you reach a small waterfall. Walk past the waterfall for 50m and at the fork, take the path to the left. Walk down for 300m until you reach a grave site. From the grave site, look for an off-beaten trail heading downwards. It leads to the top of the crag. Coming from Haneul-byeok, it will take twenty-five minutes.

Gear
10 draws and a 50m rope.

Safety
(**Seong-byeok**) - The trail to Seong-byeok 성벽 from the grave is very steep and rough. The belay ground is a bit sketchy.

Additional Comments
(**Jeok-byeok, Sumeun-byeok**) - Because of their location by the hiking trail, these crags are seldom visited. During the weekends, it's hard to find a place to belay because of the hikers.

Water and restrooms are available at the parking lot. It's hard to find great campsites, but there are a few available on the flat rocks.

Tanggeon-bawi 탕건바위

Route Name	Grade	Height
Skullcap 탕건	5.10c	10
Gold Crown 금관	5.12a	10
Reclining Dragon 와룡	5.11d	10
Initial Position 원위	5.11b	10
Prowess 무용	5.11b	10
Mother-In-Law 장모	5.10b	10
Yearning 사모	5.10d	10
China Pink 패랭이	5.10d	10
The Crown Of Thorns 멸류관	5.12a	10
Corn Hat 고깔	5.11d	10
Woven Headband 망건	5.11b	10
Bamboo Hat 삿갓	5.11a	10
Glow Of The Setting Sun 낙조	5.10d	10
Sunset 석양	5.11b	10
Daybreak 여명	5.11b	10
Mucheok 무척	5.11a	8
Courage 담력	5.10d	10
Gangtaegong 강태공	5.10c	10
The Eve Of Boot Camp 입영전야	5.10a	10
Lady B 양	5.13a	10
Baekdu 백두	5.12a	10

Tanggeon-bawi (Upper Wall) 탕건바위 상단벽

Route Name	Grade	Height
Buddhist Nun 비구니	5.11c	8
Buddha's Birthday 석가탄신일	5.12d	12
Lotus Lantern Festival 연등회	5.11a	8
Buddhist Period 불기	5.10d	8
Mercy 자비	5.10b	8

Beom-bawi 범바위

Route Name	Grade	Height
Before June 유월전	5.8	8
Lintel 인방	5.10a	8
Exodus Of The Land Of Egypt 애굽탈출	5.10b	8
Realm Of Black And White 흑암의 영역	5.11a	8
Nasreddin 나설인	5.11b	8
Unleavened Bread 무교병	5.10d	8
The City Of Refuge 도피성	5.11a	8
March In The Wilderness 광야의 행진	5.10d	8
The Reaping 열 재앙	5.12a	10

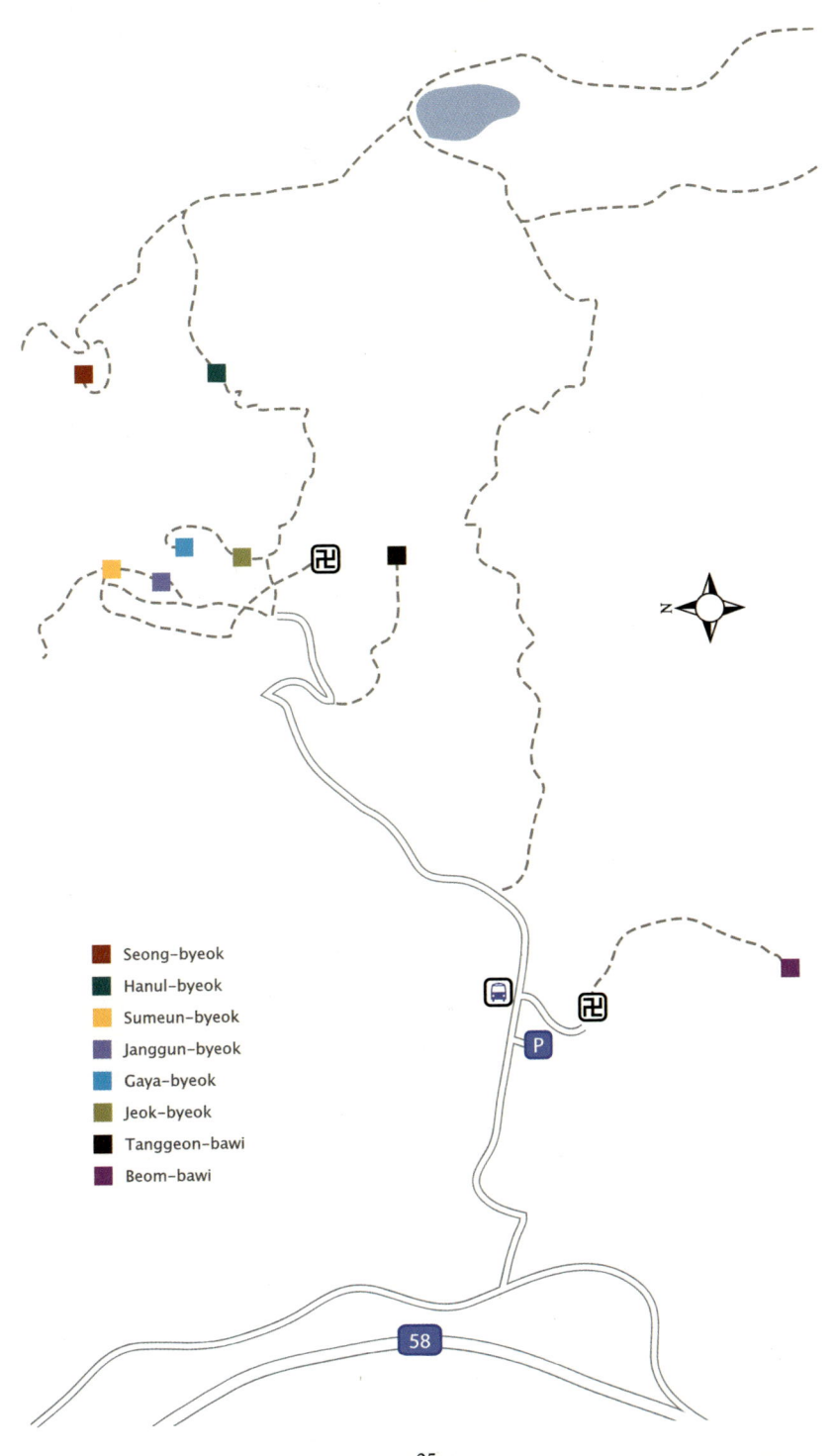

JANGGUN-BYEOK 장군바위 (1 OF 2)

Route Name	Grade	Height
Rice Planting 모내기	5.10c	7
Bodhendrum Temple 보리암	5.11a	7
Nakdong River 낙동강	5.11a	8
Iron Bridge 철교	5.11b	10
Glow Of The Setting Sun 노을	5.11d	10
Mummery 머메리	5.11a	10
Excursion Day 소풍가는날	5.10d	10
It's Snowing In Hamlet 눈나리는산마실	5.11a	10
Love Song 연가	5.12b	10
Delight 환희	5.12b	10
Smile 미소	5.11b	11
Shabby Spring 허름한봄	5.10a	8
Toddling 걸음마	5.8	9
Offering 공양	5.11b	13
Wooden Gong 목탁	5.10d	8
Pay Homage To Buddha 예불	5.11b	8
Merciful Buddha 미륵	5.10d	9
To Infinity & Beyond 하늘끝까지	5.10d	20
Together 둘이서	5.10b	20
Harvest 추수	5.10b	18
Garden Of Eden 에덴동산	5.8	8
Life Tree 생명나무	5.10b	12
Knowledge Tree 지식나무	5.10b	8
Cunning Lure 간사한유혹	5.11a	8
Broken Idol 우상다깨고	5.11d	8
Jangmangseong 장망성	5.10c	8
Goliath 골리앗	5.11b	10
Samsondrila 삼손드릴라	5.12b	10
Sodom Gomorrah 소돔고모라	5.12a	10
The Pilgrim's Progress 천조역정	5.11d	8
Adam's Apple 아담의타락	5.11c	8
Earth 땅	5.11b	8
Sky And Earth 하늘과땅	5.12b	8
The Last Supper 최후의만찬	5.12c	11

JANGGUN-BYEOK 장군바위 (2 OF 2)

Route Name	Grade	Height
The Creation 천지창조	5.12a	12
Let There Be Light 빛이있으라	5.12c	12
Saddoukai 사두경마	5.12a	12
Prodigal Son 돌아온탕자	5.10c	10

JEOK-BYEOK 적벽

Route Name	Grade	Height
Watch Your Step 발조심	5.11b	6
Pulling Under 언더뜯고	5.11b	6
Just So So 그런데로	5.10c	6

GAYA-BYEOK 가야벽

Route Name	Grade	Height
Call Wind 콜바람	5.10b	10
Ara Gaya 아라가야	5.10*	18
Crown Gaya 금관가야	5.10a	18
Goryeong Gaya 고령가야	5.9	18
Little Gaya 소가야	5.10b	10
Big Gaya 대가야	5.10d	10
Seongsan Gaya 성산가야	5.10a	10

SUMEUN-BYEOK 숨은벽

Route Name	Grade	Height
Mageolri 막걸리	5.10b	10
Soju 소주	5.10d	10
Big Unchaste Lady 큰음녀	5.10c	7
Leaven 누룩	5.9	10
Bivouac 비박	5.10c	12
Masterpiece 걸작품	5.11b	12
Oil 기름	5.12b	12
Ambition 야심	5.11d	12
Iron Man 철사장	5.12a	10
Captain Jeon 전대장	5.11c	10
Sunday Mucheok 선데이무척	5.11a	10
Pretty Pants 이쁜팬티	5.10a	10
The Way Of Rookie 초보의도	5.8	8
You Can Do It 하면된다	5.10c	10
I Can Do It 하고말거야	5.10d	10
I Did It 해냈어	5.11a	10

Bryan Hylenski (KOTRi) and Choi Byeong Ho installing a new anchor during an initiative.

Haneul-byeok 하늘벽

Route Name	Grade	Height
Virginal Purity 첫순결	5.8	6
First Meet 첫만남	5.9	7
First Pure-Hearted 첫순정	5.9	7
First Love 첫사랑	5.9	7
First Experience 첫경험	5.9	7
First Regret 첫후회	5.9	7
Seongsan Gaya 성산가야	5.10a	10

Seong-Byeok 성벽 (1 of 2)

Route Name	Grade	Height
Castle Wall 성벽	5.10c	19
Breast Wall 옹벽	5.11b	12
Rock Wall 바위성	5.12a	13
Defense Wall 철벽	5.12b	13

Seong-byeok 성벽 (2 of 2)

Route Name	Grade	Height
Castle 성곽	5.12a	13
Watch Tower 망루	5.13a	14
Barrier 장벽	5.13a	25
Impregnable Fortress 철벽	5.12d	23
Citadel 요새	5.13a	22
Strong Fortification 철옹성	5.13b	22
The Lord Of A Castle 성주	5.13c	17
Satanic Castle 악마의성	5.12c	15
Fortress 성채	5.12b	13
Watch Tower 망대	5.12c	12
Castle Gate 성문	5.12a	12
Wall 담벼락	5.10a	10

CHEONTAE-SAN 천태산

Description
Developed in 2000 with three different walls, Siru-bong is a granite bluff that overlooks the longest river in South Korea, the Nakdong River 낙동강.
(Siru-bong, Bukseo-byeok) - This wall is on the north face of Siru-bong. The routes here consists of crack and vertical climbing.
(Siru-bong, Dongnam-byeok) - This wall is on the southeast face of Siru-bong. The climbing on the far right offers overhanging routes with a great view of the Nakdong River. On the south side, there is moderate climbing of jugs and slab. The rock changes, as you ascend further up, to finger-pockets.
(Sumeun-byeok) - This crag is 100m away from the main crags. It is mostly crack climbing. It hasn't been maintained very well and the trail is overgrown.

Directions
35.384653N 128.880107E
Geomsei-ri, Samnangjin-eup, Miryang-si 밀양시 삼랑진읍 검세리

(Siru-bong) - From Samnangjin Station 삼랑진, walk southeast along the river for twenty minutes to Jakwongwan 작원관, a historic site. If you grab a cab, it will save time. From the site, follow the paved concrete that goes above the train tracks. At the end of the concrete path, there is a faint trail that leads off to the right. Keep walking on the relatively flat trail with the train tracks on your right. A pleasant tree-covered trail runs gently up and down for thirty minutes past two small concrete walls and a tiny hut. When the crag comes into view, the trail starts becoming steeper. Hike up the steep trail for ten minutes to the crag.
(Sumeun-byeok) - From the northwest end of Siru-bong, Sumeon-byeok can be seen to the north. It is a five minute walk from Siru-bong.

Gear
10 draws and a 60m rope.

Safety
The belay station on the southeast wall of Siru-bong has limited space on the steep rocky ground. Belayers should be anchored to the guide wire or to the bolts on the ground. Rock falls occasionally on the middle section of the southeast wall.

Additional Comments
Try to get everything you need at the stores by the train station. If you grab a cab, ask the driver to give you his business card so you can call him to drive you back to the train station after you finish climbing.

Dong-il Ryou, the author, on "A Room With A Good View"/5.11b

SUMEUN-BYEOK 숨은벽

Route Name	Grade	Height
Companion Taken Away 빼앗긴동지	5.10c	35
Friend's Betrayal 후배들의배신	5.11b	35
Ending Of Betrayer 배신자의종말	5.10a	23
The Road To The Great Stone 큰바위길	5.10c	10
Half & Half 반타작	5.10b	5

BUKSEO-BYEOK 북서벽

Route Name	Grade	Height
Alpine Rose 석난	5.9	17
Friend 친구	5.9	17
Incompletion 미완성	*	20
Dear Mother 어머님전상서	5.11c	20
Incompletion 미완성 3	*	20
Big-Wall Myth 빅월신화	5.11b	24
Endless Robber 끝없는도적	*	24
Mountain Over Mountain 산넘어산	5.11b	23
Thou, No Response To My Call 불러도대답없는그대여	5.10b	23

DONGNAM-BYEOK 동남벽

Route Name	Grade	Height
Quick-Witted Child 똘똘이	5.10a	13
Thunderclap 천둥소리	5.10b	40
Bbiggiri 삐끼리	5.10a	40
Millennium 밀레니엄 1	*	*
Millennium 밀레니엄 2	*	*
Millennium 밀레니엄 3	*	*
New Millennium Love 새천년의사랑	5.13	15
Big Deal 빅딜	5.13	17
Climber's Dream 클라이머의꿈	5.13	16
A Room With A Good View 전망좋은방	5.11b	22
Bat And Hammer 박지와해머	5.11*	22
Chan-Chan-Chan 찬찬찬	5.10b	20
Still I Am A Human Being 아직도내가사람으	5.11c	13
Cornus Fruit 산수유	5.12c	12
Partner 파트너	5.12*	13
Prince Outing 왕자나들이	5.12c	13

Bird's Chorus - Amjang 새들의 합창 암장

Description
This place was developed by a local climbing club in Gimhae 김해. This is a small, but cozy place to climb during winter. The easiest climbing starts at the far left and then gradually gets harder as the routes move to the right.

Directions
35.3704N 128.867826E
Doyo-ri, Sangrim-myeon, Gimhae 김해 생림면 도요리

There is no direct public transportation to the crag. From Gimhae Bus Terminal 김해, take the bus leaving for Doyo 도요. Get off at Doyo 도요 and walk towards the overpass. Walk underneath the overpass and continue on the road alongside the river for 5k until you reach a sign that says "백련암" Baekneonam. Take the unpaved road heading towards the mountain for ten minutes. There will be a sign on your right that indicates the rock climbing area. The crag can occasionally be seen to your right as you hike up.

Gear
8 draws and a 50m rope.

Additional Comments
There is a good wooden belay station and campsites with a restroom. Food and water should be purchased in town.

Bird's Chorus - Amjang 김해 새들의 합창 암장

Route Name	Grade	Height
Spring Chicken 햇병아리	5.9	10
Staggering Duck 뒤뚱대는오리	5.10a	12
Disappeared Phoenix 사라진봉황	5.10b	15
Returned Swallow 돌아온제비	5.10b	15
Magpie Hosts Guest 손님맞는까치	5.10d	15
Woodpecker Picking Rocks 바위쪼는딱다구리	5.11a	15
Swan Lake 백조의호수	5.10b	17
Eagle On A Rock 바위에앉은독수리	5.10b	17
Seagull Returned To A Mountain 산으로온갈매기	5.10b	18
Kite's Dream 솔개의꿈	5.10b	15
Owl Grabbed A Rat 쥐를움켜쥔부엉이	5.11b	15

MUNSU-SAN 문수산

Description
Munsu 문수 was developed from 1989 to 1993. It has about one hundred routes across nine different walls and is divided horizontally by the hiking trail. The routes are made of gneiss rock with various features, lengths, and grades. All of the routes face south and are in the sun all day.

Directions
35.530078N 129.213402E
Yul-ri, Cheongryang-myeon, Ulju-gun, Ulsan 울산 울주군 청량면 율리

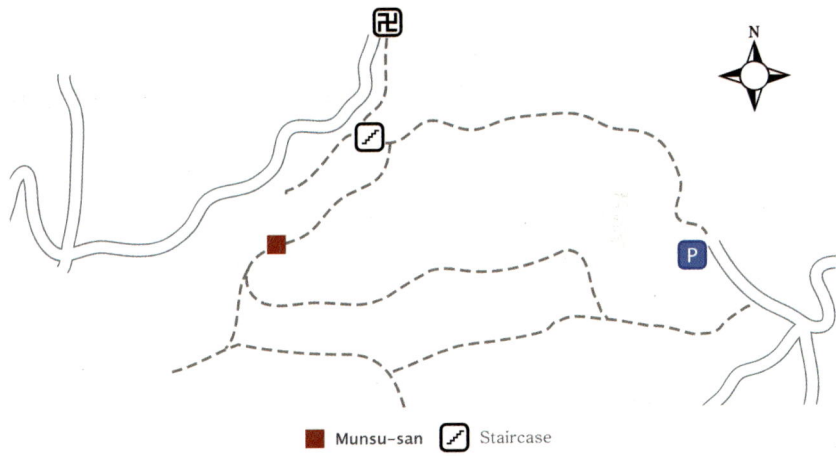

■ Munsu-san   ⧋ Staircase

From Ulsan or Busan Nopo-dong Bus Terminal, take a bus heading for Munsu 문수. Get off at Yulli, Yeonghae Maeul Bus Stop 율리 영해마을. Go towards Nonghyeop Bank 농협 and hike along the paved road that leads to the mountain for forty minutes until you reach the Munsu-sa 문수사 parking lot. From the parking lot, walk on the main trail for ten minutes until you reach stairs with a steel handrail. Look for a trail on your left, just before the stairs, and take that trail to reach the upper walls. Along the upper section trail you will pass a hut and a small cascade. Past this area is a trail to your left that heads down to the lower section walls.

Gear
10 draws and a 60m rope.

Safety
Be careful not to kick down any rocks because there may be climbers on the lower sections of the wall.

Additional Comments
There are campsites around the crag and water is available from the spring, but it may run dry during the winter. From the lower section of the wall, it will be easier to walk back down to the parking lot by following the rock stairs for ten minutes.

Munsu-San

GIJYEON-AMJANG 기존암장

Route Name	Grade	Height
Existing 기존 A	5.9	30
Existing 기존 B	5.9	34
Route For Memories 추모길	5.10b	34
Direct Course 직등코스	5.10b	34
Road To Ulsan Univ. 울대길	5.10c	34
Existing 기존 C	5.10*	34

OTTUGI BOULDER 오뚜기 볼더

Route Name	Grade	Height
Can 깡통	5.9	15
Spigot 꼭지	5.10c	15
Pipe Dream 뜬구름	5.11b/c	15
Love Affair On Weekend 주말의정사	5.10c	15
March For Beloved One 님을위한행진곡	5.11b	15
B. B II	5.10a	15

HYEONJUNG BOULDER 현중 볼더

Route Name	Grade	Height
Mt. Bamboo Road 산죽길	5.10b	10
Heat Haze 아지랑이	5.11c/d	11
Silent Of Beloved One 님의침묵	5.12a	11
Road Of Seoksu 석수길	5.10c	10

CHOSDAE BOULDER 촛대 볼더

Route Name	Grade	Height
Approach Path 진입로	5.11a	15
Lonely Star 외로운별	5.10a	15

OEDOLGAE-AM 외돌개암

Route Name	Grade	Height
Photo 포토	5.9	15

CHEONSEO HIGH-AM 천서 하이암

Route Name	Grade	Height
Photo 포토	5.9	15

GEOBYUK-AM 거북암

Route Name	Grade	Height
Orchid House 난원	5.10a	15
Lightning 번개	5.9	15
Reunion 재회	5.10c	15
Acorn 도토리	5.10a	15

HYEONSAN ROCK 현산암

Route Name	Grade	Height
Harmoniousness 아기자기	5.10b	11
Lady 레이디	5.9	11
New Generation 신세대	5.10b	13
Never Give Up 포기하지마	5.11a	13
Temptation 유혹	5.10c	13
Anna 안나	5.10b	13
Stop Being MIA 잠수하지마	5.11a	13
Hyeonja 현자	5.11c	13
Passage Of Time 가는세월	5.9	13
Quack 엉터리	5.8	13
Observatory 전망대	5.11a	12

HYEONGONG OB-AM 현공 OB 암

Route Name	Grade	Height
One-Sided Love 짝사랑	5.9	18
Toothpick 이쑤시게	5.10c	17
Doolie 둘리	5.10a	15
Refuge 안식처	5.10a	17
Boss 왕초	5.10a	17
Stand On One's Own Feet 홀로서기 1	5.11a	20
Stand On One's Own Feet 홀로서기 2	5.10c	15
Riding Surf 파도타기	5.10a	17
Morning Sunlight 아침햇살	5.12a	17
Glow Of The Setting Sun 저녁노을	5.11d	17
Nangga Base 낭가베이스	5.11c	17
Camp 1	5.11a	17
Camp 2	5.10a	17

FAMILY BOULDER 페밀리볼더

Route Name	Grade	Height
Grand Mom 할매	5.7	12
Scamp 개구장이	5.9	12
Siblings 오누이	5.10c	12
Hyeonsu 현수	5.10c	13
Uncle 삼촌	5.10a	14
Mom 엄마	5.10a	14
Dad 아빠	5.10a	14

KOTRi (Korea on the Rocks Initiatives), a non-profit volunteer group, has worked closely with the developers of Munsu-san to replace the old and rusty equipment with new bolts and anchors. (www.kotri.org)

Eunhasu-Amjang 은하수암장

Route Name	Grade	Height
Castration, Go For It 거세정진	5.10b	23
Hungry Boy 배고픈아이	5.10b	25
Husband & Wife 부부	5.10c/d	23
Chick 병아리	5.9	15
Lora 로라 2	5.11a	20
Lora 로라 1	5.10a	18
Forever Mountain Friend 영원한악우	5.11a	18
Mountain Friend 악우	5.10b	18
Guri Guri 구리구리	5.10a	18
Existing Route 기존길	5.10b	15
Simpleton & Princess 온달과평강공주	5.9	15

Hyeong Boulder 형제 볼더

Route Name	Grade	Height
Little Baby 작은애기	5.7	12
Pimple 뽀드락지	5.10a	12
Coiling 또아리	5.10a	13
Big Baby 큰애기	5.9	13
Take It Away 너줄께	5.11a	11
Mutual Pleasure 너와나의기쁨	5.10c	11
One Point 한포인트	5.12a	11

91 Boulder 91 볼더

Route Name	Grade	Height
Knocked Down 7 Times, But Got Up The 8th 7 전 8 기	5.12a	13
Heaven And Earth 천상천하	5.12b/c	16
Vision 울산	5.13*	24

Rabbit Boulder 토끼 볼더

Route Name	Grade	Height
Kiss Angel 천사와키스	5.11a	14
Yellowish 연두	5.10a	14
Green 초록	5.10b	14
Toad 두꺼비	5.10b	14
Tadpole 올챙이	5.10b	15
Fine Tree Hill 솔뫼	5.9	15
Forgotten Name 잊어진이름	5.10a	13
Spring Picnic 봄나들이	5.9	12
Kongji 콩지	5.10a	12
Patji 팥지	5.8	12
First Experience 첫경험	5.7	11
Chick 병아리	5.7	11
Oldster Doesn't Know 어른들은몰라요	5.7	11

Union Boulder 연합볼더

Route Name	Grade	Height
Young Brother 젊은오빠	5.10d	12
Unexpected Chance 우연한기회	5.12a	13
Union 연합 94	5.12b	13
Dalgubeol 달구벌	5.11d	13
Edelweiss 에델바이스	5.11a	14
Korando 코란도 9	5.11b	20
Walking To The Sky 걸어서하늘까지	5.10b	18
Windless Zone 무풍지대	5.11b	11
Wing 날개 93	5.11b	15
Little Angel 리틀엔젤	5.10c	16

BAEKUN-SAN 백운산

Description
(***Hanbaek-am***) - This granite crag was opened to the public in November 2008. It offers seventeen routes, including a few multi-pitches with one five-pitch route. It faces south and was developed to honor a member of the K2 expedition team in 2008 from Ulsan Hanbaek Mountain Club 울산한백산악회. This crag used to be called Central Wall 중앙벽.

(***Jowa-byeok***) - This small crag is 500m to the left of Hanbaek-am. It offers challenging climbs on a steep slab that faces south. The routes are relatively short and have not been named or graded because there have been multiple developers in this area. If attempting the granite routes here, the climbing is like a hard 5.11. This is a good place to warm up before climbing at the main crag.

(***Wu-byeok***) - This is a training crag for beginners. It is composed of easy, granite slab routes that have not been named or graded because there have been multiple developers in this area. This wall faces south as well.

Directions
35.589504N 128.988272E
Samyang-ri, Sannae-myeon, Miryang-si 밀양시 산내면 삼양리

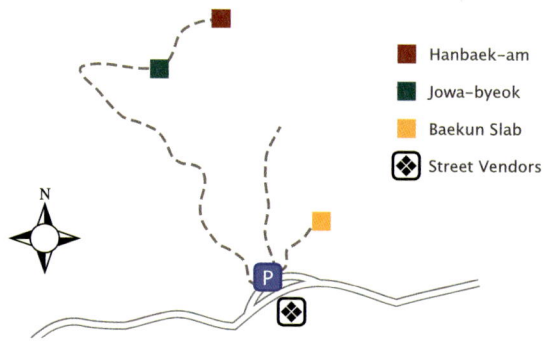

From Miryang 밀양 or Eunyang 언양, take the bus bound for Euleumgol 얼음골. Get off at the last stop Hobakso 호박소. Go back up the road along the mountain side for 5km until you see the stone sign "밀양얼음골사과주지" Miryang Euleumgol Sagwa Jusanji, by a small noodle tent called Busan Jib 부산집. Across from the noodle tent, the trailhead starts at a point where there are lots of hanging ribbons. Immediately turning right on the trail will take you to Baekun Slab. If you keep hiking up instead of turning right at the trailhead, you will end up reaching the top of the mountain. To get to the Hanbaek-am and Jowa-byeok, look for a small trail that is 7m left of the main trailhead. Follow this trail for thirty minutes.

Gear
10 draws, a 60m rope, and a full set of cams.

HANBAEK-AM 한백암

Route Name	Grade	Height
Green Fish 초록물고기 1p (5.8|25m) 2p (5.10b|30m)	5.10b	55 (2p)
Bottle Neck 보틀넥 1p (5.8|25m) 2p (5.10b|30m)	5.10b	55 (2p)
Like The First Time 처음처럼 1p (5.8|20m) 2p (5.10c|30m)	5.10c	50 (2p)
Gyeongjin Rock Friend 경진악우	5.10a	40
Sketch Youth 청춘스케치	5.10b	40
Actions Speak Louder Than Words 선행후언	5.10b	41
Dream Of K2 의 꿈	5.10b	41
Dream Of Seorak 설악의 꿈	5.10b/c	42
Hanbaek 한백	5.10c	42
S Line S 라인	5.10c/d	42
Student Surpasses His Teacher 청출어람	5.10b	30
Everything Must Go To Where It Has To Go 만절필동 1p (5.10a|30m) 2p (5.8|17m) 3p (5.10b|15m) 4p (5.8|25m)	5.10b	87 (4p)
Dream Is Only One 꿈은 하나	5.11c	30
Star 별 (**1st pitch can be climbed on 2 different routes) 1p(v1) (5.8|35m) *1p(v2) (5.6|30m) 2p (5.11b|43m) 3p (5.7|26m) 4p (5.12*|20m) 5p (5.9|28m)	5.12*	152 (5p)
Back To The Nature 귀거래사 1p (5.10b|42m) 2p (5.10c|20m)	5.10c	62 (2p)
'Delight' Ridge "환희"릿지 (*1st pitch can be climbed on 2 different routes) 1p(v1) (5.8|30m) *1p(v2) (5.6|32m) 2p (5.10a|33m) 3p (5.10a|25m) 4p (5.9|28m)	5.10a	118 (4p)
You Can Do It 할수있다 1p (5.9|30m) 2p (5.9|27m)	5.9	57 (2p)
"Dreaming Pine Tree" 릿지 "꿈꾸는 소나무" 릿지 1p (5.9|25m) 2p (5.9|25m) 3p (5.10a|20m) 4p (5.8|20m) 5p (5.9|20m)	5.10a	110 (5p)

Safety
A helmet is recommended.

Additional Comments
A good belay station is set up at Hanbaek-am and good campsites available. Food and water should be gathered beforehand.

GUMAN-SAN AMJANG 구만산 암장

Description
Development began here in 2000. It is an overhanging crag that faces west. It still offers untapped potential.

Directions
35.610156N 128.872054E
Bongeui-ri, Sannae-myeon, Miryang-si 밀양시 산내면 봉의리

From Miryang Bus Terminal, get off at Sannae Elementary School 산내초등학교. Walk along the road to Guman-san 구만산, past Bongeui Bridge 봉의교, for thirty minutes. The crag is at the beginning of the first wooden staircase. It takes ten minutes to reach the crag from the trailhead at Guman Temple 구만사.

Gear
10 draws and a 50m rope.

Safety
There is a waterfall by the crag so the routes are easily dampened and prone to rockfall. A helmet is recommended.

Additional Comments
Since it is located by a rivulet in the valley, it is a good place for a holiday trip in the summer. The crag is still under development and the route names are up in the air.

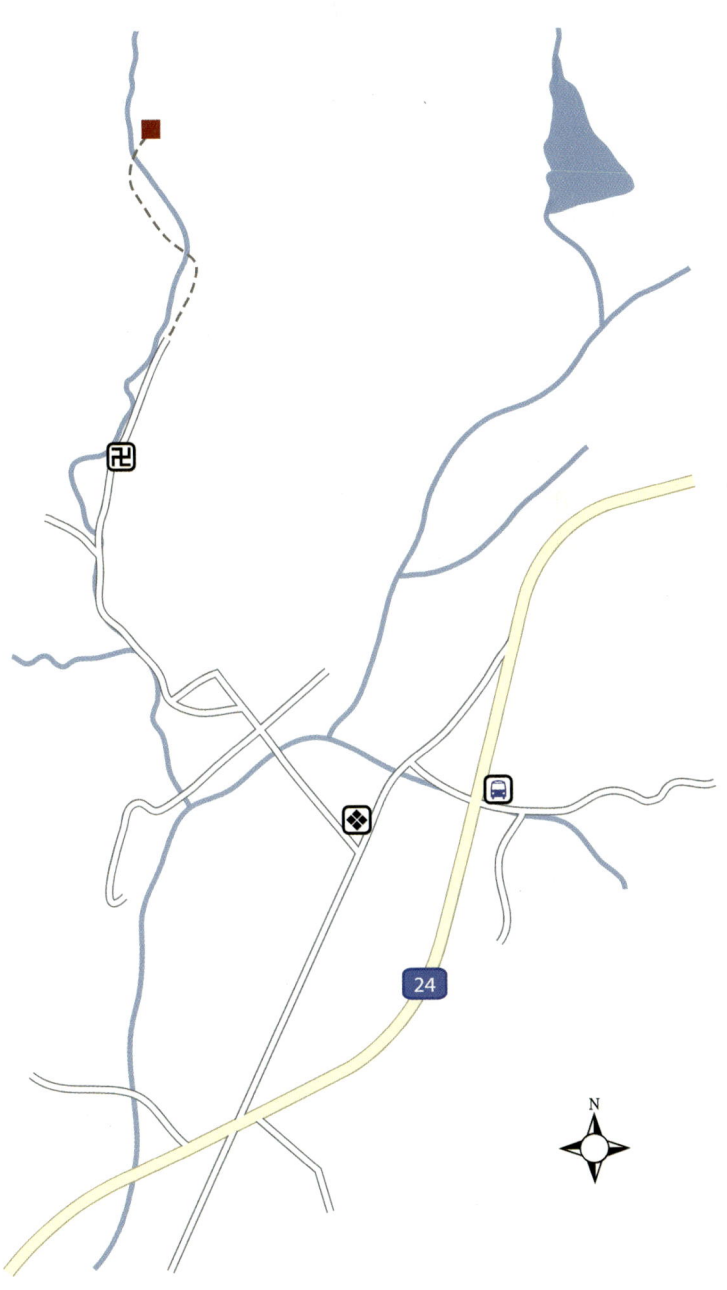

■ Guman-san Amjang　　◈ Sannae Elementary School 산내초등학교

MIRYANG, BUEONGSAE-BAWI 밀양 부엉새바위

Description
Developed from 2001 to 2002, this granite crag has vertical, overhanging, and small roof climbing. It offers various moves and requires power. There are a couple of short, easy routes on the right side of the wall. It faces northwest.

Directions
35.514806N 128.86817E
Taeryong-ri, Danjang-myeon, Miryang-si 밀양시 단장면 태룡리

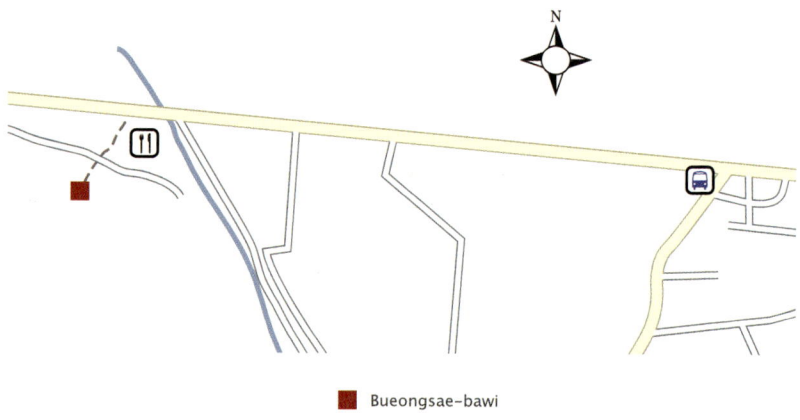

■ Bueongsae-bawi

From Miryang Bus Terminal, take the bus for Pochung-sa 표충사. Get off at Taeryong 태룡. Head east on the main road for five minutes. You'll reach the restaurant "Noblian". The crag is right behind the restaurant. It will take twenty minutes to reach the climbing wall from Miryang Bus Terminal.

Gear
12 draws and a 60m rope.

Additional Comments
This crag is on private land. In 2009, this climbing area was closed to all climbing due to the inappropriate conduct of climbers using the wall. In 2012, KOTRi (Korea on the Rocks Initiatives) finally succeeded in persuading the land owner to re-open the wall. With the help of local Busan climbers, they repaired the equipment on the wall. All the anchors were replaced with new stainless chains. All of the rusty bolts were removed and new bolts were put in.

Photo Courtesy of Lea Gang, 강레아

BUEONGSAE-BAWI 부엉새바위 (1 OF 2)		
Route Name	Grade	Height
Outing 나들이	5.10a	20
Long Leg Beach 롱다리비취	5.11b	23
Ocean Of Time 시간의바다	5.11d	29
Born 92 탄생	5.11d	29
Favorite 총애	5.12a	29
Fortune 천운	5.12c	29
Rope Man 로프맨	5.13b	23
Buffalo 버팔로	5.13*	20
Family Love 가족사랑	5.11d	22
Into One 하나로	5.12c	29

BUEONGSAE-BAWI 부엉새바위 (2 OF 2)		
Route Name	Grade	Height
Owl 부엉새	5.12d	29
Dream Of Casanova 강쇠의꿈	5.13b	29
Fake Cannon 공갈포	5.10b	13
Bizarre Virtue 엽기덕기	5.11b	29
Autumn Wind 가을바람	5.10c	23
Play Ground 놀이터	5.7	6
Mamushi Escape 살모사탈출	5.12b	23
Pipe Dream 뜬구름	5.10a	6
Camera Man 카메라맨	5.9	6
Sky 하늘	5.12a	23

PHOCHUNG-SA, JEOK-BYEOK 표충사 적벽

Description
This crag was developed in 1997 and has seven routes. It is located high in the mountain behind Phochung-sa, one of the most famous temples in Korea. There is an A2 aid climb, which can be climbed even in the rain. Jeok-byeok has a dihedral that faces southwest. The position and character of its routes will remind climbers of the climbing at Jeok-byeok on Seorak Mt.

Directions
35.532183N 128.981264E
Gucheon-ri, Danjang-myeon, Miryang-si 밀양시 단장면 구천리

From Miryang Phocung-sa Ticket Counter 밀양표충사, turn right after passing a small bridge. Hike up the main trail that follows along the creek towards Cheungcheung Falls 층층폭포 for forty minutes. Look for the area sign "마-1", right before the small wooden bridge past Heukryong Falls 흑룡폭포. Look for an off beaten trail to your left from the sign, and scramble up for 100m to the crag.

Gear
12 draws, a 60m rope, and two full sets of cams.

Safety
A helmet is recommended as a precaution against some of the loose rock.

Additional Comments
During the summer season, this area can get overgrown and there are a lot of bugs. Bring bug repellent. There are good campsites under the overhanging section. It offers great shelter when it rains.

JEOK-BYEOK 적벽

Route Name	Grade	Height
Y1	5.9	20
Y2	5.9	18
Bee 벌	5.10*	21
Lunge 런지	5.11a	19
8.15	5.11c	19
Three Pocket	5.12a	23
Terrible	5.11b	22
Gyeongjeon Route 경전길	A2	80*

*Multi-pitch info is unavailable at this time

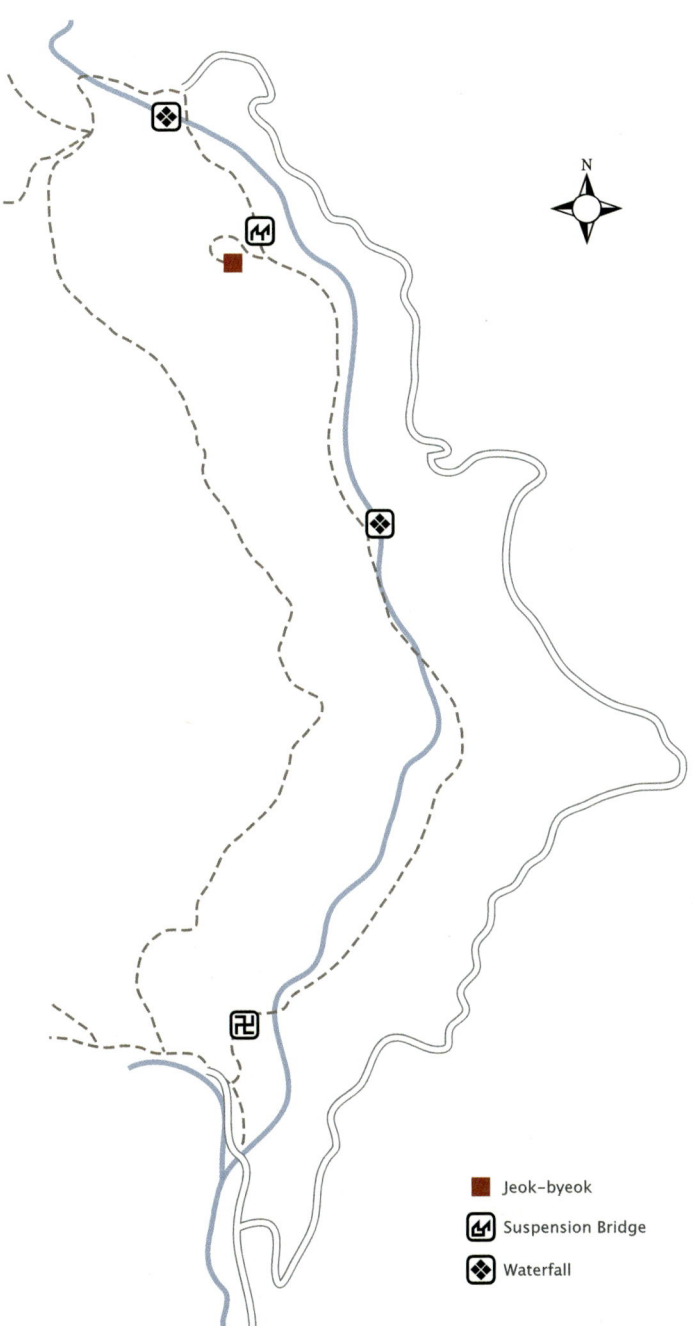

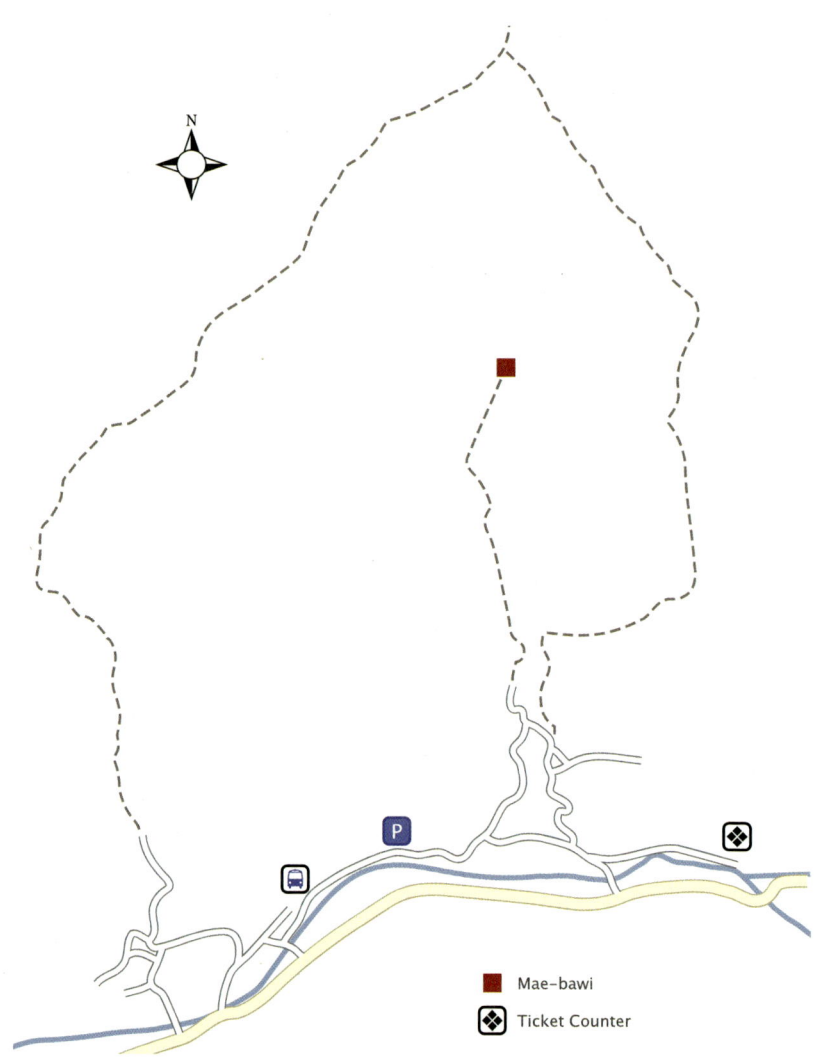

MAE-BAWI 매바위 (1 OF 2)

Route Name	Grade	Height
Creation of Myth 신화창조 **1p** (5.9|40m) **2p** (5.10a|35m)	5.10a	75 (2p)
Chat Chat 도란도란 **1p** (5.9|35m) **2p** (5.9|30m) **3p** (5.10a|45m)	5.9	110 (3p)
Wing Road 날개길 **1p** (5.9|40m) **2p** (5.10c|45m)	5.10c	85 (2p)
Moon Light Flows Through The Road 달빛 흐르는길 **1p** (5.9|35m) **2p** (5.10c|40m) **3p** (5.11a|25m) **4p** (5.9|10m)	5.11a	110 (4p)

Phyochung-sa, Mae-bawi 표충사 매바위

Description
This gigantic wall of metamorphic rock faces south and offers a great multi-pitch climb that makes you feel the high altitude. It was developed by Ulsan University. During the Japanese colonial period, rumor had it that there were treasures inside the cave at this crag. The Japanese came up to find the treasures, but all the treasure had turned into falcons. Mae-bawi is named after this story.

Directions
35.543864N 128.950449E
Gucheon-ri, Danjang-myeon, Miryang-si 밀양시 단장면 구천리

From Miryang 밀양시, take a bus bound for Phyochung-sa 표충사. Get off at the end of the line. Walk towards the Phyochung-sa Ticket Counter 표충사매표소. There is a small bridge 20m before the ticket counter. Cross the bridge and hike up until you reach the village "Mae-bawi Maeul 매바위마을". The main trail to the crag was blocked a long time ago by the local people. However, you can take the dirt road to your left, which is easily seen from the small parking lot in the middle of the village. Follow the road and take the first left at the fork. The trail starts to ascend steeply after a few minutes, scramble up the path for fifteen minutes. When you see the big crag on your right from the ridge, cross the heap of stones in the valley. It will lead you to the main trail which leads to the crag. Follow it for ten minutes to reach the crag.

Gear
15 draws, a 60m rope, and a full set of cams.

Safety
Be careful of falling rocks. A helmet and extra webbing is recommended.

Additional Comments
There are great campsites available with fresh water and restrooms. Take your food when leaving your campsite because goats may eat it! Lots of minbaks are available around the bus stop.

Please respect the local people. The farmers and villagers blocked the main trail to the crag a long time ago. You need to get permission from them to open the gate. It's really hard to get to the crag by hiking up the other trails.

MAE-BAWI 매바위 (2 OF 2)

Route Name	Grade	Height
Ulsan-Univ. Road 울대길	5.10a/A0	90 (3p)
1p (A0|35m) **2p** (5.10a|20m) **3p** (5.9|35m)		
Jeonggong Road 정공길	5.9	27
Dream of King's Friend 왕우의 꿈	5.10a	31
Road of Development 개척길	5.9	40
Bat Road 박쥐길	5.10a	40

Yang-san, Byeongpung-am 양산 병풍암

Description
Byeongpung-am was developed in 1992. Its overhanging, gneiss walls face northeast. The crag is in the sun for just a couple of hours in the morning. The rock is very solid.

Directions
35.342295N 129.056311E
Bukbu-dong, Yangsan-si 양산시 북부동

From Yang-san Bus Terminal, take the bus for Yang-san University 양산. From Busan, take the village bus #1 from Nopo-dong Subway Station 노포동. Byeongpung-am is right by the stream, 600m before the university.

Gear
8 draws and a 50m rope.

Safety
The bolts are in good shape, but a few of the anchors are suspect. Bring extra webbing for peace of mind.

Additional Comments
The hardest climb is to the far left side, which actually starts on the water. A belay station should be set up for the climb to keep the rope out of the water.

BYEONGPUNG-AM 병풍암

Route Name	Grade	Height
Annabel Lee 아나벨리	5.12a/b	10
Meditation 심사숙고	5.11a	12
Road To Birth 탄생길	5.11a/b	14
Rhinoceros 코뿔소	5.11a	14
Green Fine Tree 푸른소나무	5.11c	14
Day Dream 뜬구름잡기	5.11c	15
Mission Impossible 난공불락	5.12c/d	13
Empty Sky 허공	5.11d	15
Mountain Party 뫼무리	5.12a	14
Road To Alpine Spirit 뫼정길	5.11a/b	15
Existing 기존	5.9	15

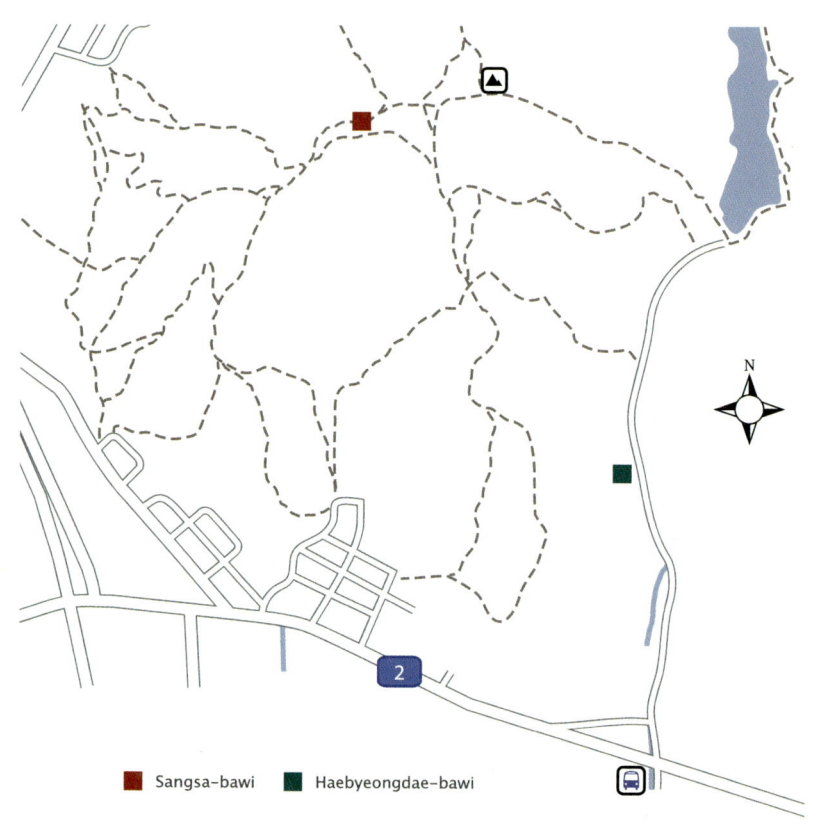

■ Sangsa-bawi   ■ Haebyeongdae-bawi

SANGSA-BAWI 상사바위

Route Name	Grade	Height
Overhang Course 오버행 A 코스 **1p** (5.11c|30m) **2p** (5.7|15m)	5.11c	41 (2p)
Overhang Course 오버행 B 코스 **1p** (5.11b|25m) **2p** (5.7|15m)	5.11b	40 (2p)
Existing Course 기존코스 1p (5.8|32m) 2p (5.8|30m)	5.8	62 (2p)
Right Wall Course 우벽 A 코스 **1p** (5.10d|30m) **2p** (5.9|20m)	5.10d	50 (2p)
Right Wall Course 우벽 B 코스 **1p** (5.9|30m) **2p** (5.9|20m)	5.9	50 (2p)

PALRYONG-SAN 팔용산

Description

(Haebyeongdae-bawi) - This crag faces west in the valley and the climbing ranges from vertical, overhanging, and slab. The Marine Corps train around here.

(Sangsa-bawi) - Sangsa-bawi sits on top of the mountain overlooking a beautiful reservoir and the industrial complex. The routes here are a mix of vertical and slab climbing.

Directions

(Haebyeongdae-bawi) - 35.225665N 128.604831E
(Sangsa-bawi) -35.232124N 128.597052E
Bongam-dong, Masanhwoiwon-gu, Changwon-si 창원시 마산회원구 봉암동

(Haebyeongdae-bawi) - From any major city, take a bus to Masan 마산. Then transfer to a bus bound for Masan Highway Bus Terminal. From there, walk five minutes towards the Export Free Zone 수출자유지역 to reach the local bus stop. Once there, take a bus bound for Changwon and get off at Sanhaewon 산해원. Follow the pavement that leads to Bongam Reservoir 봉암저수지. After five minutes, you will reach Haebyeongdae-bawi 해병대바위.

(Sangsa-bawi) - The trailhead to Sangsa-bawi starts at the southwest side of the dam at the lake. Follow the northeast bound trail towards the summit for twenty minutes.

Gear

10 draws, a 60m rope, and small to mid-sized cams.

HAEBYEONGDAE-BAWI 해병대바위

Route Name	Grade	Height
Witch Spider Road 무당거미길	5.12a	8
Brother Road 아우길	5.10b	8
White Smile Road 하얀미소길	5.9	8
Piano Road 피아노길	5.10c	8
Wing Road 날개길	5.9	8
Hanma Road 한마길	5.10a	8
Road For Memories 추모길	5.10d	8
Butterfly Road 나비길	5.9	8
Spirit of Palryong 팔용의혼	5.11c	8
Friend Road 벗길	5.11a	10
Seongmin Road 성민길	5.10d	10
Standing Crack 선크랙	5.10a	10
Union Road 합동길	5.10a	10

SINBAN 신반

(*Byeongpung-am*) - This metamorphic rock, developed in 1997, faces west. It has three walls. The middle part is hard and overhanging, the left part is a steep face, and the right side is fairly easy with vertical face climbs.
(*Keundeom-bawi*) - This crag was developed in 2009. It features sedimentary rock that faces east.
(*Jakeundeom-bawi*) - This crag is metamorphic-sedimentary rock that faces east. The 5.10's consist of vertical climbing, but the rest are overhanging lines.

Directions
(*Byeongpung-am*) - 35.466979N 128.329453E
(*Keundeom-bawi*) - 35.473707N 128.3057E
(*Jakeundeom-bawi*) - 35.467626N 128.308296E
Sinban-ri, Burim-myeon, Euiryeong-gun 의령군 부림면 신반리

(*Byeongpung-am*) - From Busan or Masan, take the bus for Burim, Sinban 부림 신반. At downtown Burim, cross the bridge Shinbangyo 신반교 and walk under the overpass towards Songam-sa Temple 송암사. The crag is visible from the street.
(*Keundeom-bawi*) - From the village Burim, Sinban 부림 신반, walk west on the main road for 600m and turn left onto a small, cement-paved road that heads towards the mountain. After you cross the stream, you'll see a small sign saying "큰덤바위" Keundeom-bawi. Take the trail to your left. Just 5m after the trailhead, look carefully for a faint path on your right and continue hiking up for five minutes.
(*Jakeundeom-bawi*) - From the village Burim, Sinban 부림 신반, walk towards the intersection by the police station. Take a left towards the elementary school and continue for 1km. Right before the bridge Seodeokgyo 서득교 turn right at Euiryeong Retirement Home 의령군민노인복지회관 and continue on the road for 1.5km. The crag is across from the small village Sangampyeong-Maeul 상암평마을. A big tree will be on your right. Walk through the rice field by the farm and cross the stream. It takes ten minutes to get to the crag from the village and the crag can be seen from the road.

Gear
10 draws and a 60m rope.

Safety
A helmet is recommended.

Additional Comments
(*Byeongpung-am*) - Good campsites and water can be sought at the temple, but always be aware of your surroundings and do not disturb the temple.
(*Keundeom-bawi*) - There are a few great campsites and a simple restroom around the crag.

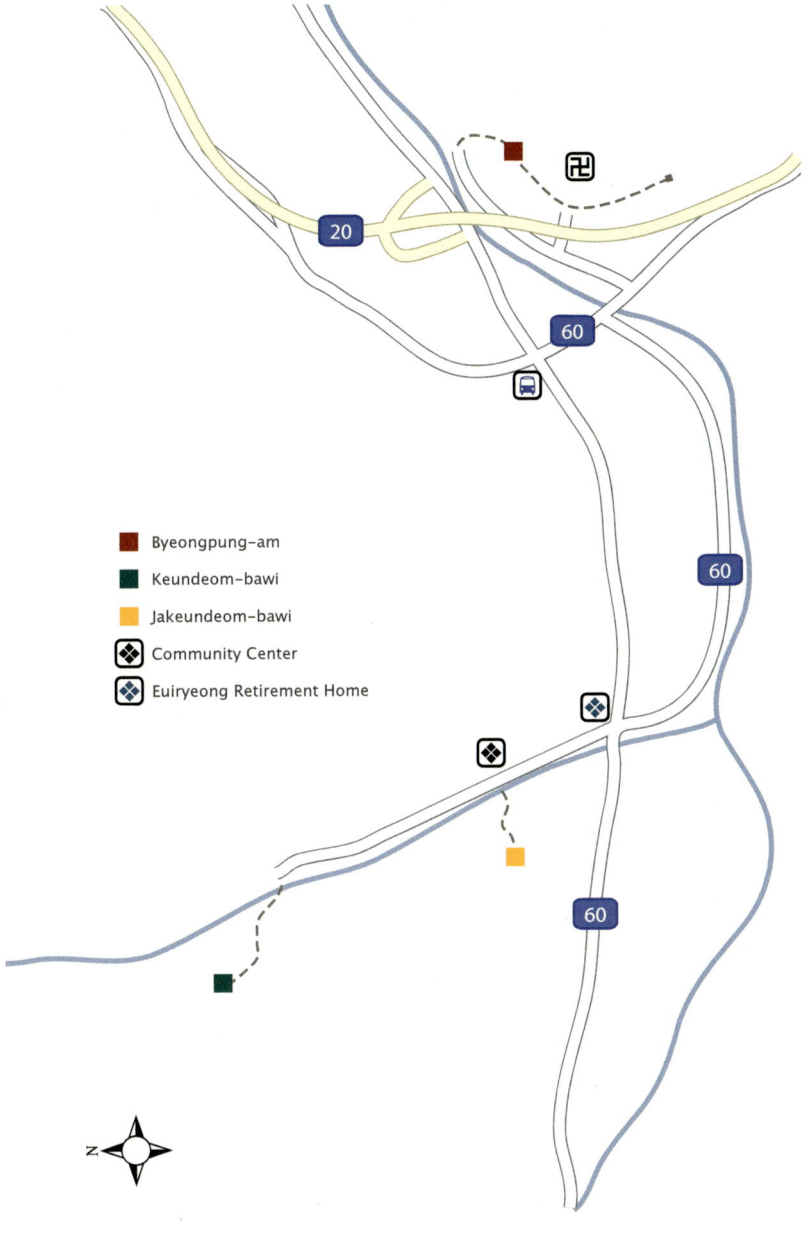

BYEONGPUNG-AM 병풍암 (1 of 2)

Route Name	Grade	Height
Long Leg 롱다리	5.11b	15
Silk Road 실크로드	5.11c	23
Mountain Over Mountain 산넘어산	5.11d	23
Calm Face 조용한얼굴	5.11c	23
Live With A Mask, Die With A Mask 폼생폼사	5.12a	23
Rock Party And Rock 록파티와바위들	5.11b	23
Broadway 신작로	5.10d	20
Still Thinking 아직도생각중	5.11a	18
In Unity There Is Life 뭉치면살고	5.11d	12
In Disunity There Is Death 흩어지면죽는다	5.11c	12
Cha-Cha-Cha All Together 다함께차차차	5.9	15
Here Comes Rookie 떳다초보	5.10a	15
Tears Of Dragon 용의눈물	5.10a	15
Lonely Rambo 외로운람보	5.10b	15
Sinban Mill 신반정미소	5.11a	15
Partner 파트너 1	5.11a	15
Partner 파트너 2	5.11b	15
We Are One 우리는하나	5.11c	15
Fun & Merry 신난다 재미난다	5.10b	12
Live Straight 똑바로살아라	5.11c	12

BYEONGPUNG-AM 병풍암 (2 OF 2)

Route Name	Grade	Height
Searching For A Dream 꿈을찾아서	5.12c	12
Summer 1997	5.11d	12
Songam-sa 송암사	5.10c	20
Proud Country 장한나라	5.10d	20
Twenty Forty 이십사십	5.10d	20
Pride 4874 프라이드 4874	5.10d	20
Swallowtail 호랑나비	5.9	20
Always Be There 늘그곳에	5.10a	20
One Point 한포인트	5.10c	20
Blackish 시커먼스	5.10a	20
Winter Story 겨울이야기	5.10a	20
Brush Killer 브러쉬킬러	5.10a	20
Like Flying Leaf 날으는풀잎처럼	5.8	10
Like Flowing Water 흐르는물처럼	5.9	10
Heart In Agony 고뇌하는마음	5.10a	20
Soaring Wing 비상하는날개짓	5.10a	20
Seeing Me, You Smile 나만보면웃는그대	5.10b	20
What Is The Reason 이유가뭘까	5.10b	17

JAKEUNDEOM-BAWI 작은덤바위

Route Name	Grade	Height
To The Sky In Lying Down 누워서하늘까지	5.12c	17
Beautiful Memory 아름다운추억	5.12a	15
In Coma 혼수상태	5.12b	15
Go Away IMF 가거라 IMF	5.11a	14
Sinban Community Worker 신반공익요원	5.10d	14
One More Time Even If It's Hard 힘들어도다시한번	5.11b	14
Perhaps We Should Go Sinban 우리는아무래도신반으로	5.11a	14
Our Dream Go To Where 우리의꿈은어디까지	5.11b	14
It's Up To You Brother 형님이알아서하이소	5.11a	14
Hyeji Born 탄생혜지	5.11b	16
Rope Die-Hard 로프불패	5.10b	17
Breaking 5.14 가자 5.14	5.10b	18
Pretty Faces 아름다운얼굴들	5.10b	18
Happiness Of The Poor 가난한사람들의행복	5.10d	18
Top Climber 톱클라이머	5.10b	18

KEUNDEOM-BAWI 큰덤바위

Route Name	Grade	Height
Dinosaur Egg 공룡알	5.11b	30
Feigned 무늬만 13	5.11b	30
Untitled Subject 미제	*	30
Greeting 상견례	5.10c	30
Safe Climbing 안전등반	5.10b	30
First Intention 초심	5.10b	30
White Loneliness 흰고독	5.10d	26
Mountain High River Long 산고수장	5.10d	30
Mimicking Iron Man 철인따라하기	5.10b	26
Karma 인연	5.10a	30
Chick 병아리	5.9	30
NEPA	5.9	25
Chameleon 카멜레온	5.10b	28
Brother First 아우먼저	5.10c	28
Jagalchi 자갈치	5.11c	28
Black Loneliness 검은고독	5.12a	28
Be	5.11b	28
Acacia 아카시아	5.11b	28
Pendulum 펜듈럼	5.11b	28
Quick Draw 퀵드로 13	5.11b	28
Gorgeous Movement 화려한무브	5.11b	30
Don't Look At The Other Holds 남의홀드를탐하지마라	5.11b	30
Being One In Flesh & Spirit 일심동체	5.12a	30

WARYONG-SAN, SANGSA-BAWI 와룡산 상사바위

Description
Sangsa-bawi 상사바위 used to be a cliff where people jumped off because of unfulfilled love. Sangsa means to anguish over a lover, so Sangsa-bawi is the place to sit and wait for your lover. It was developed from 1980 to 1990. The crag is divided into five walls and faces southeast with an amazing view of the ocean.

Directions
34.978463N 128.097469E
Jukrim-dong, Sacheon-si 사천시 죽림동

From Jinju Bus Terminal 진주, take a bus heading for Samcheonpo 삼천포. The buses run every ten minutes. From there, take the bus for Namyang-dong 남양동. Walk through the small town and continue to the trailhead, past Namyang Reservoir 남양저수지, for twenty minutes from Namyang-dong Bus Stop. At the trailhead, hike up the Minjae-bong 민재봉 trail for twenty minutes until the trail reaches a fork. Take the trail to the right for ten minutes.

Gear
15 draws, a 60m rope, and a full set of cams.

Safety
Rock falls occasionally and a bit of the crag is chossy. A helmet is recommended.

Additional Comments
There are campsites available by the crag.

SANGSA-BAWI 상사바위 (1 OF 2)

Route Name	Grade	Height
Right Slab 슬랩우	5.10b	20
Slab Bolt 슬랩볼트 A	5.8	20
Slab Bolt 슬랩볼트 C	5.10a	20
Slab Bolt 슬랩볼트 D	5.7	20
Road To Languish 상사길	5.10a	104 (4p)
1p (5.10*|24m) 2p (5.10b|30m) 3p (5.9|20m) 4p (5.8|30m)		
Road To The Peak 정상길	5.7	93 (4p)
1p (5.10*|24m) 2p (5.10*|30m) 3p (5.9|19m) 4p (5.8|20m)		
Maeksan Road 맥산길	5.7	20
Solo Route 단독길	5.8	20
Existing 기존 B	5.10a	25
Existing 기존 A	5.11b	20
Zzazzaroni 짜짜로니	5.9	6

SANGSA-BAWI 상사바위 (2 OF 2)

Route Name	Grade	Height
Headwall Route 정면길	5.10a	45
Route Of Friendship 우정길	5.8	40
1p (5.10b|20m) 2p (5.10c|20m)		
Flying Dragon 비룡 B	5.10b	50 (2p)
1p (5.10b|20m) 2p (5.10*|30m)		
Flying Dragon 비룡 A	5.8	50 (2p)
1p (5.10*|20m) 2p (5.9|30m)		
Road Of Mt. Friendship 산우길	5.10a	10
Maeksan Road 맥산길	5.10b	10
Marcha 마차 D	5.10c	15
Marcha 마차 A	5.11a	15
Marcha 마차 B	5.10c	15
Marcha 마차 C	5.10b	15

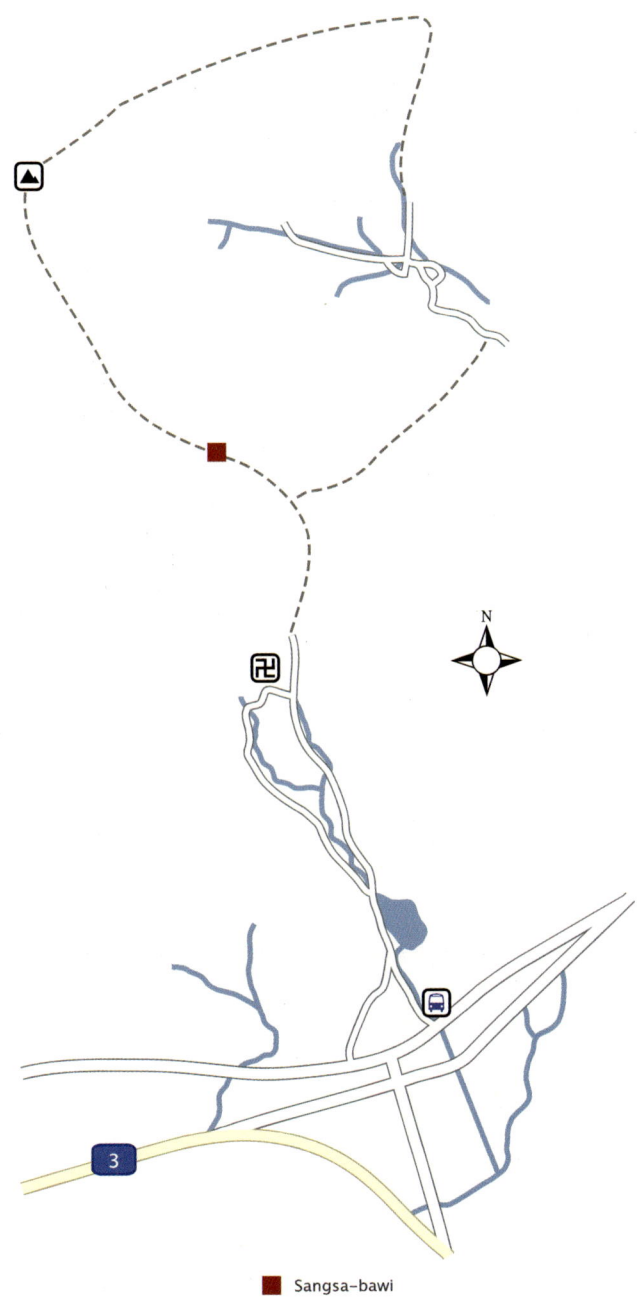

■ Sangsa-bawi

AE-BAWI 애바위

Description
Ae-bawi 애바위 stands tall and overlooks the captivating coastline of the south sea. It was developed in 2001 and is located on Geoje Island. It is granite rock of mostly multi-pitch routes with face climbing on the first pitches and slight overhangs on the second pitches. The longest route is 62m and the crag faces southeast.

Directions
34.809839N 128.657455E
Mangchi-ri, Ilun-myeon, Geoje-si 거제시 일운면 망치리

From Jangseungpo 장승포, take the bus to Youn Dol 윤돌. It will stop at the Mangchi Samgeori 망치 삼거리 three-way intersection, between Gujora Beach 구조라 해수욕장 and Mangchi Beach 망치 해수욕장. From there, take the north road that leads up to the mountain for forty minutes and there will be a sign to your left, located on the top of a hill, that says "황제의길" Hwangjeeuigil. There will also be a small open area for car parking. Look for a white arrow mark in this area, labeled "애바위" Ae-bawi. Following the arrow, hike past the open area and up the trail for fifteen minutes. Ae-bawi will be on the left side of the trail. For an alternate route, exit at Mangchi 망치 Bus Stop, which is three stops after Youn Dol 윤돌. 400m southwest from the bus stop is a pension house called "박하향기" Bakhahyanggi. There is a trail on the south side of the house. Follow this trail for forty minutes up to the crag, which will be on your right side.

Gear
16 draws and a 50m rope.

Safety
The bolts and anchors have been well maintained. However, some of the rock is loose so a helmet is recommended.

Additional Comments
The view from the crag overlooking the ocean is amazing and there are many campsites around the crag that offer a great stay.

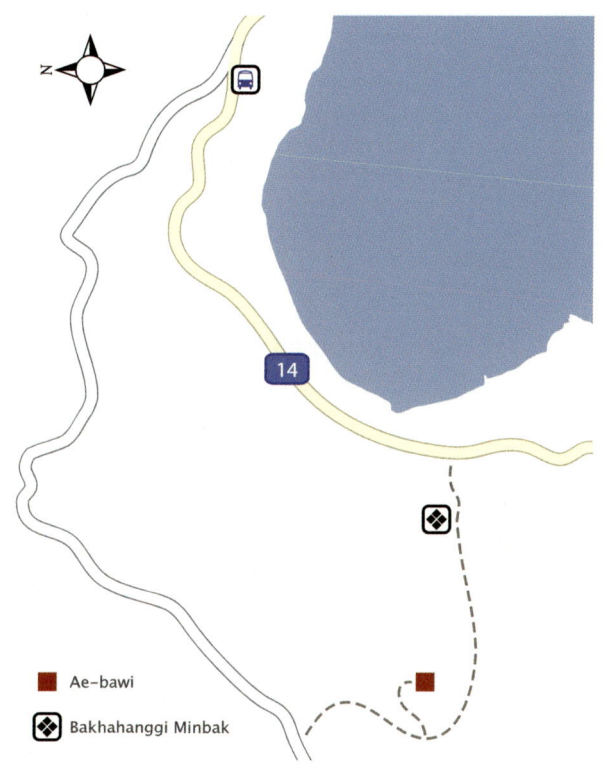

AE-BAWI 애바위 (1 OF 2)

Route Name	Grade	Height
Silver 실버 A	5.9	43 (2p)
1p (5.8|23m) **2p** (5.9|20m)		
Silver 실버 B	5.9	45 (2p)
1p (5.8|25m) **2p** (5.9|20m)		
Mong Dol 몽돌	5.9	47 (2p)
1p (5.9|27m) **2p** (5.8|20m)		
Hot Pepper 땡초	5.11a	50 (2p)
1p (5.11a|30m) **2p** (5.8|20m)		
Sky 하늘	5.11a	50 (2p)
1p (5.11a|30m) **2p** (5.8|20m)		

AE-BAWI 애바위 (2 OF 2)

Route Name	Grade	Height
Friendship 우정	5.11b	50 (2p)
1p (5.11b|30m) **2p** (5.9|20m)		
Alpine 알파인	5.10a	62 (2p)
1p (5.10a|32m) **2p** (5.10a|30m)		
Fine Tree 소나무	5.10c	57 (2p)
1p (5.10c|30m) **2p** (5.10c|27m)		
Thunder & Lightning 천둥과번개	5.12a	44 (2p)
1p (5.10a|22m) **2p** (5.12a|20m)		
Fantasy 환상	5.10d	43 (2p)
1p (5.10b|23m) **2p** (5.10d|20m)		
Mangchi 망치	5.10c	47 (2p)
1p (5.10a|27m) **2p** (5.10c|20m)		

TONGYEONG 통영

Description
Tongyeong is known as the "Naples" of Korea because of its beautiful coastal scenery. All of the climbing here is similar. The granite rock features crack, overhanging, and vertical climbing with holds ranging from small porous pockets to fist-sized jugs. The main crag here is Ssangsa-bawi. There are two other crags that sit next to Ssangsa-bawi.
(**Ssangsa-bawi**) - This granite crag is 50m wide and 80m high with an amazing view of the ocean from the top. There are a total of eight routes. Its name means "Two Snakes", named for the snake-like cracks running up its face.
(**Buchae-bawi**) - It is located 20m southeast (left) of Ssangsa-bawi and is mainly vertical climbing.
(**Mumyeong-am**) - This crag sits 10m east (right) of Ssangsa-bawi. Unlike the other two, this wall also offers slab climbing.

Directions
34.92901706694599N 128.42039108276367E
Tongyeong-si, Gwangdo-myeon, Deokpo-ri 통영시 광도면 덕포리

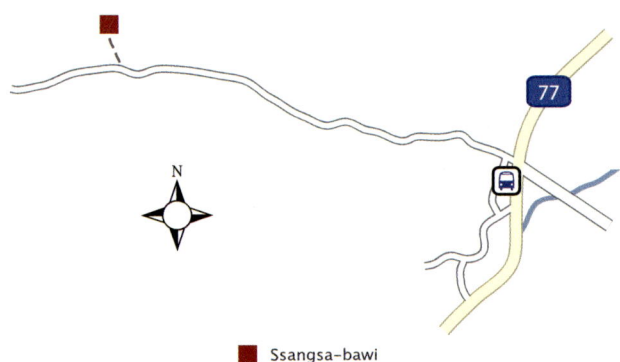

From Tongyeong Bus Terminal, take a bus to Deokpo-ri. The bus runs every hour. Get off at Jeokdeokmaeul Samgeori 적덕마을삼거리. Follow the concrete pavement in the middle of the small village for fifteen minutes, until you reach a small dike on your right. There is a little opening for parking to your left. Mantle up the start of the tiny dike and continue up for five minutes. The crag can be seen from the village.

Gear
15 draws with a 60m rope. There is one trad route available here. Bring a rack of mid-sized cams for it.

Additional Comments
Restrooms are available at the crag. There is a map of the routes leaning against Ssangsa-bawi, at the center of the crag.

SSANGSA-BAWI 쌍사바위 (1 OF 2)

Route Name	Grade	Height
Seokhyeong 석형	5.13c	8
Jaegyeong 재경	5.13b	8
Guibyeom 규범	5.13a	8
Giuk 기욱	5.12d	7
Seongmin 성민	5.13c	8
Mouse 생쥐	5.10a	17
Bull 황소	5.10c	18
Tiger 호랑이	5.10d	18
Rabbit 토끼	5.11a	18
Yong Yong 용용	5.11b	15
Friendship 우정 A	5.10b	25
Friendship 우정 B	5.10a	25
Ssangsa 쌍사	5.11c	23
Camp 5.14	5.11c	22
Cone Head 짱구	5.12b	18
Goat 산양	5.12b	18
Donkey 조랑말	5.12c	18
Monkey 원숭이	5.11c	18
Hen 암닭	5.11b	20
Mutt 똥개	5.10c	18
Oint Oint 꿀꿀	5.10c	18
Boss 왕초	5.10a	20
Trap 함정	5.10a	20
Dasol 다솔 2	5.12a	20
Dasol 다솔	5.10c	20
The Altair & The Vega 견우와직녀	5.11a	20

SSANGSA-BAWI 쌍사바위 (2 OF 2)

Route Name	Grade	Height
Palsong 팔송	5.11d	15
Eagle 독수리	5.10a	22
Crow 까마귀	5.10a	23
First Trip 초행길	5.9	21
Armful 한아름 1	5.9	21
Armful 한아름 2	5.10a	22
Born For Farewell 이별을위한탄생	5.10c	20
Naerincheon 내린천	5.10d	18
National History 국사	5.10d	20
Dilemma 난제	5.11c	20
Byeokpa 벽파	5.12a	14
Diagonal Line 사선	5.11c	14

MUMYEONG-AM 무명암

Route Name	Grade	Height
Daewoo 대우	5.10d	18
Shipbuilding 조선	5.10d	20
Namhae 남해	5.11c	20
Ocean 해양	5.12b	14
Trust 신뢰	5.11c	14

BUCHAE-BAWI 부채바위

Route Name	Grade	Height
Eagle 독수리	5.10a	23
Crow 까마귀	5.10a	23

SOMAEMUL-DO 소매물도해벽

Description
The island Somaemul-do 소매물도 is located in Tongyeong-si Hansan-myeon 통영시한산면, which is on the southern tip of the Korean peninsula. Somaemul-do consists of the main island and a smaller island to the south which can be reached on foot at low tide. The island has been featured on many TV commercials for its spectacular settings. There are two crags on this island, the one on the main island is called Goraegae Sea Cliff 고래개해벽. Also, there are five monoliths scattered around the island. Goraegae Sea Cliff gets sun all day long. This island is great place for a summer holiday climbing trip.

Directions
34.62879832674262N 128.55185687541962E

From Busan, take an intercity bus heading to Tongyeong or Geoje-do. At the passenger boat terminal, get on a ferry bound for Somaemul-do 소매물도. Once you arrive on the island, walk up the main trail that heads south. When the fork splits, take a left to go to Goragae and the Monoliths. The path to the Monoliths is only accessible during low tide. During any other time, you can hire a fisherman to take you there by saying "Chotdae-bawi gabsida", which means "Can you take me to the Monoliths?"

Gear
12 draws, a 50m rope, and a full set of cams.

Safety
A lot of the rock is loose. A helmet is recommended.

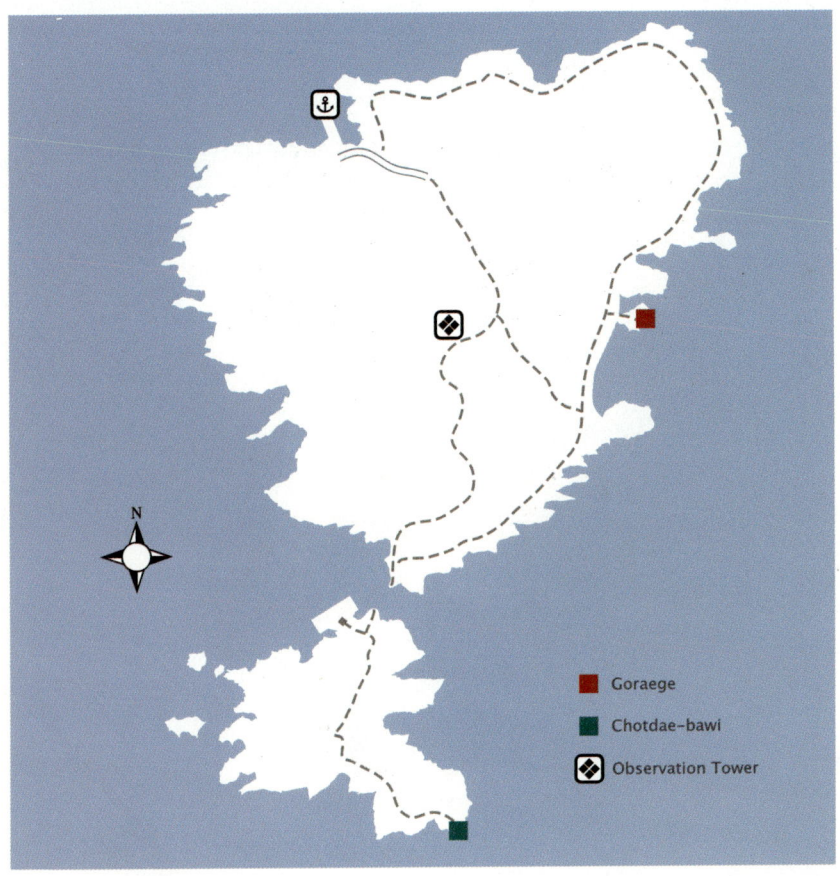

Additional Comments

The routes here are not established routes. There are anchors at the top and a few bolts on the routes, but there are many variations to each route. Goragae can easily be set up for top-rope and may be the best solution for most climbers because of the loose rock and undefined routes. Also, with the changing beta, grades are not set. However, the difficulty will usually be under 5.11a.

Goragae 고래개

Route Name	Grade	Height
Beautiful Days 아름다운날들	5.10a/b	20
Gate To Hell 지옥문	5.9	20
Oedae Route 외대길	*	20
Suri A Route 수리길	*	20
Landscape 풍경길	5.10a/b	20

Chotdae-bawi 촛대바위

Route Name	Grade	Height
Daewoo 대우	5.10d	18
Shipbuilding 조선	5.10d	20
Namhae 남해	5.11c	20
Ocean 해양	5.12b	14
Trust 신뢰	5.11c	14
Eagle 독수리	5.10a	23
Crow 까마귀	5.10a	23

JEOLLANAM-DO

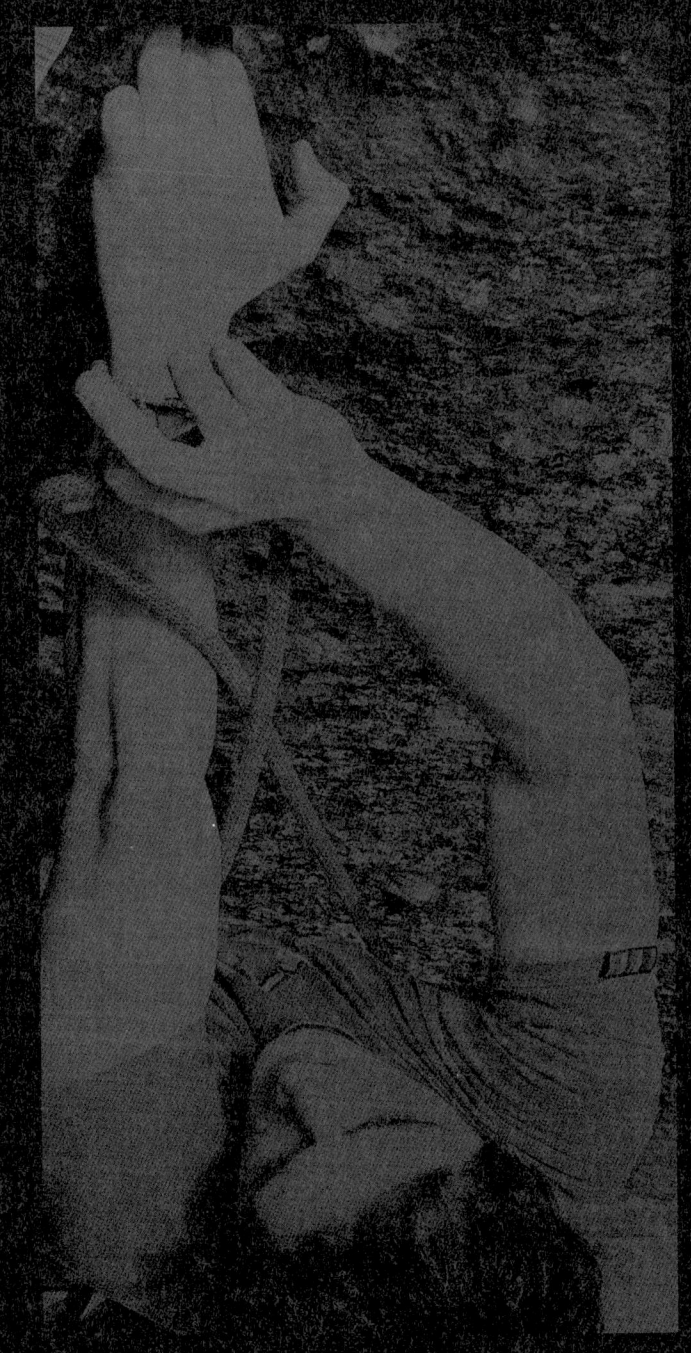

전라남도

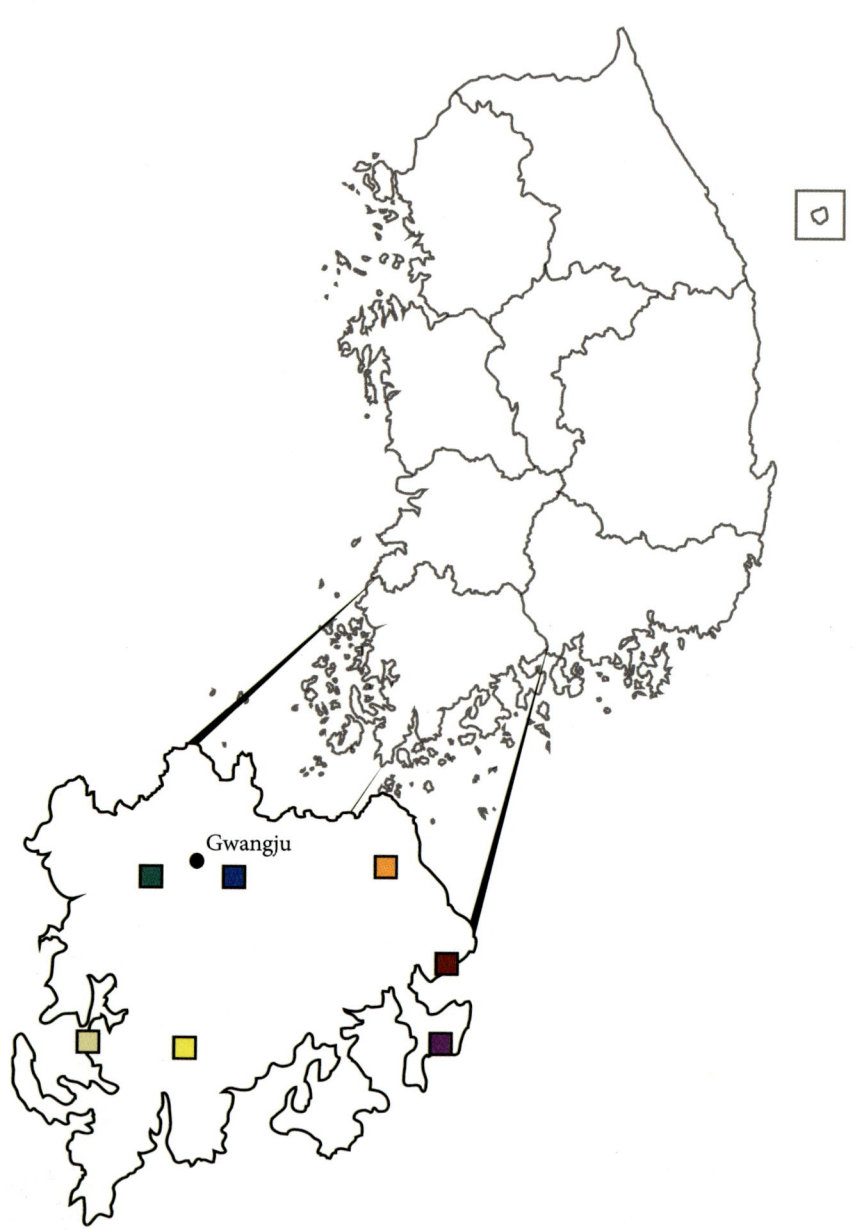

Jeollanam-do Province 전라남도

- Saein-bong
- Seonbi-bong
- Seokmun-san Amjang
- Yongseo Pokpo
- Gaya-san
- Baealdo
- Horang-am
- Siru-bong
- Mae-bong
- Yeonsil-bong
- Koggiri-bawi
- Iron Palms Wall

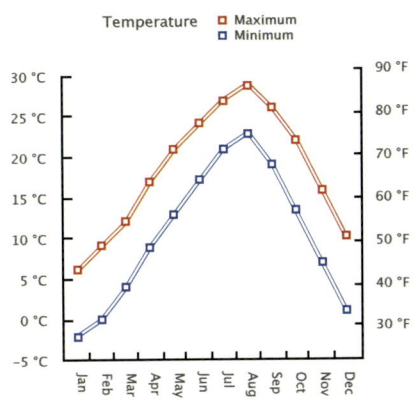

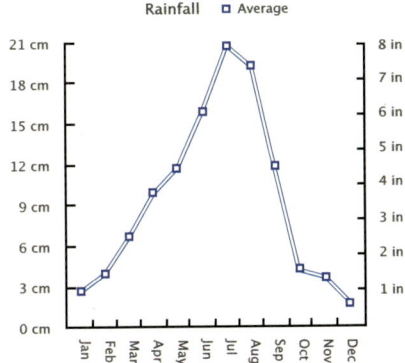

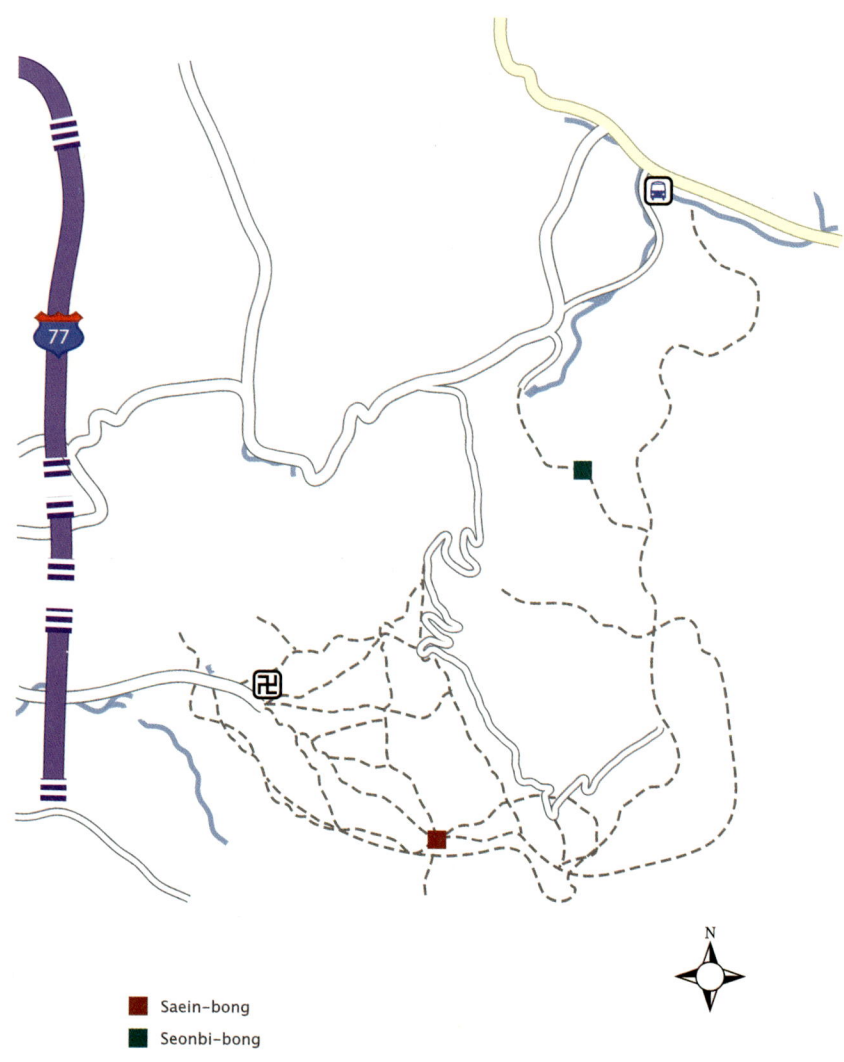

Mudeung-san, Saein-bong 무등산 새인봉

Description
This was one of the first crags developed by Gwangju 광주 local climbers. It is composed of a variety of climbs including face, crack and a few overhanging routes on granite rock. It is located on Mudeung-san 무등산 and offers a vast view of downtown. Saein-bong faces southeast.

Directions
35.11882N 126.984572E
Hakun-dong, Dong-gu, Gwangju 광주 동구 학운동

From downtown Gwangju, take a bus bound for Jeungsim-sa 증심사. At the entrance of Jeungsim-sa 증심사입구, take the trail for Yaksa-am 약사암 and continue on for twenty-five minutes until you reach a fork called "Saein Samgeori 새인삼거리". Take the right trail and continue for twenty minutes. The top of the crag will be on your left next to a fence. To start the routes, you need to rappel down from the top anchors on the trail because there is almost no way to scramble down to the bottom.

Gear
12 draws with a 60m rope.

Safety
Hikers may cause rocks to fall above the crag. A helmet is recommended.

Saein-bong 새인봉

Route Name	Grade	Height
Sunneong Gil 선능길	5.12*	35
Seeking A Partner 파트너구함	5.13*	10
For A Woman 한 여인을 위하여	5.13*	15
Kongjun Gil 공전길	5.9	35
Medical Department Gil 의대길	5.9	35
Direct 다이렉트 1	*	35
Over 오버 2	5.10*	37
Biennale 비엔날레	5.11*	18
Over 오버 3	5.11*	18
Direct 다이렉트 2	5.10*	37
New Sword 신검	*	10
Sirasony 시라소니	*	10
Bright Beginning With A Dull Ending 용두사미	5.11*	15
Vertical Wall 직벽	5.10*	9
Shower 소낙비	5.10*	20

MUDEUNG-SAN, SEONBI-BONG 무등산 선비봉

Description
Developed in 1998, this crag is 40m high and 150m wide. It faces northwest and is a mix of granite and andesite. At this wall, there is vertical, overhanging, and crack climbing. There are a few boulder lines as well in the middle of the wall.

Directions
35.157916N 127.004871E
Geumgok-dong, Buk-gu, Gwangju 광주 북구 금곡동

Take a bus heading for Chunghyo-dong 충효동 and get off at Geumgok-dong 금곡동. At the three-way intersection, turn right towards the ceramic museum and walk down the unpaved road for five minutes. You will reach a fork and there will be a sign for "광일목장" Gwangil Mokjang. Take a left at the fork and continue up the winding cement-paved road for twenty-five minutes. The trailhead for the crag is 20m off the road and can be seen while walking up the road.

Gear
13 draws and a 60m rope.

Additional Comment
Most of the climbs look vertical, but once you get on the routes they reveal themselves as hard, overhanging climbs. The village is known for Mudeung-san Watermelon 무등산수박. So enjoy the famous watermelon afterwards, and shake off all the sweat from your hard climbing.

SEONBI-BONG 선비봉 (1 OF 2)

Route Name	Grade	Height
Thou in My Heart 그대를 내 품 안에	5.13*	27
When Ginger Blossom 생강 꽃 필 무렵	5.13*	26
Sacred Democratic Area 민주성지	5.12b	14
Sprit Of Mystery 신비의 혼	5.11b	10
Agada 아가다	5.10c	10
Sunshine When The Sun Goes Down 저녁노을 질 때면 햇살이	5.11b	20
Carrier 케리어	5.13*	20
March 16th, Rain 3 월16 일 비	5.12c	16
Embracing Scent 향기를 안으면	5.13*	16
One More Step 한 걸음만 더	5.12a	16
Out Of Fun 심심 풀이	*	7
Is That One A Climber? 재! 클라이머 맞아?	*	7
Mango Crag 망고 크랙	*	7
Chun-Hyang's Swing 춘향이 그네	5.13*	13

Photo Courtesy of Lea Gang, 강레아

Seonbi-bong 선비봉 (2 of 2)

Route Name	Grade	Height
Like Flowing River 흐르는 강물처럼	5.12c	14
Pink Love 진달래빛 사랑	5.12a	12
Scenic Of Summer 여름풍경	5.12b	22
This Or That	5.12b	12
Just Try It!	5.12a	12
Road To Seoul 서울 가는 길	5.11a	23
Y Route Y 길	5.10b	19
Honeymoon 신혼 여행	5.13*	34
My Way 마이웨이	5.11c	14
Salty Mackerel on the Rock 돌판위의 간 고등어	5.11c	16
Classroom No.2 in 4th Grade 4 학년 2 반	5.11c	16
Space In City 도시의 여백	5.10a	16
In Sabbatical Leave 휴직 기간에	5.10b	13
Sunflower 해바라기	5.10d	12
Sorry For Saying Good-Bye 떨어지기 아쉬워	5.12c	23
Dolsoi's Love Story 돌쇠의 사랑이야기	5.12c	23
Still Love Is Not Over 아직은 사랑은 끝나지 않았네	5.12c	22

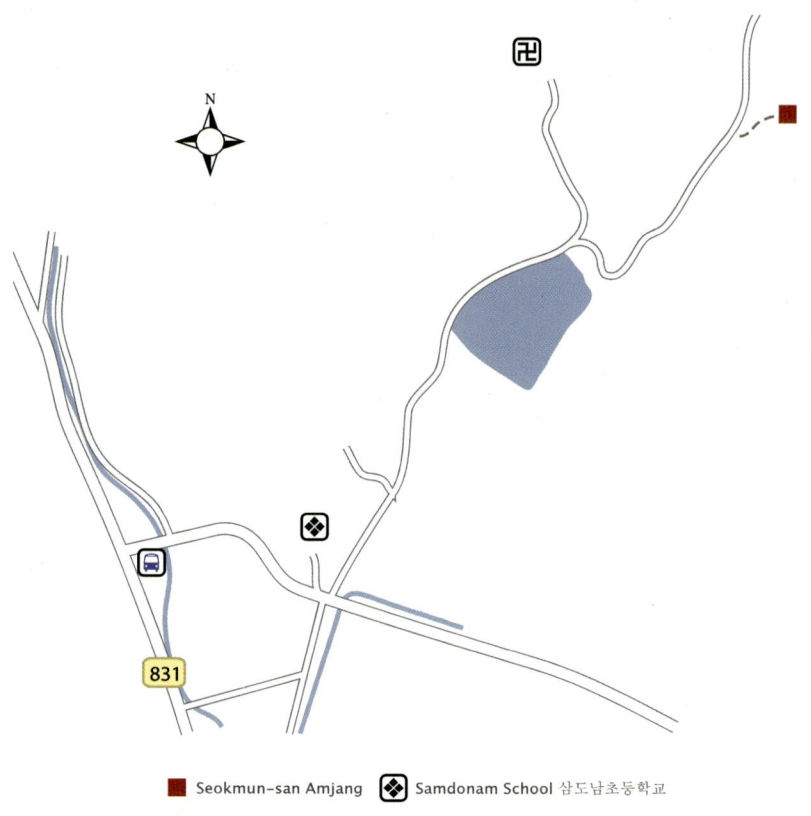

■ Seokmun-san Amjang ◈ Samdonam School 삼도남초등학교

SEOKMUN-SAN AMJANG 석문산 암장

Description
This crag is volcanic rock with mostly moderate face climbs. It faces south.

Directions
35.133887N 126.689025E
Samdo-dong, Gwangsan-gu, Gwangju 광주시 광산구 삼도동

From downtown Gwangju, take a bus heading to Daesansamgeori 대산삼거리. Get off at Samdo 삼도 and walk towards Saenalhakgyo 새날학교, which used to be Samdonam Elementary School 삼도남초등학교. Turn left towards Gwaneumjeong-sa 관음정사 and continue walking on the road until you reach a reservoir. At the end of the reservoir, there is a farm. Take the path to the right, in front of the farm, and walk up the road towards the mountain for ten minutes. The crag will be on your right.

Gear
10 draws and a 50m rope.

Safety
Some of the bolts and anchors appear unsafe. A helmet is recommended.

SEOKMUN-SAN AMJANG 석문산암장

Route Name	Grade	Height
Greeting Rock 인사바위 1	5.10a	8
Greeting Rock 인사바위 2	5.9	9
Greeting Rock 인사바위 3	5.10b	9
Goof-Off 농땡이	5.11a/b	9
Practice 연습 1	*	10
After Meeting 만남이후	5.10c	19
Junior 후배	5.8	19
Novice 초보	5.7	15
Because Of You 너때문에	5.7	14
Wedding March 결혼행진곡	5.11a	19
Stone Orchid 석란	5.10a	18
Bee 벌	5.10a	20
Azalea 진달래	5.11a	9
Practice 연습 2	*	8

YONGSEO POKPO 용서 폭포

Description
Developed from 1995 to 1998, Yongseo Pokpo is sedimentary rock with seventy-four routes offering loads of features. It faces southeast and boasts a beautiful waterfall right in the middle of the crag. The crag is divided into five walls: Yong-bawi 용바위 (upper and lower part); Waterfall left 폭포좌벽; Waterfall right 폭포우벽; Akdong-byeok 악동벽; and Euidae-byeok 의대벽.

Directions
35.1506N 127.469569E
Geumpyeong-ri, Hwangcheon-myeon, Suncheon-si 순천시 황천면 금평리

From Gurye-gu Station 구례구, take a bus bound for Geumpyeong-ri 금평리 to Yongseo Village 용서마을. Buses run every hour or so. It will save time if you take a taxi. However, if there are several of you, it is a pleasant walk that passes through the countryside and villages, which have certain rustic charm. It takes twenty-five minutes on foot from the station. Walk out the station and turn right. Follow the road towards Yongseo Village. Once you arrive at the village, it is only another five minutes to reach the small restaurant called "Yongseo Pokpo Garden 용서폭포가든". Follow the trail behind the restaurant. Ideally, the best way to get to the crag is grab a taxi at Gurye-gu Station and ask the driver to take you to Yongseo Pokpo 용서폭포.

Gear
12 draws and a 60m rope. If attempting the multi-pitch route, bring 17 draws, two 60m ropes, and two full sets of cams.

■ Yongseo Pokpo　◆ Chicken Restaurant & Minbak

Additional Comment
On the ground, by the waterfall, there are good campsites available and a make-shift restroom. Be cautious of rockfall. While developing all the routes, the locals climbers cleaned the waterfall area, which used to be a mess. This place is now a great spot for climbers and vacationers.

Yongseo Pokpo

Yongseo Pokpo 용소 폭포 (1 of 4)

Route Name	Grade	Height
Hornet 말벌	5.11d	33
Ladybug 무당벌레	5.11a	31
Moonlight Sonata 달빛소나타	5.11d	25
Squirrel 다람쥐	5.11c	30
Eurasian Red Squirrel 청설모	5.11a	28
Batman 베트맨	5.10d	30
Aksooni Upper 악순이상	5.11c	27
Akdong Upper 악동상	5.12a	27
Akdoli Upper 악돌이상	5.12a	28
Rambo 람보	5.12b	30
Owl Upper 올빼미 상	5.11b	25
Fairy & Lumberjack 선녀와 나무꾼	5.10c	25
Puppy 강아지	5.8	22
Bore 멧돼지	5.10d	22
Rock Love 바위사랑	5.11a	*
Quince 모과나무	5.10a	20
Stubble Spirit 그루터기혼	5.12a	*
Aksooni Lower 악순이 하	5.10d	20
Yo-Heave-Ho! 으라챠아차!	5.10a	*
Akdong Lower 악동 하	5.10b	22

Yongseo Pokpo 용소 폭포 (2 of 4)

Route Name	Grade	Height
Akdoli Lower 악돌이 하	5.10c	22
Jeildae Route 제일대길	5.10d	*
Juliet 줄리엣	5.10a	22
Owl Lower 올빼미 하	5.10a	22
Fairy 선녀	5.10b	22
Lumberjack 나무꾼	5.9	22
Haejeong 해정 1	5.10a	20
Haejeong 해정 2	5.10a	20
Little Prince 어린왕자	5.10c	20
Youjeong 유정	5.9	20
Peter Pan 피터팬	5.10c	20
Go! Nanga Parbat 가자! 낭가파르밧으로	5.10b	*
Sinbad 신밧드	5.11c	20
My Love Stubble 내사랑 그루터기	5.12a	*
Janggong 장꽁	5.10c	18
Unmarried 독신	5.9	18
Cinderella 신데렐라	5.10a	18
Nolbu 놀부	5.9	8
Heungbu 흥부	5.8	7
Beast 야수 1.5	5.12b	35

Yongseo Pokpo 용소 폭포 (3 of 4)

Route Name	Grade	Height
Bamboo 바자울	A3	50
Start 스타트	5.8	20
Yosemite 요세미테	5.12a	30
Shinbok 신복	5.12b	26
Janghwan 장환	5.12a	26
Mincheol 민철	5.13*	25
Jiyeon 지연	5.11a	14
Haeryong 해룡	5.10b	14
Gyeonghyeon 경헌	5.13*	20
Yonggyeong 용경	5.10c	16
Hyeonran 현란	5.12a	17
Jaeseung 재승	5.12c	17
Tanseong 탄성	5.10c	17
Hongman 홍만	5.11d	13
Hyeonjik 현직	5.10c	12
Woohyeong 우형	5.11d	14
Jeonguk 전국	5.12b	14
Hyeonggil 형길	5.11a	14
Seunghwan 승환	5.11c	14
Hoisan 회산	5.10c	14
Bongju 봉주	5.10b	14

Yongseo Pokpo 용소 폭포 (4 of 4)

Route Name	Grade	Height
Hyeoncheol 현철	5.11b	14
Yongbae 용배	5.10b	13
Yeonggoun 영균	5.11b	13
CUMSAC	5.11d	8
Before Matured 철들기전에	5.10c	9
Hooya Hooya 후야후야	5.10b	11
Son Of Moon 달의아이	5.10c	10
Dream Of Hippocrates & Nightingale 히포크라테스와 나이팅게일을 꿈꾸며	5.10d	24
Star In My Heart 별은 내가슴에	5.9	26
Art Teacher Likes Sugar 미술선생님은 설탕을 좋아합니다	5.12a	26
Fear Of Roosevelt 루즈벨트의 두려움	5.11a	27
Something Happened At 22 22 살에 생긴일	5.10d	27
I Will Rest At The Mountain 나 산에 잠드리오	5.10c	25
(No Name) 무명 1	*	*
(No Name) 무명 2	*	*

GAYA-SAN 가야산

Description
(**Gaya-san Amjang**) - There are around seventy routes scattered along the west side of the mountain, ranging from 5.6 to 5.12. The rock is granite and varies from face climbing to crack lines and overhanging routes. It faces southwest.
(**Bueungi-bawi**) - This granite crag is 18m high and 22m wide. There are only six routes.

Directions
(**Gaya-san Amjang**) - 34.959059N 127.697021E
(**Bueungi-bawi**) - 34.958963N 127.710207E
Ma-dong, Gwangyang-si, Jeollanam-do 전남 광양시 마동

(**Gaya-san Amjang**) - From Gwangyang City Hall 광양시, walk east along the main road for fifteen minutes towards the mountain until you reach Jungma High School 중마고교. On the street by the high school, cross the pedestrian bridge. The trailhead begins here. At the end of the pedestrian bridge, take the lefthand trail and continue up, following the signs that read "적벽" Jeok-byeok. After thirty minutes, you'll reach a wooden staircase with a hand rail. 5m before the top of the stairs, look to the left for a trail. Follow it to reach the crag.

(**Bueungi-bawi**) - From the road, under the pedestrian bridge mentioned above, keep walking east until you reach a tunnel (there is a parking area and a golf course before the tunnel). Walk up to the trail above the tunnel, turn left and continue for ten minutes. You'll be able to see the crag from the approach.

Gear
10 draws and a 50m rope.

Additional Comment
(**Gaya-san Amjang**) - Sometimes people call the crag Byeongpung-am 병풍암, however, there are seven to eight separate crags around Jeok-byeok 적벽 and only one of them is Byeongpung-am. Get everything you need from downtown beforehand.
(**Bueungi-bawi**) - Since the golf course was set up, it is harder to get to the crag. It has not been maintained well.

BUEUNGI-BAWI 부엉이바위

Route Name	Grade	Height
First Love 첫사랑	5.11a	15
Prince 황태자	5.11c	15
Stubble 그루터기	5.11a	14
Excelsior 비상	5.12c	15
Companion 동반자	5.11b	12

GAYA-SAN AMJANG 가야산 암장

Route Name	Grade	Height
Goam 고암 A	5.7	6
Goam 고암 B	5.7	6
Sea Of Clouds 운해	5.8	6
Turtle 거북	5.8	7
Perennial Youth 불로	5.8	7
White Crane 백학	5.9	10
Milchum 밀춤	5.9	10
Deer 사슴	5.10c	9
Crystal Water 옥수	5.7	11
Green Mountain 청산	5.8	10
Perpetuity 영구	5.6	8
Old Pine Tree 노송	5.8	8
Cross Star 십자성	5.10c	9
Dawn 여명	5.10a	10
Freedom 자유	5.9	10
The Creation 개벽	5.10b	10
The Empty Air 허공	5.11a	11
Adventure 모험	5.11a	11
Ordeal 시련	5.10c	11
Challenge 도전	5.10b	10
Courage 용기	5.12a	12
Cooperation 협동	5.11c	12
Escape 탈출	5.11a	8
Hanwool Ga 한울가	5.9	10
Hanwool Na 한울나	5.9	10
Hanwool Da 한울다	5.10a	10
Hanwool Ra 한울라	5.11b	10
Hanwool Ma 한울마	5.11b	10
One Family 한가족	5.10c	9
No Pain, No Gain 고진감래	5.9	9
Noteworthy Progress 괄목상대	5.9	9
Bouldering Course 볼더링코스	Boulder	
No Choice But To Carry On 기호지세	5.10c	10
Life Is Full Of Ups & Downs 새옹지마	5.11b	10
Panic-Stricken 전전긍긍	5.11c	8
Neck-And-Neck 난형난제	5.11c	8
Groping My Way 암중모색	5.10a	8
Deep In The Mountains 첩첩산중	5.10c	10
(No Name) 무명	5.11a	9
Recasting 환골탈퇴	5.10c	9
Blue Thread 청실	5.9	12
Red Thread 홍실	5.10a	12
Stump 그루터기	5.11c	12
Black Pearl 흑진주	5.11b	12
Perfect Beginner 왕초보	5.9	12
Pearl 진주	5.10c	12
Free Of Charge 공짜	5.10b	12
Predestined Relation 천생연분	5.10a	10
Baby 베이비	5.11a	14
Honeymoon 허니문	5.11b	15
Love 러브	5.10d	15
Date 데이트	5.10c	15
Friend 프렌드	5.10b	15
Chinese Alphabet 천자문	5.8	10
Johnny Reb 남부군	5.10b	20
Old Man & The Sea 노인과바다	5.10a	20
Taebaeksanmaek 태백산맥	5.9	20
Mokminsimseo 목민심서	5.9	20
Jirisan 지리산	5.11a	20
Practice 연습 1	5.9	20
Practice 연습 2	5.9	20
Weekend Trip 주말여행	5.8	10
Weekend Hiking 주말산행	5.10a	10
Weekend Love 주말사랑	5.11b	10
Weekend Widow 주말과부	5.11c	7
Fortress 산성	5.9	10
Etiquette 싸가지	5.11a	14
Hiker 산꾼	5.11a	14
Climber 산쟁이	5.11c	14
Alpine Climber 산악인	5.12b	14
Mountaineer 산사나이	5.11a	14
Bandit 산적	5.10c	14

BAEALDO 배알도

Description
Baealdo is located on the opposite side of the beach. All the climbs here are steep and overhanging, requiring power and strength. It faces southeast.

Directions
34.9621N 127.752714E
Mangdeok-ri, Jinwol-ri, Gwangyang-si 광양시 진월면 망덕리

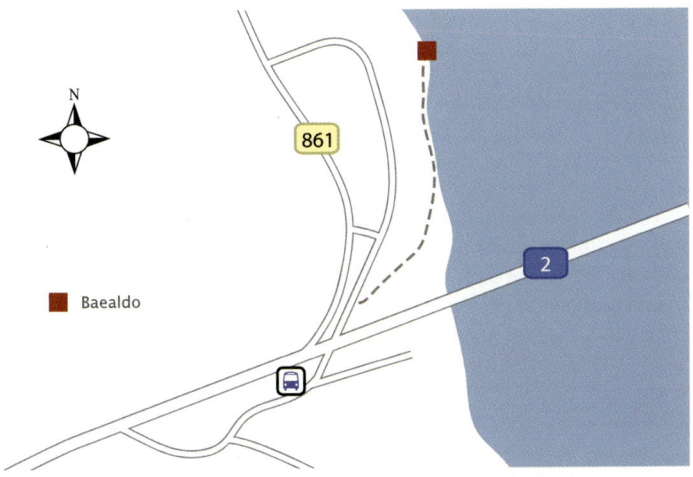

From Gwangyang City 광양, take a bus heading for Baealdo Beach 배알도 and get off at Mangdeok 망덕. At the end of the north bound bridge, walk down to the beach on your left for five minutes.

Gear
8 draws and a 50m rope.

Safety
Most of the anchors are bad and there are rusty bolts on the unkempt wall. The path to the crag is overgrown as well.

BAEALDO 배알도

Route Name	Grade	Height
Alien 이방인	5.10*	14
Stubble 그루터기 B	5.11b	14
Stubble 그루터기 A	5.10c	10
Roly Poly 오뚜기	5.11b	10
Cintamani 여의주	5.12a	14
Brother & Sister Road 남매길	5.11b	8

HORANG-SAN, HORANG-AM 호랑산 호랑암

Description
In 1991, the Yeosu Hyangam Mountain Club started developing Horang-am at Horang-san. It opened to the public in 2004. The crag has fifteen routes with a couple of unfinished projects. It faces southeast on a mix of granite and basalt rock, and offers face and overhung climbing with a scenic view of Yeosu 여수 harbor, the site of Expo 2012.

Directions
34.791004N 127.696495E
Bonggye-dong, Yeosu-si 여수시 봉계동

From downtown Yeosu 여수, take a bus for Dundeok Intersection 둔덕삼거리 or Yeodo Elementary School 여도초등학교. There are two trails to the crag. One option is to take the trail on the right side of the elementary school, passing a survival training area at the foot of the mountain, and hike up for twenty-five minutes until you reach a marker for "신동아아파트 0.8k" Shindonga Apt and "정상 0.7k" Jeongsang. Just 5m before the marker, look for a faint trail on your right. Follow the trail for five minutes. Another option is to walk through the elementary school grounds to the mountain side and turn left at the parking area, passing a small playground, to a path with an apartment complex on your left. Take the main trail, that has a map of the mountain and continue hiking up until the marker mentioned above.

Gear
13 draws and a 60m rope.

Additional Comment
There is one good campsite and a great bivouac site at the base of the crag. At the top of the crag is a great view of the sea and the city.

HORANG-AM 호랑암

Route Name	Grade	Height
Existing 기존 A	5.8	12
Existing 기존 B	5.8	12
Fairway 뱃길	5.7	12
Existing 기존 D	5.8	13
160	5.8	13
Face 페이스	5.8	13
Rain 레인	5.7	12
Cho Oyu 초오유	5.8	18
Bottled Water 생수	5.10b	26
The End & The Beginning 끝과시작 **1p** (5.9|16m) **2p** (5.9|22m)	5.9	38 (2p)
Good-Bye Anna 굿바이안나	5.10b	26
Little Brother 리틀브라더	*	33

WOLCHUL-SAN 월출산

Description
These crags at Wolchul-san 월출산 have been at the forefront of the climbing community in this province and climbers still frequent this beautiful rocky mountain even though a lot of young climbers are flocking to the clip-and-go sport climbing areas.

(Siru-bong) - This crag features primarily slab climbs and crack climbing on granite rock with multi-pitch routes. It faces east.

(Mae-bong) - As the largest crag in Wolchul-san, the crag offers crack and slab climbing on good quality granite. This crag is divided into an upper and lower section. In the middle of the crag, there are some bushes. It faces southeast.

(Yeonsil-bong) - This crag consists of relatively easy routes for training beginners on slab.

Directions
(Siru-bong) - 34.767687N 126.715214E
(Mae-bong) - 34.767351N 126.712832E
(Yeonsil-bong) - 34.766329N 126.714914E
Gaesin-ri, Yeongam-eup, Yeongam-gun 영암군 영암군 개신리

(Siru-bong) - Take a bus that heads for Yeongam 영암 and then transfer to a bus for Wolchul-san 월출산. At the parking lot, walk up the main trail to the temple Cheonhwang-sa 천황사. Facing the temple, take the trail to the left and continue up for twenty minutes until you get close to the pedestrian pass. The crag can be seen as you hike up. It is next to the main trail on your right.

(Mae-bong) - Hike straight up the main trail towards the peak, to the huge rock standing tall near the top. It takes fifteen minutes to get here from Siru-bong 시루봉.

(Yeonsil-bong) - It sits on the left side of Siru-bong and in front of Mae-bong.

Gear
12 draws, a 60m rope, and a full set of cams.

Safety
The bolts and anchors have been replaced on many of the routes. A helmet is still recommended.

Additional Comments
Officially, climbing at this mountain requires a permit. Visit the ranger office to get a permit. There is another crag, called Hyeongje-bong 형제봉, located across from these crags. It can be reached by the trail that branches off to the right at the temple, but is being visited less and less.

Siru-bong 시루봉 (1 of 2)

Route Name	Height
Habeom Route 하범길 1p (*|37m) 2p (*|35m)	71 (2p)
Whale's Back Route 고래등길 1p (*|40m) 2p (*|38m)	78 (2p)
Honeymoon Route 신혼길 1p (*|40m) 2p (*|35m) 3p (*|40m)	115 (3p)
Route For Memories 추모길 1p (*|40m) 2p (*|25m) 3p (*|10m)	75 (3p)
Crack Route 크랙길 1p (*|33m) 2p (*|31m)	64 (2p)
Dawn Route 새벽길	40
Existing 기존 A 1p (*|31m) 2p (*|34m) 3p (*|35m)	100 (3p)
Central Route 중앙길 1p (*|19m) 2p (*|32m) 3p (*|38m)	79 (3p)

Siru-bong 시루봉 (2 of 2)

Route Name	Height
Gongjeon Route 공전길 1p (*|27m) 2p (*|23m) 3p (*|35m)	85 (3p)
Existing 기존 B 1p (*|27m) 2p (*|28m) 3p (*|35m)	90 (3p)

Yeonsil-bong 연실봉

Route Name	Height
Existing 기존 A 1p (*|37m) 2p (*|38m)	75 (2p)
Existing 기 B 1p (*|37m) 2p (*|38m) 3p (*|33m)	108 (3p)
Existing 기존 C 1p (*|22m) 2p (*|32m)	54 (2p)
Under Route 언더길 1p (*|20m) 2p (*|31m)	51 (2p)

Photo Courtesy of Lea Gang, 강레아

MAE-BONG 매봉

Route Name	Grade	Height
Mountain Friend Route 악우길 ABC	*	100 (5p)*
Hana Route 하나길	*	200 (5p)*
Bamboo Fence Route 바자울길	*	200 (5p)*
Snow Ridge Route 설릉길	*	100 (5p)*
Friendship Route 우정길	*	200 (5p)*
Gongjeon Route 공전길	*	200 (5p)*
Route for Memories 추모길	*	200 (5p)*
Medical School Route 의대길	*	100 (3p)*
Competition Route 대회길	5.11a	35

NOTE: At this time, most of the route information for Wolchul-san is not available.

YOUDAL-SAN, KOGGIRI-BAWI 유달산 코끼리바위

Description
This crag is granite rock with 25m high walls that stretch out over 60m. This crag offers moderate face climbs with finger pockets and faces southeast. It is located on the west side of Youdal-san 유달산.

Directions
34.794021N 126.369579E
Jukgyo-dong, Mokpo-si 목포시 죽교동

To access the crag, take a train to Mokpo 목포. From the station, take a bus to Daeban-dong 대반동 and get off at Mokpo Maritime University. Walk north for five minutes, with the sea to your left, until you reach a sharp switchback in the road. Look for a couple of buildings across the road. Hike up the trail that passes through the houses. It will take ten minutes to reach the crag. The crag is visible to the left from the trail.

Gear
7 draws and a 50m rope.

Additional Comments
A route map is available at the base of the crag. Water and food can be bought at the trailhead.

KOGGIRI-BAWI 코끼리바위

Route Name	Grade	Height
First Love 첫사랑	5.10a	11
When The Sun Goes Down 일몰과함께	5.9	14
Along A Waterway 물길따라	5.9	16
Tumbler's Route 오뚝이길	5.10b	17
I Like Abnormal 변태가좋아	5.11c	17
I Hate Abnormal 변태가싫어	5.11c	17
Delight Of Spring 봄의환희	5.10a	17
Stairways Of Heaven 천국의계단	5.10b	18
Legends Of The Fall 가을의전설	5.9	17
Nameless Route 무명길 2	5.10c	16
Cat Claw 고양이발톱	5.10b	17
Wooden Ferry 나무나루 1	5.10b	18
Wooden Ferry 나무나루 2	5.10a	18
Snowstorm 눈보라	5.10b	18
Beautiful Memory 아름다운추억	5.10b	20
Homesick 고향생각	5.11a	19

YOUDAL-SAN, IRON PALMS WALL 유달산 아이언팜스월

Description
This granite crag offers overhanging and vertical climbs of cracks and porous holds. It is divided into an upper and lower level with climbs from easy 5.8 to 5.14's. It faces southeast.

Directions
34.789272N 126.372425E
Jukgyo-dong, Mokpo-si 목포시 죽교동

From the main gate at Mokpo University, walk south on the main road for five minutes. The sea will be on your right. Hike up the trail that leads to Soyojeong 소요정 until you reach a stone staircase that heads to the peak. At the bottom of the staircase, take the lower trail that goes east and there will be a faint trail to your left that leads to the crag.

Gear
10 draws and a 60m rope.

Additional Comments
The crag dries quickly after it rains and is climbable in the winter. During summer, the path is overgrown and it may be difficult to reach the crag.

IRON PALMS WALL 아이언팜스월 (1 OF 2)

Route Name	Grade	Height
Guardian Angel 수호천사	5.12b	15
Stairways Of Heaven 천국의계단	5.11a/b	15
Mokpo Going Backward 뒤로가는목포	5.11b	12
To You, Going Down With The Sunset 석양과함께지는그대들에게	5.11a	12
Fairy & Lumberjack 선녀와나무꾼	5.10a	9
Garden Of Heaven 하늘정원	5.10d	10
First Feeling 첫느낌	5.9	12
Running Fight 추격전	5.12d	12
Mountains, Streams, Plants & Grass 산천초목	5.12b	10
Two Lunge	5.12a	10
Strong Boy	5.13a	15
Fighting Spirit 투혼	5.13b	17
Sola's Dream 솔아의꿈	5.12b/c	21
Story Of You & The Rain 비와당신의이야기	5.11b	22
Aram 아람	5.12d	25
I Am A Legend	5.13d	27
Masterpiece Of J	5.14a/b	28
Graduation Trip 졸업여행 2	5.12b	20

■ Koggiri-bawi   ■ Iron Palms Wall   卍 Mokpo Maritime University

Iron Palms Wall 아이언팜스월 (2 of 2)

Route Name	Grade	Height
Rock Master	5.12c	22
Seungmin~ing 승민~ing	5.11a	20
1-4	5.12b	22
Graduation Trip 졸업여행 1	5.12a	18
Noggang Route 노깡길	5.10c	18
Reason For Being 존재의이유	5.10d	18
Rock Lake 바위호수	5.10c	12
Rock Surgery	5.12b	15
Traverse Instruction 입문트레버스	5.8	9
Thunder Storm	5.12a	9
Love Song 사모곡	5.8	30

JEOLLABUK-DO

전라북도

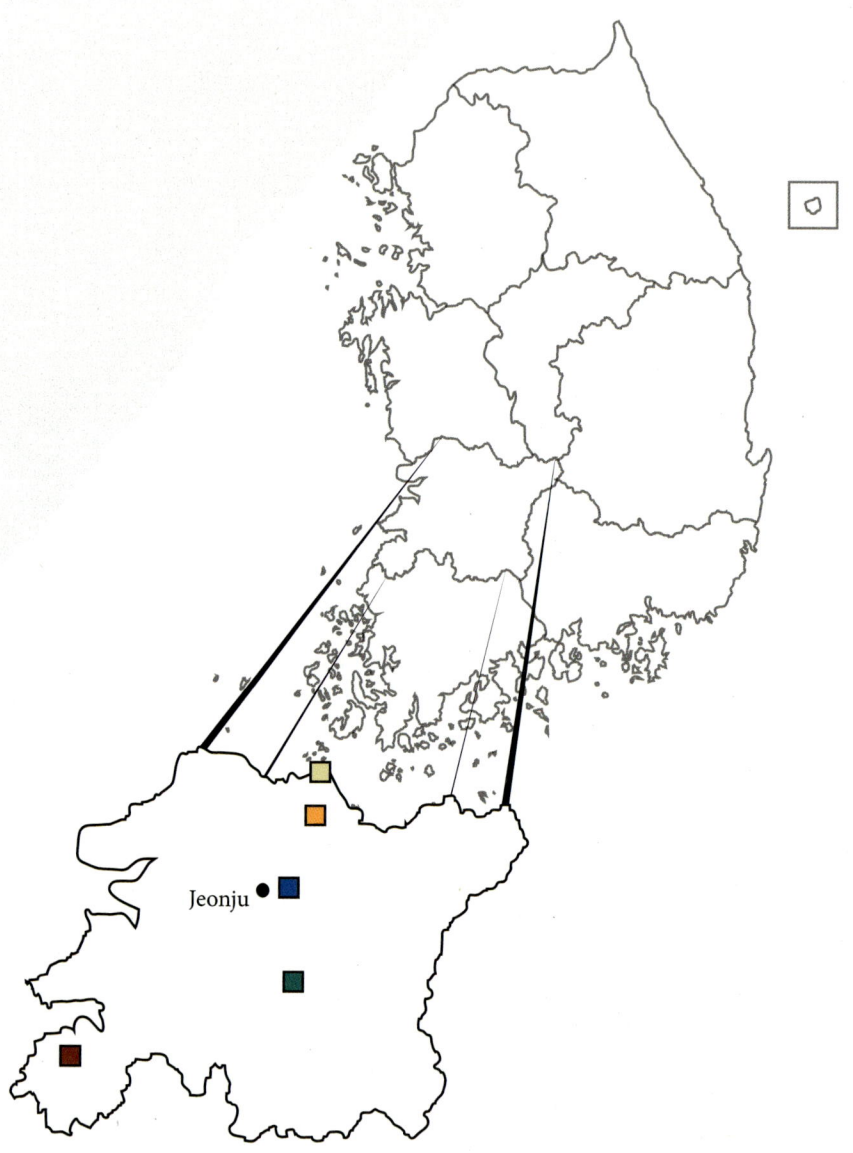

JEOLLABUK-DO PROVINCE 전라북도

- Sin-ri Amjang
- Siru-bawi
- Soksal-bawi, Seonun-san
- Tugu-bawi, Seonun-san
- Mun-bawi, Seonun-san
- Dosol-am, Seonun-san
- Halmae-bawi
- Janggun-bawi
- Samcheon-bawi
- Sinseon-bawi, Daedun-san
- Dwaeji-bawi, Daedun-san
- Chag-bawi, Daedun-san
- Wimungongyeon-bawi, Daedun-san

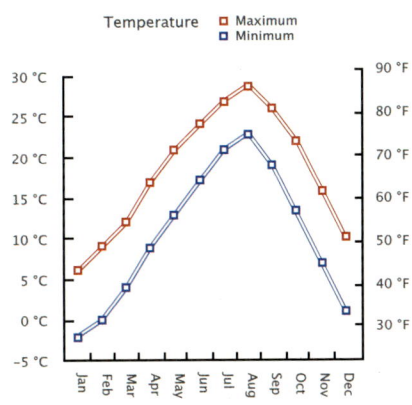

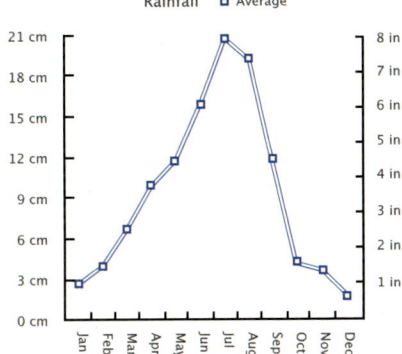

Sin-ri Amjang 신리 암장

Description
This crag consists of vertical and crack climbing. It faces southeast.

Directions
35.768069N 127.21241E
Sin-ri, Sanggwan-myeon, Wanju-gun 완주군 상관면 신리

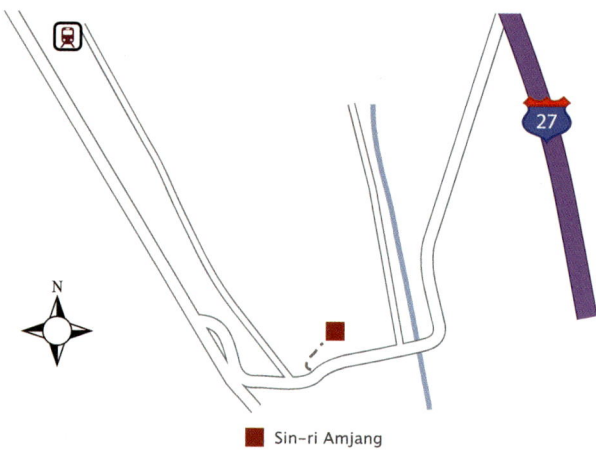

From Jeonju, go to Sinri Station 신리. Take the bridge over the railway and turn left immediately after the bridge. The crag is ten minutes from the station.

Gear
10 draws and a 50m rope.

Safety
Although the crag is located in the city, the ground may be overgrown. The bolts and anchors are not in very good shape.

Sin-ri Amjang 신리 암장 (1 of 2)

Route Name	Grade	Height
Collapse 허탈	5.10d	10
Three Days 삼일	5.10b	12
Rock Palm 바위손	5.10c	15
Bolt Route 볼트길 A	5.10b	15
Bolt Route 볼트길 B	5.10a	17

Sin-ri Amjang 신리 암장 (2 of 2)

Route Name	Grade	Height
Crack 크랙 A	5.9	20
Crack 크랙 B	5.9	20
F	5.10b	20
Artificial 인공	5.11a	20
Opening 개막	5.12a	18

Siru-bawi 시루바위

Description
This crag was developed in 2001. It is sedimentary rock that faces south and has a black stripe on the wall. The climbs start on a steep overhang face and morphs into face climbing after a couple of hard pulls. Most of the routes have lots of pocket holds, side pulls and underclings.

Directions
35.609581N 127.203698E
Hagam-ri, Unam-myeon, Imsil-gun 임실군 운암면 학암리

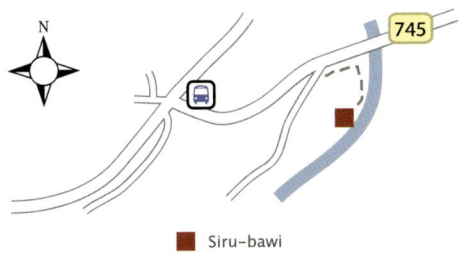

From Jeonju or Wanju, take a bus bound for Unam-myeon 운암면, and get off at Hagam-ri 학암리. From there, walk towards the bridge Singigyo 신기교. Don't cross the bridge. Walk down the side of the bridge to reach the river and then follow it south.

Gear
10 draws and a 50m rope.

Additional Comments
This crag is in the sun all day and is a nice place for family summer outings. Get water and snacks at the village.

Siru-bawi 시루바위 (1 of 2)

Route Name	Grade	Height
3004	5.10b	10
Buyeong 부영	5.11a	12
Shrewd Fellow 뺀질이	5.12b	13
In My Youth, Challenging The Mountains 내청춘산에걸고	5.12a	14
Hidden Pictures 숨은그림	5.12c	14
Autumn Fairy Tale 가을동화	5.12c/d	14
Uh Oh 어어	5.12	14
Subsurface Warfare 수중전	5.12c/d	14
Flush 물빼	5.11a	9

Siru-bawi 시루바위 (2 of 2)

Route Name	Grade	Height
Asymmetrical Line 비대칭라인	5.11b	11
Bbae Bbae Ro 빼빼로	5.11a	11
Hate Me Only 나만미워해	5.11b/c	13
One More Time If You Hate Me 미워도다시한번	5.10b	11
Black Hole 블랙홀	5.10b	11
Dec 19th 12월 19일	5.10c	11
Mason 석수쟁이	5.10c	10

SEONUN-SAN 선운산

Description
Deep in the valley of Seonun-san Provincial Park 선운산, climbers and outdoor enthusiasts alike visit this park frequently. It holds some of the country's best sport climbing. The climbing in Seonun-san is world-class and even the likes of Chris Sharma have tested the overhanging, pock-marked limestone. Developed in the early 90's, this area houses steep test pieces where local hard men battle their egos. With four crags and about two-hundred fifty routes, this place has created the standard of hard climbing in Korea. It is definitely worth a visit that will have you coming back for more. Since this area is within a provincial park, we ask you to be mindful and to respect the temple culture upon your visit.

(*Soksal-bawi*) - Soksal-bawi faces southwest and although the routes are within meters from each other, each one does have its own unique peculiarities. The steep limestone here will entice the warrior within you to observe, focus and commit.

(*Tugu-bawi*) - Within the wind tunnel, aptly named for its hair-swirling, skirt-lifting authority you'll find both sides curving inwards providing constant shade throughout the day. The right side of wall holds the arduous overhung climbs, but the left side is moderate.

(*Mun-bawi*) - While not exactly the same as other crags in this mountain, this crag offers a lot of variety on a vertical face.

(*Dosol-am*) - The routes are scattered around the temple and have been less and less visited by climbers because the monks here are strongly against the climbing in their area. However, there are still great routes to climb further away from the temple where an intricate carving of Buddha is etched on a rock outcropping.

Directions
(*Soksal-bawi*) - 35.485759N 126.571915E
(*Tugu-bawi*) - 35.48634N 126.571662E
(*Mun-bawi*) - 35.486161N 126.57119E
(*Dosol-am*) - 35.480994N 126.563079E
Samin-ri, Asan-myeon, Gochang-gun, Jeonbuk 전북 고창군 아산면 삼인리

(*Soksal-bawi*) - To access the crag, take the main trail from the parking lot until you reach the reservoir. Continue on the main trail to the west and up the steel staircase. Follow the path as it climbs up the hill and you will come to a small fork. You may choose either direction. Soksal-bawi, Tugu-bawi and Mun-bawi adjoin each other.
(*Tugu-bawi*) - Follow the directions for Soksal-bawi, until you reach the fork with a small sign. Veer to the right and then head left at the top of the hill towards the rock formations.
(*Mun-bawi*) - There is a trail at the north and south end of Tugu-bawi that wraps around the crag and leads to Mun-bawi.
(*Dosol-am*) - From Tugu-bawi, take the trail at the bottom of the crag to the west. At the trail intersection, turn left towards the temple. There are routes all around the temple and marked on the rock at the beginning of each route. The approach time will be thirty minutes.

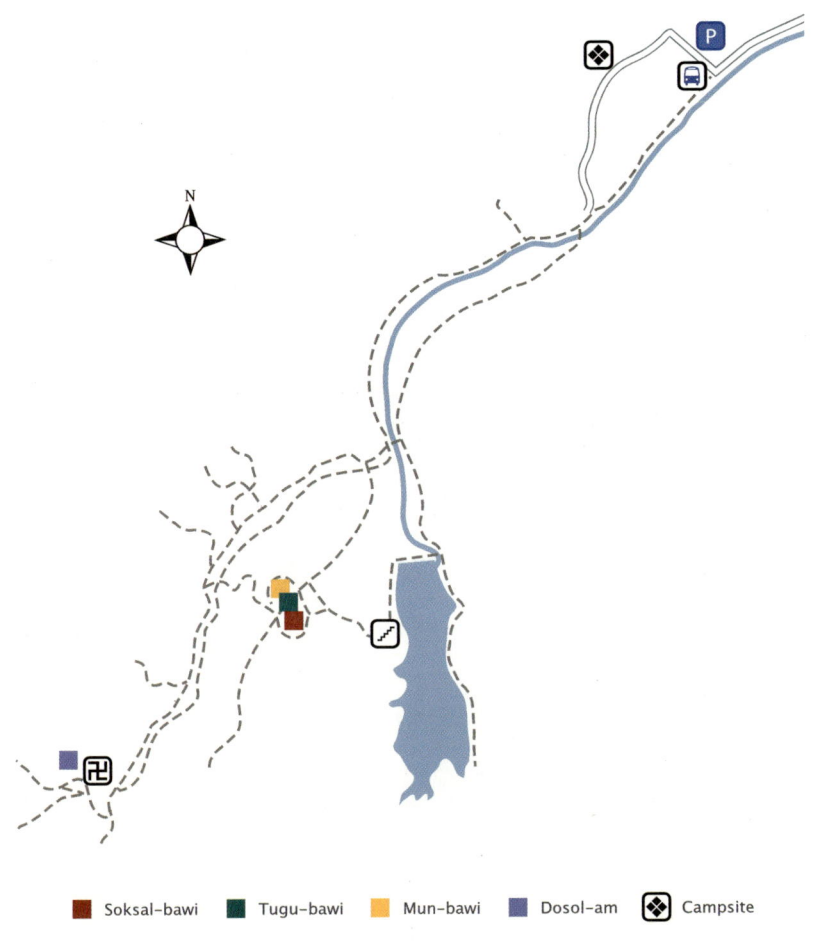

Gear
(***Soksal-bawi, Tugu-bawi, Mun-bawi***) - 12 draws and a 60m rope.
(***Dosol-am***) - 15 draws and a 60m rope.

Additional Comments
Camping is not allowed inside of the park. There is a campsite with a restroom available at the entrance of the park.

SOKSAL-BAWI 속살바위 (1 OF 2)

Route Name	Grade	Height
From Solo To Duet 솔로에서듀엣으로	5.9	7
Baegam 백암 1	5.10c	10
Baegam 백암 2	5.10d	11
Baegam 백암 3	5.10b	13
Like Sunshine Falling On A Stone Wall 돌담에비친햇살같이	5.11d	15
Original Resolution 초심	5.11a	18
Abnormal 변태	5.11c	20
Road For A Lady I Loved 내가사랑한여자를위한길	5.12b	19
Uam's Road 우암길	5.12a	19
Woman's Preliminary 96 여자예선	5.12a	13
Sad Monologue 슬픈독백	5.12b	16
Spent Countless Nights, But Memories Of You Remains 수많은밤을지세웠지 만너의기억은그대로	5.13a	15
Always Stand By You 언제나너의곁에서	5.13a/b	16
Last Woman 마지막여인	5.12d	13
Love Not in Possession 소유하지않는사랑	5.11c	12
Extempore Separation 준비없는이별	5.12c	10
If You Go Away 그대떠나가도	5.12a	10
Baegam 백암 4	5.11b	13
Ojakgyo In Sunshine 햇살속오작교	5.12b	18
Baegam 백암 5	5.11a	16
Man's Preliminary 96 남자예선	5.12b	16
Hard Workers 노력하는사람들	5.12b	17

SOKSAL-BAWI 속살바위 (1 OF 2)

Route Name	Grade	Height
Late Bloomer 늦깍이	5.11d	17
Freshman 새내기	5.11b	17
JCC	5.11a	15
Fantastic Travelers 환상의트레버스	5.13b	12
JCC2	5.11b	17
JCC3	5.11c	21
ZOO	5.12a	20
Puzzle 수수께끼	5.12b	19
KCU	5.12d	20
New Generation 신세대	5.12b	20
April Revolution	5.13b/c	20
Father & Son 준수랑아빠랑	5.13a	20
Somewhere Over The Rainbow 어딘가너머무지 개가	5.12c	22
Good Bye 안녕	5.13b	21
Best Of The Best 베스트오브베스트	5.13b	21
Up Version 업버전	5.13c	21
Won't Forget Precious Memory Of You 잊지않을께소중한너 의기억	5.11c	16
Sometimes It's Hard 때로는힘들지만	5.13a/b	18
Cutting In 꼽살이	5.13b	18
Seonun-san Rambo 선운산람보	5.12d	18
Gomdoli Zoo 곰돌이주	5.13a	15
Buddy 버디	5.13b	15
Speed 스피드	5.13a	18
Story Of The Lady 그여자의이야기	5.12c/d	18
Pampas 팜파스	5.12c	17
Breakfast At Tiffany's 티파니에서아침을	5.12a/b	14

TUGU-BAWI 투구바위

Route Name	Grade	Height
Yeongsan Road 영산길	5.10a	23
Seoknan Road 석난길	5.10b	27
Dream Of Autumn 가을의꿈	5.10d	27
What A Wonderful World 아름다운세상	5.12b	30
J's Life 제이의 인생	5.11b	14
Back Gear 후진기어	5.11b	20
Casanova Of Dosol Mt. 도솔산강쇠	5.12a	20
The End Of Eternity	5.11c	32
New Spring Country 새봄나라	5.11a	23
Searching for Freedom 자유를찾아서 1p (5.10d|22m) 2p (5.12a|20m)	5.12a	42 (2p)
Jack & Jill 별남별여	5.12a	30
Crazy Man 크레이지맨	5.13b	16
Secret Of Pretty Woman 아름다운여인의비밀	5.11c	20
Blossom In The Wind Of Beautiful Flowers 꽃바람속에피어난꽃	5.12c	26
Little By Little 시나브로	5.12b	22
Under Frog 언더개구리	5.12b	20
Ho Waiting 호기다림	5.12d/5.13a	20
Hungry Gang 헝거리강	*	20
Joker 조커	5.14a/b	20
Present 선물	5.13a	20
Sosahyeon 소사현 2	5.12b	18
Sosahyeon 소사현 1	5.12a	18
Worming Up 워밍업	5.11c	12
Art Climbing 아트클라이밍	5.12a	10
Unexplored Chimney 비경의침니	5.10a	10
Easy Route 쉬운길	5.10c	10
More Easy Route 더쉬운길	5.13a	10
Sorrow Of Ssang-bawi Bear 쌍바위곰의슬픔	5.12a	20
Sand Wall 샌드월	5.13a	20
Dance Of Azalea 진달래탈춤	5.13b	20
(No Name) 미상	*	20
Automatic 오토매틱	5.14a	20
Winter Rambo 겨울람보	5.13d	21
Morning Sunshine 아침햇살	5.13c	16
Kim You 김유	5.12b	13

TUGU-BAWI 투구바위 (2 OF 2)

Route Name	Grade	Height
Kim You 김유	5.12b	13
Vanted 밴티드	5.12d	12
Snow Orchid 설난	*	10
One Summer Night 한여름밤	*	10
Power Power 파워파워	5.14b/c	10
Under Wall 언더월	5.13b/c	10
Monthly Renting Room 월셋방	5.10c	11
Energetic Kid 힘돌이	5.12b/c	10
Wearing Dark Lipstick 립스틱짙게바르고	5.11a	9
Miran Road 미란길 2	5.7	7
Miran Road 미란길 3	5.8	7
Miran Road 미린길 4	5.8	7
My Dog Day Afternoon 개같은나의오후	5.11b	10
Renounce The Filthy World 더러운세상을버리고	5.11a	8
Aquamarine Country 물빛나라	5.11a	8
Pamir 파미르	5.11b	10
Yountag Road 윤택길	5.11a	*
Jungneung & Seonwoo Road 중능과선우길	5.11a	12
Legend Of Autumn 가을의 전설	5.11a	10
Just Walked 그냥걸었어	5.12a	9
Seokgyeongmin's Guest 석경민손님	5.10b	11

MUN-BAWI 문바위 (1 OF 2)

	Grade	Height
Sad Reason 슬픈사연	5.8	10
Beautiful Reminiscence 아름다운추억	5.7	10
Between Truth & Hypocrisy 진실과위선의사이	5.9	10
Blossom In The Snow 눈속에핀꽃	5.7	12
Eundeok Road 은덕길	*	12

MUN-BAWI 문바위 (2 OF 2)

Route Name	Grade	Height
Asphalt 아스팔트	5.8	11
Adieu 아듀	5.9	12
Happy Boss Day 해피보스데이	5.10a	19
Shower 소나기	5.10d	13
Period 마침표	5.11b	23
Thou Become Bird 그대새가되어	5.10d	25
Borken Gimbap 터진김밥	5.11a	19
Scorching Sun 땡볕	5.10a	22
Rock Hand 바위손	5.10b	22
Liaison Office 연락사무소	5.10d	15

DOSOL-AM 도솔암 (1 OF 4)

Route Name	Grade	Height
Winter Vagabond 겨울나그네	5.11b	18
Road For A Girl 소녀를위한길	5.11a	18
Ilyeon's Road 일연길	5.10b	18
Mountain Friend 악우	5.10b	18
Camellia 동백꽃	5.10b	18
Fate 운명	5.11b	18
Exodus of Chaos 카오스탈증	5.11a	18
Two Sex 투섹스	5.10c	22
Sex 섹스	5.10c	22
Little Prince 어린왕자 1	*	24
Little Prince 어린왕자 2	5.13a	24
The Sorrow Of Young Werther 젊은베르테르의슬픔	*	*
Handeung Road 한등길 1	5.11c	20
Handeung Road 한등길 2	5.12*	20
Passionate Rose's Evening 정렬의로우즈이브닝	5.12d	17
Miran's Road 미란길	5.9	9
Gang's Vine & Kim's Moss 강녕쿨과김이끼	5.11a	10
Light Up, Ilyeon 일연아불밝혀라	5.11d	10
Tears That I Want To Give Away 주고싶은눈물	5.11d	10

Route Name	Grade	Height
Merry Christmas 메리크리스마스	5.10a	9
Taehyeon's Road 태현길	5.10a	9
Road For Lady 여자를위한길	5.11a	5
The Woman Who I Dumped 내가버린여자	5.10a	5
Tico 티코	*	10
For The Future 내일을향하여	5.11c	10
Even It's Windy 바람은불어도	5.11b	10
Rock Group 돌무리 3	5.11a	10
Rock Group 돌무리 2	5.11a	10
Rock Group 돌무리 1	5.12a	10
Doggotag Heeyoun 독고탁희윤	5.11a	10
Papa 아비 1	5.10a	7
Taejin's Road 태진길	5.10a	7
Indiscreet Time 철부지시절	5.10b	8
Bouldering 볼더링 1	5.10a	7
Bouldering 볼더링 2	5.10a	7
Bouldering 볼더링 3	5.10a	7
Seoul, Gwangju & Turn 서울광주찍고턴	5.10a	7
Seoul, Busan & Turn 서울부산찍고턴	5.10a	7
Sorrow Of Rock 바위의슬픔	5.11a	10
Stallion Lady 종마부인	5.10a	10
Cherished Horse Of Lady 애마부인	5.11c	10
Road Of Jongsik's Brother 종식이형길	5.11b	10
Papa 아비 2	5.11a	10
Food Stall 포장마차	5.11c	10
Dongga 동가	5.11b	10
Purse 장지갑	5.11a	10
Heeyoun's Road 희윤길	5.11d	10
Rock & Heeyoun 바위와윤희	5.11b	10
Brother Gang's Road 강형길	5.11a	9
108 Torments Of Mankind 백팔번뇌	5.12a	25

Route Name	Grade	Height
On To You 너에게도	5.12d	25
Man's Final 96 남자결승	5.13b	25
Excelsior 저높은곳을향해	5.12c	15
Beatles 비틀즈	5.12b	30
Seungjae's Road 승재길	5.12b	30
Gyeongo's Road 경오길	5.10b	25
Gyeonghee & Jinhee 경희와진희	5.11a	25
Chohee 초희	5.11a	25
Virus 바이러스 2	5.11d	12
Virus 바이러스 1	5.12b	12
Moonlight Sonata 달빛소나타	5.11a	30
EM	5.11a	20
Jungbong Road 중봉길	5.12b	20
Super Mario 슈퍼마리오	*	25
Dream 꿈	*	25
Our Star 2 우리별	5.13b	20
Our Star 1 우리별	5.13c	20
Will Fall In Love 사랑하리라	5.12d	20
I Don't Like You 난네가싫어	5.13a	20
I Like You 난네가좋아	5.12b	18
Seokei Road 석이길	5.10a	8
(No Name) 미상	*	25
Jump 점프	5.12b	18
Beauty & Beast 미녀와야수	5.13*	25
Piece Of Cake 그림의떡	5.10c	10
Free Zone 자유공간	5.10b	12
Hibernating Stage 월동기	5.10b	12
Wang Wang 왕왕	5.10a	10
Tree Frog In A Pond 한우물의청개구리	5.9	10
Mosquito 모기	5.10a	12
One Pond 한우물	5.10a	12
Pastoral Song 목가 2	5.11a	10
Pastoral Song 목가 1	5.10a	10
Suwon 수원 1	5.11a	9
Suwon 수원 2	5.12a	9

Dosol-am 도솔암 (4 OF 4)

Route Name	Grade	Height
Suwon 수원 3	5.12a	9
Suwon 수원 4	*	9
Turned The Half Round Of The Earth To Meet You 너를만나기위해지구를반바퀴돌아왔다	5.13a	9
One String 한줄	5.10a	13
First Greeting 첫대면	5.11b	25
Silver Fox 은여우	5.10a	20
Assistant 도우미	5.10d	13
Expo 엑스포 93	5.11a	13
Dreamer 꿈돌이	5.12a	13
Hee 희	5.11a	11
Seon 선	5.11a	7
Clove Hitch Knot 까베스통	5.11a	8
Side Thinking 모로생각	5.10a	20
MiMi 미미	*	*
Cheolsu 철수	5.12a	*

HALMAE-BAWI 할매바위

Description
This crag was developed between 1994 and 1998. Halmae-bawi is 22m high and has twenty-five routes. It is made of limestone rock with many pockets and jugs on the face and some overhanging rock.

Directions
35.478967N 126.618419E
Gyeosan-ri, Asan-myeon, Gochang-gun 고창군 아산면 계산리

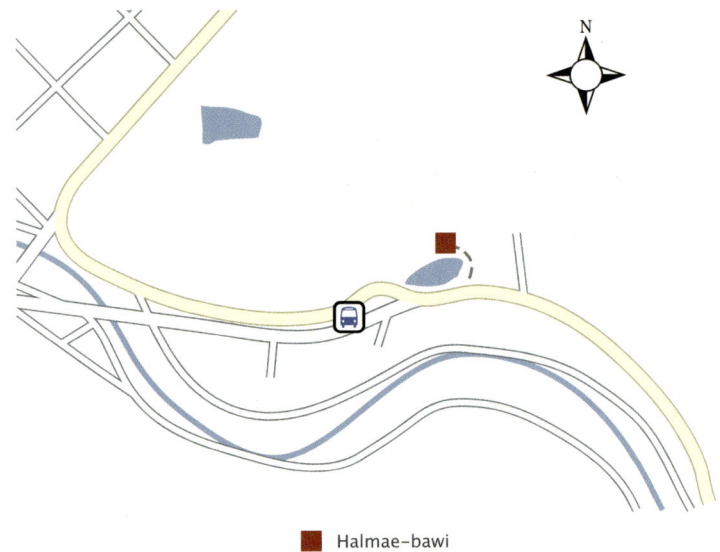

Halmae-bawi

From either Gochang 고창 or Seonun-san Bus Terminal 선운산, take a bus heading to Byeonam Intersection 병암교차로. Walk along the pond by the rice fields to the crag. It will take five minutes from the bus stop and the crag can be clearly seen from the road.

Gear
10 draws and a 60m rope.

Additional Comments
This crag was closed for a while because of issues between climbers and the land owner. Be mindful to respect the locals and leave no trace.

Halmae-bawi 할매바위 (1 of 2)

Route Name	Grade	Height
Excursion 나들이	5.9	12
Expert 전문가	5.10a	12
Forfeit 범칙금	5.10b	18
Wangpho 왕포	5.10a	12
Seokpho 석포	5.10d	12
Salty Road 곰소길	5.10c	22
Wand 뽠트 94	5.11a	22
Ladder 사다리	5.12a	13
Snake & Rat 꽃뱀과사마귀	5.12b	13
Red Land	5.11a	12
Arirang Grandmother 아리랑할머니	5.10b	12
Iron Ash Tree 쇠물프레	5.11c	8
Orcher Color 황토빛	5.12c	8

Halmae-bawi 할매바위 (2 of 2)

Route Name	Grade	Height
Wand 뽠트 19	5.11c	8
Samgok 삼곡	5.11a	7
Chinese Scopes Owl 소쩍새	5.11a	8
Isragi 이스라지	5.11b	13
Sir Baby 애기나리	5.11a	13
Shriek 비명	5.10d	13
Big Spider 왕거미	5.10d	13
Big Spider 왕거미 2	5.10c	12
Finishing 마무리	5.11c	15
Making Sweetheart 애인만들기	5.11a	20
Marriage Story 결혼이야기	5.10c	20
Honeymoon 허니문	5.11b	20

BUAN, JANGGUN-BAWI 부안 장군바위

Description
This crag was developed in 2000 and is armed with the most 5.14 routes in Korea. It is mostly steep, overhanging granite and faces southwest.

Directions
35.693169N 126.633954E
Seoksang-ri, Haseo-myeon, Buan-gun 부안 하서면 석상리

From Gimjae 김제, take a bus bound for Buan 부안 and then transfer to a bus heading to Seoksang-ri 석상리. Get off at Yongwamaeul 용와마을 and walk towards Yeongeun-sa 영은사 for ten minutes. Follow the trail along the temple grounds for another ten minutes. The crag will be on your right.

Gear
15 draws and a 60m rope. Most of the overhanging routes have permanent draws in place.

Additional Comments
Many of the routes here are still projects and require a lot of strength. There are good campsites available around the temple.

JANGGUN-BAWI 장군바위 (1 OF 2)

Route Name	Grade	Height
I Don't Know 난몰라	5.12a	9
Mother 엄마	5.11b	9
Terrifying 10m 공포의 10m	5.11b	10
True Friend 의벗	5.10a	16
Dinosaur Egg 공룡알	5.12d	27
Yosemite 요세미티	5.13c	28
Jewel 쥬우얼	5.14*	28
St. Peter 베드로	5.14*	28
Start 시발	5.13c	28
Shock Troops 돌격대	5.14*	25
Troubleshooter 해결사	5.14*	25
Freedom 자유 2000	5.14*	32
Rerun 재연	*	27
Dyno 다이노	5.13c	25
Black Hole 블랙홀	5.14*	24
Go 5.14	5.14*	26
Bomb Crack 폭탄맞은크랙	5.13c	25

JANGGUN-BAWI 장군바위 (2 OF 2)

Route Name	Grade	Height
Cobra Twist 코브라트위스트	5.13a	20
Doll Baby 이쁜이	5.12c	17
Yulmok 율목	5.12b	17
Wooden Haken 우드하켄	5.12a/b	14
Incheon 미추홀	5.11c	12
Obstinacy 무대포	5.12a	15
Blackmail 공갈	5.11a	12
Untitled 무제	5.11b	12
Yeongsimi 영심이	5.11c	12
KG	5.10b	12

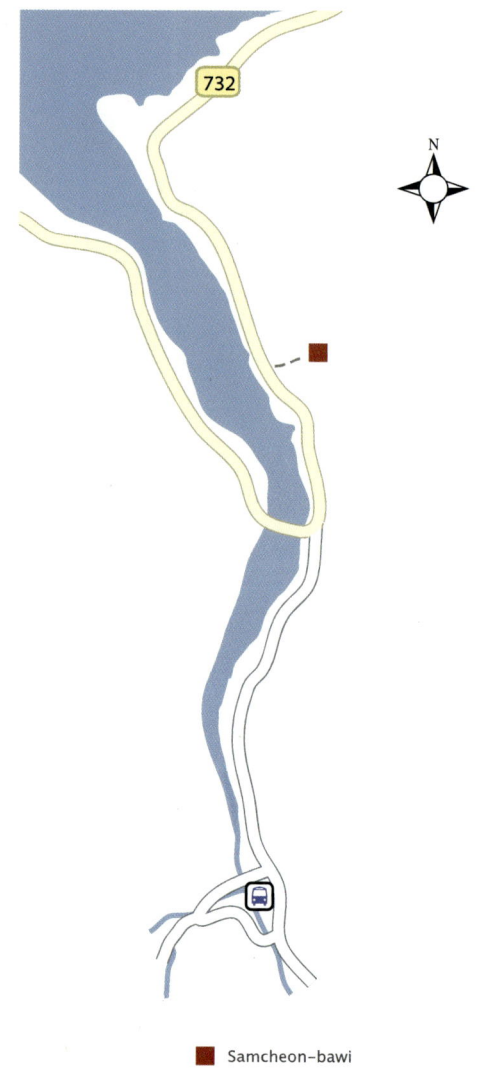

Samcheon-bawi

SAMCHEON-BAWI 삼천바위 (1 OF 2)

Route Name	Grade	Height
Hope 희망	5.10b	13
Condition 상태 1	5.10b	12
Seeing Off Milky Way 은하수를보내고	5.10c	13
The Ten Commandments 십계명	5.9	12
Condition 상태 2	5.9	13

Samcheon-bawi 삼천바위

Description
This crag lies at the foot of the mountain that is close to the road. It faces every direction. Samcheon-bawi has huge overhanging climbs on the north and south side. On the east side, the routes are relatively moderate with jugs and pockets.

Directions
35.978805N 127.284036E
Daea-ri, Dongsang-myeon, Wanju-gun 완주군 동상면 대아리

From Wanju 완주, take a bus to Daesumokwon 대아수목원. Get off at Daesamgeori 대아삼거리, next to the bridge Daeagyo 대아교. From there, walk back 500m to where the bus came from. Look for a small restaurant sign "만골" Mangol. With the lake to your left, there will be a trail to the right that leads to Samcheon-bawi.

Gear
10 draws and a 50m rope.

Additional Comments
There are no stores or restaurants so get everything in town before getting on the bus.

Samcheon-bawi 삼천바위 (2 of 2)

Route Name	Grade	Height
Spirit Of Samcheon 삼천의혼 1	5.10*	10
Spirit Of Samcheon 삼천의혼 2	5.10*	8
90 CC	5.11a	10
Is Today The Day? 오늘만 날이가 3	5.12a	10
Tarzan 타잔	5.12c	11
Outsider 아웃사이더	5.13c	12
Hangawi 한가위	5.13b	12
Candle Light 촛불	5.14*	14
Incredible King	5.14*	15
Once Upon A Time 옛날옛적에	5.14a	15
Legend 전설	5.14*	14
Three Thousand People 삼천명	5.13a	14
Last 라스트	5.12b/c	13
Is Today The Day? 오늘만 날이가 2	5.11a	8
Is Today The Day? 오늘만 날이가 1	5.10d	11
Ugly Duckling 미운오리새끼	5.13b	10
When Going To High Mountain 고산에가면	5.13c	10
Dream TN Tower	5.12d	13

Daedun-san 대둔산

Description
Daedun-san 대둔산 is one of the most scenic provincial parks in Jeollabok-do. Within it exists many crags. This is a very rewarding place to climb. However, as of publication, hikers and climbers are prohibited to use the trail that leads directly to the crag. Wildlife preservation and precaution against falling rocks are the main reasons the trail is closed. This mountain has four major crags located around Yongmun Valley 용문골, featuring everything from sport climbing and aid-climbing, to multi-pitch trad climbing.
(*Sinseon-bawi*) - This crag is a moderate granite slab with many multi-pitch climbs. Most of the routes are well bolted and less run out than other crags, which makes this crag a good place for beginners. It faces southeast.
(*Dwaeji-bawi*) - Most of the climbs are single pitch and offer crimpy climbing. It requires balance and finger strength.
(*Chag-bawi*) - This crag offers the most challenging routes in Yongmungol area. The climbs vary from overhanging to face climbing.
(*Wimungongyeon-bawi*) - This crag offers good face climbing.

Directions
(*Sinseon-bawi*) - 36.127234N 127.326543E
(*Dwaeji-bawi*) - 36.127476N 127.326264E
(*Chag-bawi*) - 36.127182N 127.326200E
(*Wimungongyeon-bawi*) - 36.122927,127.324265
Sanbok-ri, Unju-myeon, Wanju-gun 완주군 운주면 산복리

(*Sinseon-bawi*) - From Daejeon 대전 or Jeonju Intercity Bus Terminal 전주, take a bus bound for Daedun-san 대둔산. Get off at Daedunsan. From there, the crag is reached by either taking the main trail or walking 500m up the road where an off limits sign is located on the side of the road. To access the crag by way of the main trail, walk towards the cable car station for thirty minutes until you reach a fork, before the area where the cable car stops. Take the right hand trail heading to Yongmungol 용문골, that says "off limits". Continue for fifteen minutes to Sinseon-am 신선암, which is a small mountain temple built halfway into a cave. To access the crag by way of the secondary trail, walk past the off-limits sign and hike the trail for forty minutes until you reach Sinseon-bawi. From Sinseon-bawi, the steep trail to the crag is located to the right.
(*Dwaeji-bawi*) - This crag sits slightly to the left of Sinseon-bawi.
(*Chag-bawi*) - This crag is to the right of Sinseon-bawi. It has a dihedral crack that looks like an open book.
(*Wimungongyeon-bawi*) - Facing the temple, take the main trail to the right for ten minutes. It will be on your right, next to the trail.

Gear
(*Sinseon-bawi*) - 10 draws, a 60m rope, and a full set of cams.
(*Dwaeji-bawi*) - 15 draws and a 60m rope.
(*Chag-bawi*) - 11 draws and a 50m rope.
(*Wimungongyeon-bawi*) - 10 draws and a 50m rope.

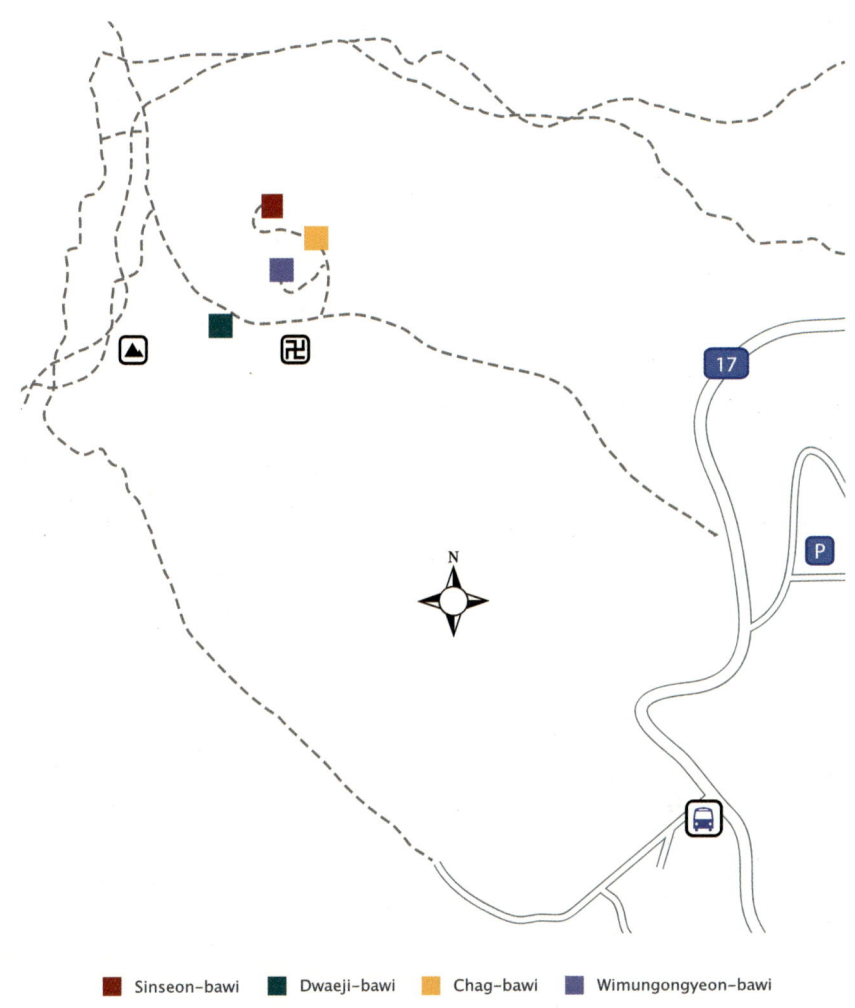

Additional Comments
There are many warning signs all over the mountain that say "Rock climbing is not allowed". The fine is 500,000 KRW. If you choose to climb here, please respect the flora and fauna along the Yongmungol 용문골 trail (the secondary trail). Climbers in Korea look forward to the day that the authorities re-open the trail and create a permit system like those in other National Parks throughout the country.

Daedun-san

Sinseon-Bawi 신선바위

Route Name	Grade	Height
Harmony 화합	5.10b	20
Youth 청춘	5.10a	20
Beginning 시초	5.11a	20
MC Road MC 로드	5.10b	120 (5p)*
Jodo 조도	5.10d	20
Sinseon 신선 A	5.10b	120 (4p)*
Husband & Wife 부부	5.10d	60 (2p)*
Somri 솜리	5.11a	60 (2p)*
Union 연합	5.9	60 (2p)*
Training 교육 A	5.8	30 (2p)*
Training 교육 B	5.8	15

Dwaeji-Bawi 돼지바위

Route Name	Grade	Height
Hoyasan 호아산	5.10a	40 (2p)*
Gongik Road 공익길	5.10c	40
Erogenous Zone 성감대	5.11d	20
Diving Fisher-Girl 비바리	5.11c	20
What Is Happiness? 행복이란?	5.11b	20
Two Become One 두리하나	5.10c	45 (2p)*
Nameless Road 무명길	5.10a	45
Original Resolution 초심	5.10a	45
Road To Gomso 곰소로 가는길	5.9	40
Country Duck 컨츄리덕	5.10b/c	40

Chag-Bawi 책바위

Route Name	Grade	Height
Baekdu 백두	5.10d	40 (2p)*
Hangawi 한가위	5.11b/c	13
Foxhole Circuit 위문공연	5.10b	13
Party 파트너	5.10b/c	13
Date 데이트	5.10d	13
Butt 엉뎅이	5.11a	13
Buttocks 방뎅이	5.11b	13
Bottom 궁뎅이	5.12c	13

Photo Courtesy of Lea Gang, 강레아

Wimungongyeon-bawi 위문공연바위

Route Name	Grade	Height
First Experience 첫경험	5.11c	18
Tap 꼭지	5.11b	18
Frog 개구리	5.10d	70 (3p)*
Portrait In Younger Time 젊은날의 초상	5.11b	18
Girl 가시내	5.13a	15
Y Road Y 로드	5.11a	20
V Crack V 크랙	5.10a	40 (2p)*
Road General 길장군	5.10c	70 (3p)*
One Mountain 한뫼	5.9	15 (2p)*
Thumb 엄지	5.9	15 (2p)*
Short Tree 키작은 나무	5.8	15

*Multi-pitch info is unavailable at this time

Gyeongsangbuk-do

경상북도

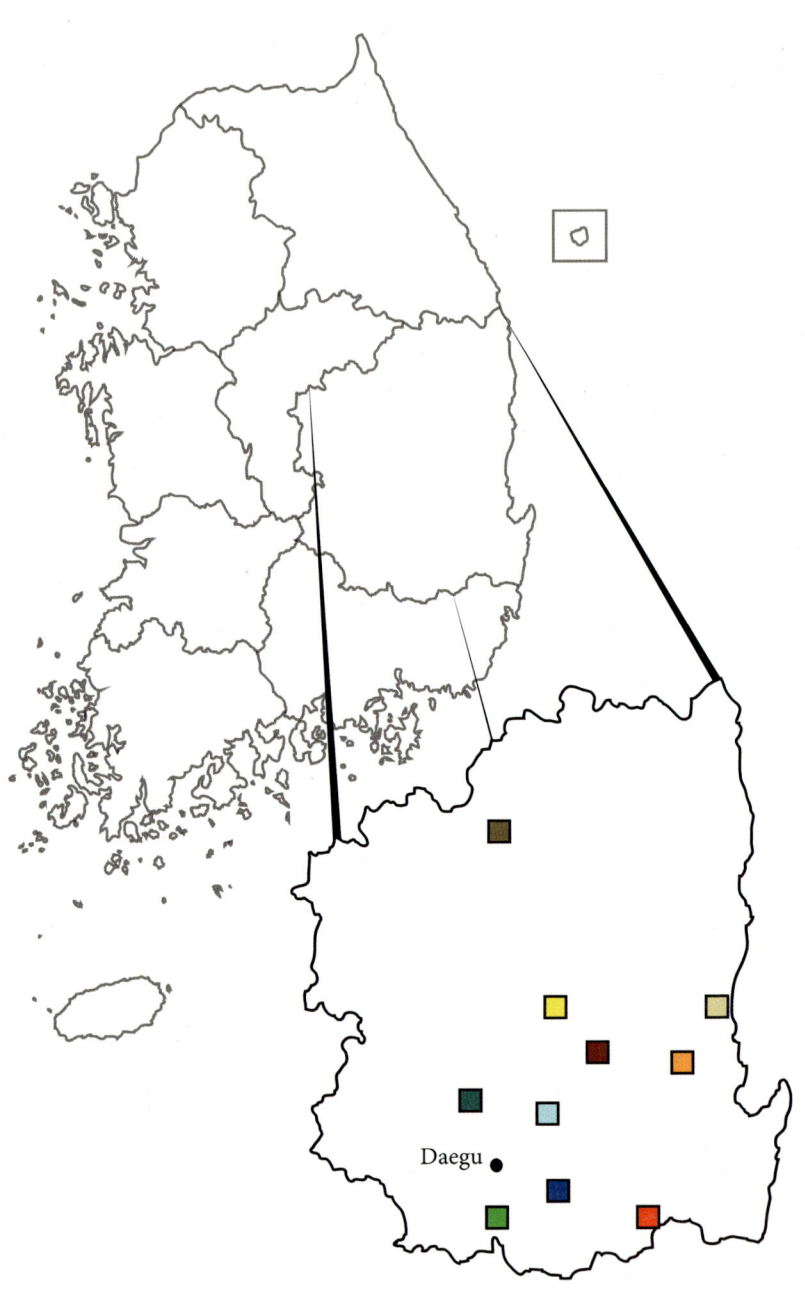

GYEONGSANGBUK-DO PROVINCE 경상북도

- Byeongpung-bawi, Palgong-san
- Bawitgol-amjang, Palgong-san
- Doyak-dae
- Yong-bawi, Do-dong
- Uksugol-amjang, Gyeong-san
- Surideum-bawi, Biseul-san
- Hak-bawi, Youhak-san
- Dungji-bawi, Youhak-san
- Duerin-bawi
- Seoksan-am, Ami-san
- Mujigae-bawi, Geumseong-san
- Jukjang, Hakdam-am
- Gwaneum-am, Naeyeon-san
- Naeyeon-am, Naeyeon-san
- Sinseondae, Naeyeon-san
- Guimyeon-am, Naeyeon-san
- Arirang Boulder, Naeyeon-san
- Seoun-am, Naeyeon-san
- Sangsa-bawi, Hakga-san

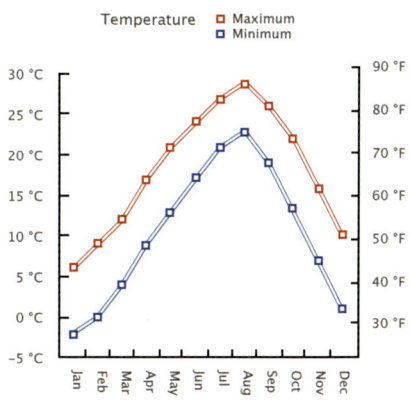

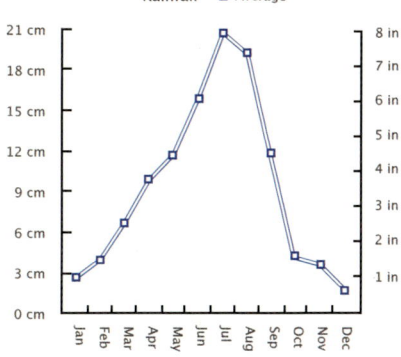

PALGONG-SAN 팔공산

Description
(***Byeongpung-bawi***) - This crag is located close to the top of Palgong Mt. and faces the south. The peak is called Dong-bong 동봉. Byeongpung-bawi 병풍바위 has eleven granite routes, from 20m to 166m long. It was developed between 1969 and 1987. The climbs mostly consist of face and slab climbing.
(***Bawitgol-amjang***) - Bawitgol-amjang is westbound from Donghwa-sa 동화사 and is separated into three smaller walls. The south wall has eleven routes ranging from 12m to 31m long. Among them is an old aid route. The three 5.7 routes on the crag are perfect for beginners to practice leading for the first time. The slab wall is about 80m long and is also great for beginners. The north face has five routes approximately 30m long. They are mainly crack climbs.

Directions
(***Byeongpung-bawi***) - 36.009655N 128.707345E
(***Bawitgol-amjang***) - 35.997139N 128.683119E
Dohak-dong, Dong-gu, Daegu 대구 동구 도학동

(***Byeongpung-bawi***) - From Daegu 대구, take a bus bound for Palgong-san Donghwa-sa 팔공산동화사 and get off at the entrance of Donghwa-sa 동화사입구. Walk east on the road towards Donghwa-sa Temple until you reach the trailhead by the parking area. Hike, for ten minutes, to Budo-am Temple 부도암 and then take the trail to the right to Yangjin-am 양진암, for ten minutes. Take the trail that veers to the right and up to the ridge. The crag is on your left before the ridge. You'll be able to see the crag when you hike up from the last temple.
(***Bawitgol-amjang***) - From Daegu 대구, take a bus bound for Palgong-san Donghwa-sa 팔공산동화사. Get off at the entrance of Donghwa-sa 동화사입구 and then transfer to the bus bound for Sutaegol 수태골. If you walk from Donghwa-sa Bus Stop 동화사, it will take thirty minutes to get to Sutaegul. Bawitgol-amjang is thirty minutes from the Sutaegol Rest Area 수태골 휴게소.

Gear
(***Byeongpung-bawi***) - 10 draws, a 60m rope, and a full set of cams.
(***Bawitgol-amjang***) - 12 draws, a 60m rope, and a set of mid-sized cams.

Safety
(***Byeongpung-bawi***) - There are still old pitons and rusty bolts on some of the routes. Some of the routes are also run out. A helmet and extra webbing is recommended.
(***Bawitgol-amjang***) - On the north wall, rope drag can be a problem so bring a few slings. The drag may also cause rope management to be difficult and it may be hard to communicate with your belayer as well. To descend, rappel from the tree on the face.

Additional Comments
Detailed route beta is currently not available.
(***Byeongpung-bawi***) - You can rappel down from each pitch at the anchor or you can walk down from the top. There are campsites available near the bus stop. Make sure to get water at the temple.

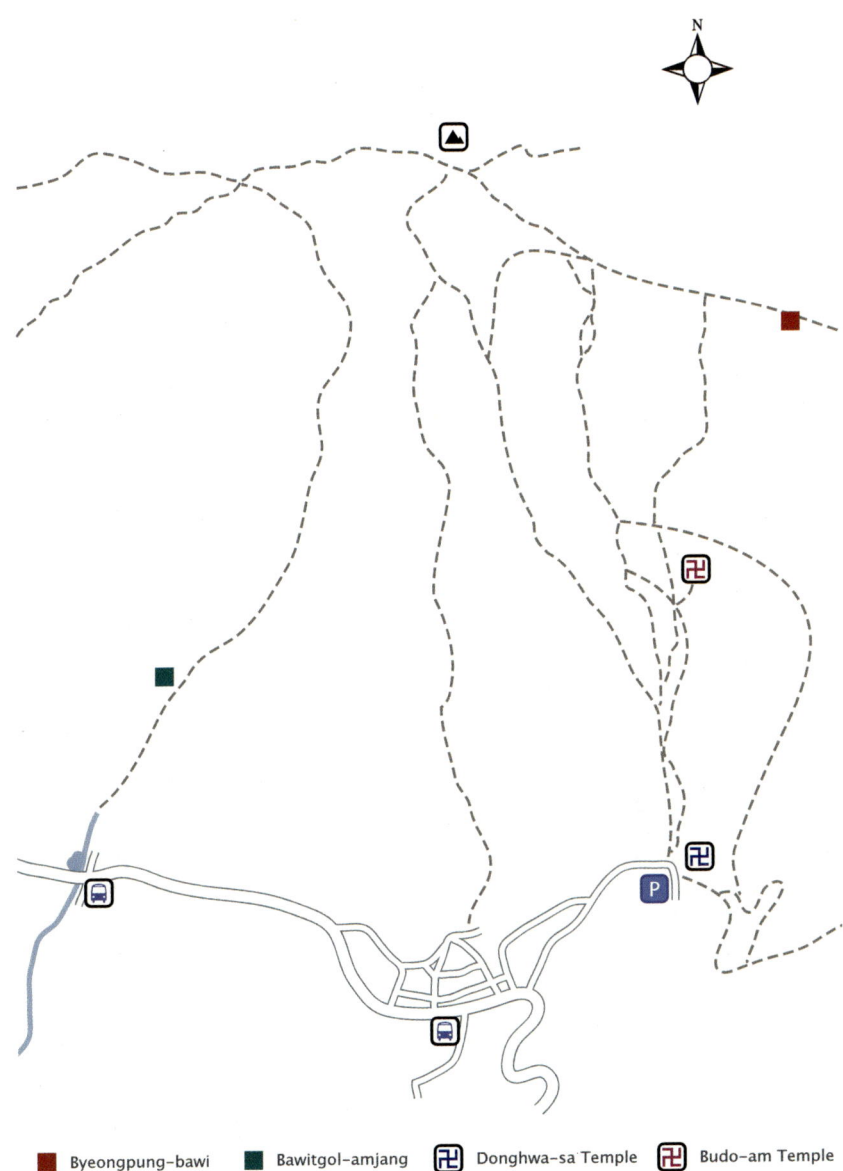

DOYAK-DAE 도약대

Description
Doyak-dae 도약대 has five different walls and includes fifty-one routes between 8m and 20m high. It has face, crack, slab and overhung climbing. The wall faces northeast.

Directions
35.970418N 128.629341E
Jimyo-dong, Dong-gu, Daegu-si 대구시 동구 지묘동

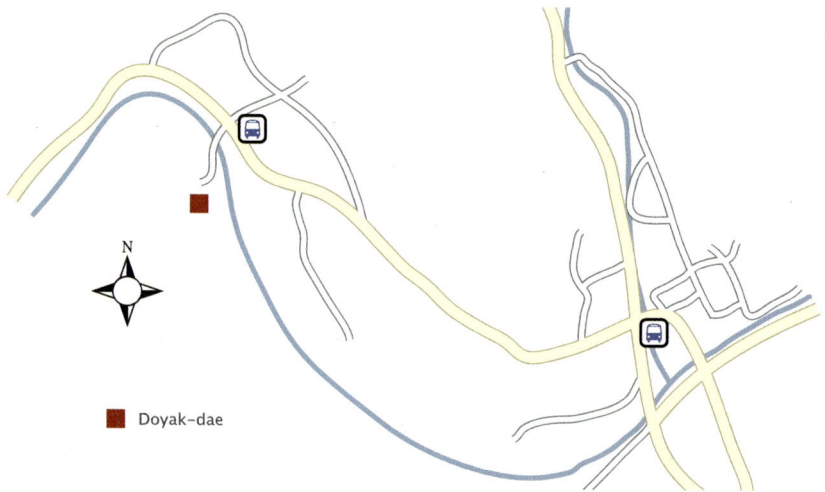

The crag may be approached either from Jungri-dong 중리 or by taking buses bound for Yeonggyeong-dong 연경동. Buses for Jungri-dong, from downtown Daegu 대구, run much more frequently than buses for Yeonggyeong-dong 연경동. From Jungri-dong, walk along the stream for twenty minutes to Daewon-sa Bus Stop 대원사. If you take a bus bound for Yeonggyeong-dong 연경동 in downtown Daegu 대구, get off at the Daewon-sa Bus Stop 대원사 and cross the stream towards the crag. The crag is right by the stream.

Gear
9 draws and a 50m rope.

Additional Comments
Given the easy access to the crag, it is one of the most popular sport climbing areas in Daegu 대구. On top of this, this place has lights that can be lit at night. At the entrance of the crag, there is a switch box where you can turn on the lights. However, they automatically turn off at midnight.

DOYAK-DAE 도약대 (1 OF 2)

Route Name	Grade	Height
Easy Route 쉬운길	5.9	8
Rainbow 무지개	5.10b	11
Cloven World 갈라진세상	5.8	11
People Who Like Rock 바위를좋아하는사람들	5.12a	11
Crosswalk 횡단도로	5.11a	18
Ddaebbang 떼빵	5.9	12
Variation Of Wing 날개변형	5.12b	10
Wing 날개	5.11c	9
Gateway To Success 등용문	5.10c	14
Mask Dance 탈춤	5.11a	14
Milky Way 미리내	5.10d	15
Nameless Route 무명길	5.12a	15
Duck Egg 오리알	5.10b	11
Sunday Driver 초보운전	5.9	11
Lie 거짓말	5.10c	11
Oh My Back 아이고허리야	5.10d	12
Having A Guess 미루어짐작	5.10c	12
Air Supply 에어서플라이	5.11a	10
Take-Off 이륙 2	5.11c	9
Forty Leader 40 대의기수	5.10a	9
Gloomy & Rainy 날은흐리고비는내리는데	5.10d	10
Crazy Fella 미친놈	5.11c	11
Hurray 만세	5.11c	12
Plus 1 Minus 1	5.11b	10
Easy 이지	5.11d	10
Eros 에로스	5.7	10

DOYAK-DAE 도약대 (2 OF 2)

Route Name	Grade	Height
Twin Rock Left 쌍바위좌	5.8	8
Twin Rock Right 쌍바위우	5.8	8
Requiem 진혼곡	5.10c	20
Taegu Sport climbing 96	5.9	20
Bear Does The Stunts 재주는곰이넘고	5.10c	16
Mabbag Route 마빡길	5.10a	18
Idleness 안일 97	5.11a	10
Four Musketeers 4 인방	5.10d	8
Leon Baek 레옹백	5.10a	13
Women's Bath 여탕	5.10a	15
Incompletion 미완성	5.9	15
Ddaebbang 때빵	5.9	15
Live Like Dandelion 민들레꽃처럼살아야한다	5.10a	15
On One's Own 홀로서기	5.10a	15
Last Road 마지막길	5.10c	10
When Green Mountain Shouts 청산이소리쳐부르거든	5.10d	18
Vertical Climber 직벽등인	5.10b	16
Searching For Freedom 자유를찾아서	5.12a	16
Splendid Start 화려한출발	5.10c	16
Treasure Hunt 보물찾기	5.10a	16
Papillion 빠삐용	5.11b	10
Robinson Crusoe 로빈슨크루소	5.11d	10
Dead Point 데드포인트	5.13a	10
To Infinity & Beyond 솟구쳐일으나라	5.11c	10
Treasure Island 보물섬	5.10a	11

DO-DONG, YONG-BAWI 도동 용바위

Description
Yong-bawi is located by the stream at Pyeonggwang-dong 평광동 in Daegu 대구. It was developed in 2002 and offers loads of features on vertical, crack, and overhung routes. It faces north and is good for summer climbing.

Directions
35.931734N 128.682024E
Phyeonggwang-dong, Dong-gu, Daegu 대구, 동구, 평광동

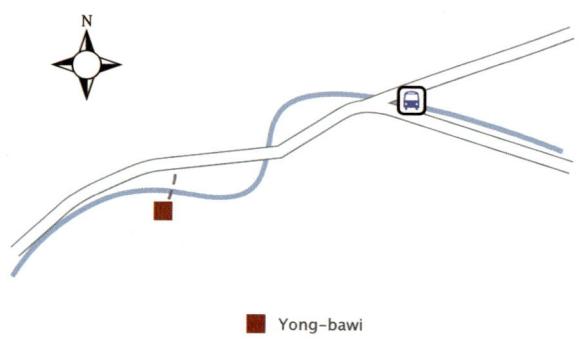

Yong-bawi

From downtown Daegu 대구, take a bus heading to Pyeonggwang-dong 평광동. Get off at the entrance of Pyeonggwang-dong 평광동입구. From there, head back to where the bus came from for 100m. Keep the stream to your left. Cross the stream at the small dike and scramble up for five minutes. The crag can be easily seen on your left from the road.

Gear
12 draws and a 60m rope.

Safety
The rock is a bit loose. A helmet is recommended.

Additional Comments
The area here is overgrown and the wall is unkempt with a lot of vines running up the face. Bug repellent is recommended during the summer. A metal board is screwed onto the rock in the middle of the wall with the route beta. It's a good place for climbing in the summer, but it seems that the crag hasn't been maintained well.

YONG-BAWI 용바위

Route Name	Grade	Height
Flake King 왕삐돌이	5.10c	9
Just Climb 막오름	5.10b	11
Wishes 희망사항	5.10c	10
On The Road Of Life 살다보면	5.8	11
Mountain 마운틴 119	5.10a	17
Only For Ddeang-Chili 땡칠이전용	5.11d	20
Freedom From All Ideas & Thoughts 무념무상	5.11c	20
Terrapin Rock 자바라위	5.9	9
Song Of Fighting Spirit 투혼의 노래	5.10d	19
Somehow 그럭저럭	5.10a	19
Late-Bloomer 대기만성	5.8	13
Silver Wheel 은륜	5.9	13
Excelsior 더높은곳을 향하여	5.10a	14
People Who Count Stars 별헤는 사람들	5.10b	28
Dragon Rock 용바위	5.10b	28
24K	5.10d	15
Black Rubber Shoes 깜장고무신	5.11b	17
Yousimjo 유심조	5.11d	17
Sky Route Of Mirr 미르의 하늘길	5.12b	19
The Power Of Dalgubeol 달구벌의 위력	5.12a	19
Jinsun and Jungyo 진선이와 준교	5.12d	18
Theme 테마	5.12a	18

GYEONG-SAN, UKSUGOL-AMJANG 경산 욱수골암장

Description
This crag was opened to the public in 2006. Uksugol-amjang is relatively small and short, but it offers a few challenging climbs on good overhangs. It faces southeast.

Directions
35.814994N 128.705156E
Uksu-dong, Suseong-gu, Daegu-si 대구 수성구 욱수동

From Daegu 대구, take a bus to Siji 시지. Get off at Deokwon Highschool 덕원 고등학교 or take the subway to Sinmae Station 신매 (Line #2, Exit 4). Walk towards Deokwon High School. It will take twenty-five minutes from the subway and five minutes from the bus stop. At the intersection, turn right and walk past Arima Castle (sauna and jjimjilbang), by Deokwon Middle School, and continue walking down the road that leads to the mountain. The crag will be on your right by the road, past the pond.

Gear
8 draws and a 50m rope.

Additional Comments
The belay stations are a bit uncomfortable. Recently, the bolts and anchors were fixed by KOTRi.

UKSUGOL-AMJANG 욱수골

Route Name	Grade	Height
Hill Of Autumn 가을의 언덕	5.10a	12
500 CC	5.10a	12
Edel 에델	5.10a	11
Uksu 욱수	5.10a	15
Rock Love 바위사랑	5.10b	10
Beomseo 범서	5.11a	9
TCS 2006	5.10b	10
Princess Wolreong 월령공주	5.11b	11
Challenger 챌린져	5.12b	10

*Routes start from the far left of the wall

BISEUL-SAN, SURIDEUM-BAWI 비슬산 수리듬바위

Description
Surideum-bawi has four routes of 5.10 difficulty. It is granite rock with face and crack climbing that ranges from 50m to 70m high. It faces southeast.

Directions
35.729792N 128.541884E
Jeongdae-ri, Gachang-myeon, Dalseong-gun, Daegu 대구 달성군 가창면 정대리

From Daegu, take a bus heading to Jeongdae-ri 정대리 and get off at the last stop. Walk along the road leading towards the hill until you reach a security gate. Walk through the iron gate (you need a permit from the guard for climbing) and follow the trail along the stream for ten minutes until you see the crag on your right. Look for the trail that leads to the crag and scramble up for fifteen minutes.

Gear
12 draws and a 60m rope, and a full set of cams.

Safety
The rock is loose. Some of the bolts and anchors are rusty and suspicious. A helmet is recommended.

Additional Comments
The crag doesn't seem to have been climbed for years and most of the protection is bad. The trail in the valley is closed for preservation.

SURIDEUM-BAWI 수리듬바위

Route Name	Grade	Height
Friend Route 프렌드길 1p (5.10*|35m) 2p (5.10*|15m)	5.10*	50 (2p)
Hansol Route 한솔길 1p (5.10*|35m) 2p (5.10*|15m)	5.10*	50 (2p)
Carpenter Bee Route 왕벌길 1p (5.10*|35m) 2p (5.10*|35m)	5.10*	70 (2p)
Going Up Route 오름길 1p (5.10*|35m) 2p (5.10*|35m)	5.10*	50 (2p)

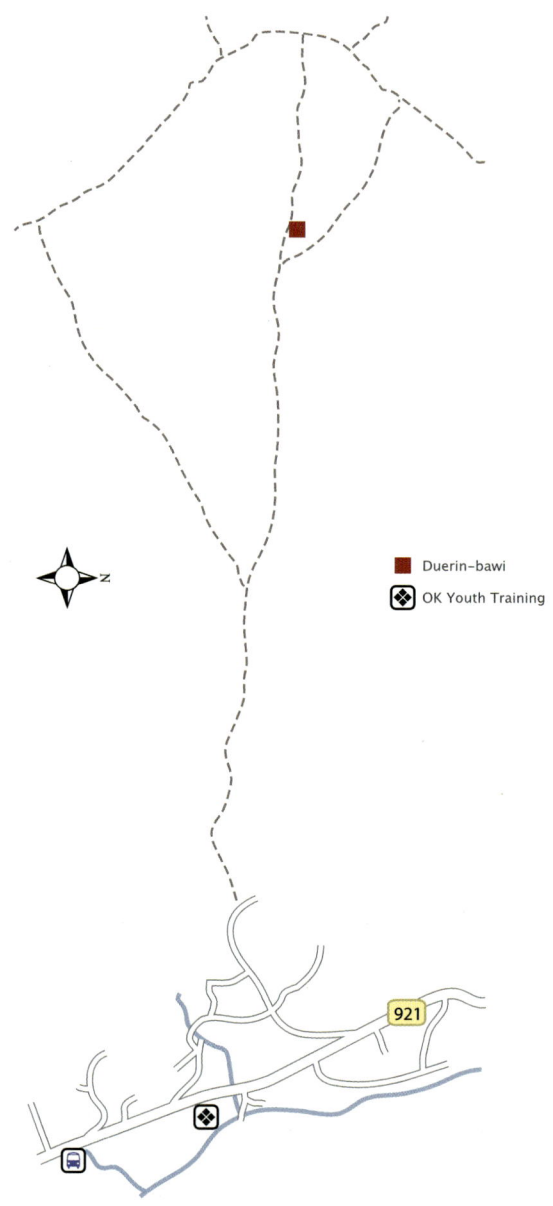

Munbok-san, Duerin-bawi 문복산 드린 바위

Description
Duerin-bawi 드린바위 is 130m high and 100m wide. It was first developed in 1975. In May 1998, it was redeveloped with the addition of five routes, including a couple of aid routes. This crag looks a bit creepy. It is dark granite and the climbs vary from face, slab, crack, and overhanging routes. This is a good place to train for big-wall expeditions.

Directions
35.675252N 129.037364E
GyeongJu Sannae-myeon Jung-ri 경주 산내면 중리

It is hard to get to the base of this mountain by public transportation. From EunYang Bus Terminal 언양, take a bus heading for Jung-ri 중리마을. Buses run every ninety minutes. At Jung-ri 중리, follow the street that runs through the small alleyway across the street from the OK Youth Training House. The trail starts at the end of the alley. The crag can be clearly seen from the trailhead. Instead of taking the more obvious gorge-side trail, take the trail to the right, that heads towards the ridgeline. Continue on until you reach a fork. Follow the trail to the left and you'll reach the crag in five minutes.

Gear
10 draws, a 60m rope, and a full set of cams. Aid climbing equipment is also needed for the multi-pitches.

Safety
The rock is loose and some of the bolts are suspicious. A helmet and extra webbing is highly recommended.

Additional Comments
There are good campsites available.

Duerin-bawi 드린 바위

Route Name	Grade	Height
Memories Of Mountain Friend 산선배의 추억 1p (*|30m) 2p (*|25m) 3p (*|35m)	5.10b	90*
Gall Bladder Of A Bear 웅담 1p (*|30m) 2p (*|30m) 3p (*|30m)	5.10c/d | A1	90*
Period Of Spring Poverty 보릿고개 1p (*|25m) 2p (*|20m) 3p (*|30m) 4p (*|25m)	5.10c/d	100*
Yo-Heave-Ho 으라차차 1p (*|30m) 2p (*|35m) 3p (*|40m)	5.11d	105*
Haken Party 하켄잔치 드린바위길 1p (*|30m) 2p (*|35m) 3p (*|40m)	5.9	105*

*Multi-pitch info is unavailable at this time

GUEMSEONG-SAN, MUJIGAE-BAWI 금성산 무지개바위

Description
Mujigae-bawi, located on Guemseong Mt. 금성산 무지개바위, has sixteen routes. The rock looks exactly like a triumphant arch. The routes vary from crack, face, and arête climbing.

Directions
36.263809N 128.71258E
Sujeong-ri, Geumseong-myeon, Euseong-gun, Kyeongsangbuk-do
경북 의성군 금성면 수정리

From Top-ri Station 탑리, take a bus heading to Gaeum 가음 and get off at Sujeonsa 수정사. Walk along the road that leads to the temple for twenty minutes. At the parking area, before the reservoir, cross the small bridge that leads to the sanctuary. Walk along the fence next to the house and continue up for twenty-five minutes until you see the crag on your left. When you see the crag, look for a trail on your left. You may find a few trails, but only take the trail that you can see the crag from. Hike up for fifteen minutes to reach the crag.

Gear
10 draws and 50m rope.

Additional Comments
Around the crag, there are 160 degree overhanging boulders and a few routes which barely get wet, even in the rain. The base of the crag is overgrown by various wild plants.

MUJIGAE-BAWI 무지개바위 (1 OF 2)

Route Name	Grade	Height
Butter Prince	5.9	10
Wind That Can't Be Caught in Net 그물에걸리지않는바람	5.12a	12
I Can Do It 하고말거야	5.11a	12
A Plate Of Pizza 피자한판	5.10a	13
Get Up After Knocked Down Seven Times 칠전팔기	5.10a	12
Front Line 사선에서	5.10c	13
Rainbow 무지개	5.13b	20
Well 잘	5.9	10
Golden Bat 황금박쥐	5.12a	12
Shelter 대피소	5.11b	13
Mountain Eagle 수리뫼	5.11b	10
Seok 석	5.10b	8
Seol 설	5.9	8

■ Mujigae-bawi

MUJIGAE-BAWI 무지개바위 (2 OF 2)

Route Name	Grade	Height
Comes To My Mind 생각나면	5.13b	15
Rock Lover 바좋사	5.12a	13
Sun 순	5.11c	13

YOUHAK-SAN 유학산

Description
(*Hak-bawi*) - This crag is a mixture of gneiss and moraine rock with forty-eight routes. It is 50m high and 60m wide. It was developed from 1996 to 1997. The dihedral wall is divided into four parts. The far left wall, that is separated a little from the main wall, has seven routes. On the main wall, the left side has seventeen routes. The middle wall has ten routes, plus two aid climbs. The right wall has twelve routes. The crag faces southwest.

(*Dungji-bawi*) - Developed in1998, this crag has twenty-four routes between 22m and 52m high. There are a couple of multi-pitches that would be good for beginners and intermediates to train on. Refer to the gear and safety concerns in this book with care.

Directions
(*Hak-bawi*) - 36.065856N 128.486202E
(*Dungji-bawi*) - 36.065808N 128.486288E
Seonggok-ri, Seokjeok-eup, Chilgok-gun 칠곡군 석적읍 성곡리

(*Hak-bawi*) - At Waegwan Bukbu Bus Terminal 왜관북부, take the bus bound for Dogyeo/Chumpyeong 도계/청평 and get off at Haksansamgeo-ri 학산삼거리. Follow the road that leads to Dobong-sa 도봉사 for twenty minutes. Continue past the Potjae Parking Area 팥재 주차장 and hike towards Dobong-sa 도봉사 for another ten minutes. At the temple take the trail to your right. Hike up until you reach a fork. Take the Youhakjeong 유학정 trail on your left. There will be a small trail to your right 5m after the fork. Continue on the path for five minutes to reach the crag.
(*Dungji-bawi*) - Continue on the trail past Hak-bawi to reach Dungji-bawi.

Gear
12 draws, a 60m rope, and a full set of cams.

Additional Comments
There are good campsites around the crags and a restroom is available before Dungji-bawi 둥지바위. Water can be found at the temple.

Route Name	Grade	Height
Windy Zone 유풍지대	5.9	12
Windless Zone 무풍지대	5.10d	9
Wind Of The Flower 꽃바람	5.10b	11
A Good Windy Day 바람불어좋은날	5.9	10
Whistle 휘파람	5.9	8
Spring Wind 봄바람	5.9	7
Mountain Wind 산바람	5.9	6
A Road New To One 초행길	5.10b	25
The Road On The Sea Of Clouds 해운길	5.11a	20
A Song Of The Crazy Wind 미친바람의노래	5.12b	18
In The Storm 폭풍속에서	5.10d	18
Rock Village 바위마을	5.10a	25
Sorrow Of A Mirror 거울애상	5.10b	27
Dream Of Five People 5인의꿈	5.12c	25
Millennial Attachment 천년지정	5.13*	25
The Adventure Of Super Monkey 서유기 2	5.11c	25
Where Is My Dream 꿈이어디메뇨	5.10c/d	45
Lady's Caprice 여자의변덕	5.10b	50
Even Moss Is A Hold 이끼도홀더	5.10c	50
Rock Performance	5.11c	47
Master Board 마스터보드	5.13*	15
Highway Crack 하이웨이크랙	5.11d	15
General's Dream 장군의꿈	5.12c	45
Wash With Moss 이끼로세수하고	5.10a	45
Climbing Is Destiny 오름짓은숙명	5.11b	40
Nowhere To Stay 머물곳이없어라	5.13*	45
A Good Old Slab 그리운슬랩	5.13*	45
I Miss The Sky 하늘이그립구나	5.13*	45
Don't Have A Wing 날개도없는데	5.11d	42
Confession 고백	5.12c	27
X File X 파일	5.13a	35
Rock Fairy 바위요정	5.12a	30
Restoration of TK TK 의부활	5.10c/d	30
Jamming Machine 재밍머신	5.12b	35
TKC	5.10a	35
Drought-Ridden Milky Way 말라붙은은하수	5.11d	35

HAK-BAWI 학바위 (2 OF 2)

Route Name	Grade	Height
With All My Heart 온몸으로	5.11a	35
Coup 쿠데타	5.11c	23
It's Jeongok 정옥이꺼	5.8	20
It's Junseok 준석이꺼	5.11c	18
To Kill Time 심심풀이	5.8	11
It's Jongguk 종국이꺼	5.11c	17
Sorry	5.11c	16
It's Ogong 오공이꺼	5.10c	18
It's Seonggi 성기꺼	5.12a	18
It's Jojang 조장꺼	5.12b	17
Bbogga Bbogga 뽀까뽀까	5.10a	12
Antenna 더듬이	5.10c	11

DUNGJI-BAWI 둥지바위

Route Name	Grade	Height
Ashamed When History Calls Up 역사의부름앞에부끄러운자되어	5.10d	22
Landslide 산사태	5.9	22
Fate 운명	5.11a	23
It's Snowing In A Hamlet 눈내리는산마실	5.11a	25
Blue Tree & Green Bamboo 청송녹죽	5.10d	25
Winter Out, Spring In 동거춘래	5.10b	30
Valley With Perch Blossom 복사꽃우거진골	5.9	30
Father & Two Sons	5.10a	30
Woman In The Rain 우중의여인	5.7	23
Korack & Ice 10	5.9	23
March For A Lover 임을위한행진곡	5.10a	22
Father & Son 부자지간 1p (5.6|20m) 2p (5.12b|27m)	5.12b	47 (2p)
Playground On The Gravy Train 신선놀이터 1p (5.6|20m) 2p (5.10b|23m)	5.10b	43 (2p)
Generous Friend 마음넉넉한친구 1p (5.6|20m) 2p (5.10b|28m)	5.10a	48 (2p)
Rainy Morning In Dabu-dong 비오는다부동의아침 1p (5.11b|30m) 2p (5.10d|15m)	5.11b	45 (2p)
A Road For The Lady 그여자를위한길 1p (5.10d|25m) 2p (5.10d|21m)	5.10d	46 (2p)
Now We Met 지금은우리가만나서 1p (5.10a|20m) 2p (5.9|23m)	5.10a	43 (2p)
Just Spaced-Out 아무생각없었네 1p (5.7|23m) 2p (5.8|25m)	5.8	48 (2p)
People Who Like Rock 98 바위를좋아하는사람들 98 1p (5.10c|22m) 2p (5.11d|22m)	5.11d	44 (2p)
No One Told Me To Go On The Road 누가나에게이길을가라하지않았네 1p (5.10a|22m) 2p (5.10a|20m) 3p (5.10a|10m)	5.10a	52 (3p)
Dosolcheon 도솔천 1p (5.9|22m) 2p (5.10a|20m)	5.10a	42 (2p)
Savage 미개인 1p (5.7|22m) 2p (5.10a|20m)	5.10a	42 (2p)
The Two Of Us Are Of One Mind 둘이서한마음 1p (5.6|20m) 2p (5.8|22m)	5.8	42 (2p)
Breaking Through The Barricade 바리케이트를넘어서	5.8	35

JUKJANG, HAKDAM-AM 죽장 학담암

Description
Hakdam-am 학담암 is divided into three walls. It is a metamorphosis granite crag that is 100m wide and 45m high. It has forty-five routes. The middle part of the wall has loads of 5.10 face climbs and the left side of the wall is mostly overhanging 5.11's and 5.12's. It faces northeast.

Directions
36.164367N 129.109011E
Maehyeon-ri, Jukjang-myeon, Bukgu, Pohang-si 포항시 북구 죽장면 매현리

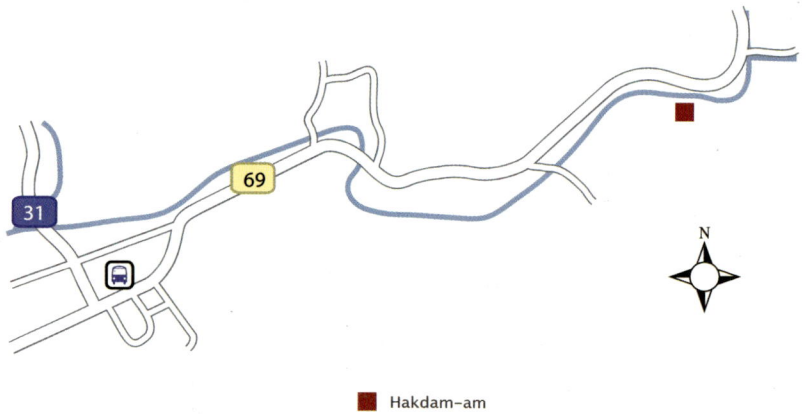

■ Hakdam-am

From Phohang Intercity Bus Terminal, take a bus for Gigyeo-myeon 기계면, Jukjang 죽장, Sangok 상옥. It takes about an hour and the buses usually run every hour. From the bus stop, walk east along the main road for fifteen minutes. As you walk along the stream, you'll be able to see Hakdam-am to your right. You will have to ford the stream to reach the crag. The water can get waist deep during the rainy season.

Gear
10 draws and 60m rope.

Safety
All of the anchors are cables with rings.

Additional Comments
There are many campsites available by the stream and a restroom on the road. Food and water can be bought at the stores in the village close to the bus stop.

HAKDAM-AM 학담암 (1 OF 2)

Route Name	Grade	Height
15 Reunion 15 동기회	5.11a	11
X-1	5.12b	12
Black Box 블랙박스	5.12a/b	12
Terrorist 테러리스트	5.12b	12
P-1	5.9	12
Little Sisyphus 리틀시지프스	5.10b	13
Individual Combat 각개전투	5.10d	13
Feast 주연	5.10c	14
Playground 놀이터	5.9	7
Party For The Elderly 경로잔치	5.8	18
Childhood 어린시절	5.8	20
Wandering 800 Miles 방랑삼천리	5.11c/d	21
Son Of God 신의아들	5.12a	18

HAKDAM-AM 학담암 (1 OF 2)

Route Name	Grade	Height
The Spirit Of Phocheol 포철의혼	5.13a	17
Fantasy 환상	5.12c	17
Trojan Horse 트로이목마	5.12b	15
Bright Boy 똘이	5.11d	16
Ulcleyeon 울클연	5.12b	15
Fantastic 판타스틱	5.11b/c	14
Soul 영혼	5.12a/b	17
Bat 박쥐 2	5.10a	21
Bee 벌	5.9	21
Birth 탄생	5.10b	19
Mr. You 유형	5.10c	18
OB Lager OB 라거	5.10c	18
Stone Water 석수	5.10b	17
Always Together 늘함께	5.11a	18
To A Friend 친구에게	5.11*	19
Against The Sun Setting 석양에등지고	5.10b	16
Cow Sole 소발바닥	5.9	18
Snail 달팽이	5.9	16
Paradise 무릉도원	5.7	18
Wedding March 웨딩마치	5.9	15
Hoya 호야	5.11a	10
2, 3 Companion 이삼동기	5.11c	10
Upper Hoya 호야상단	5.11b	16
Upper 2, 3 Companion 이삼동기상단	5.10a	14
Upper Paradise 무릉도원상단	5.7	12
1, 6 Companion 일육동기	5.10c	10
Tum-Tumming Tum-Tum 꿈따리사바라	5.10b	11
Bear IQ 곰 IQ	5.10c	11
Dinosaur IQ 공룡 IQ	5.1b	11
Turning Back To A Three-Way Intersection 돌아가는삼각지	5.10c	14
A Full Bosom 풍만한앞가슴	5.12c	12
Moist Lip 촉촉한입술	5.12a	12

NAEYEON-SAN 내연산암장

Description
(*Gwaneum-am*) - This area has many crags of gneiss rock. The biggest crag, and the main crag for Pohang climbers, is Gwaneum-am 관음암. It is the closest crag to Yeonsan Waterfall 연산폭포. This crag offers crack, chimney, and vertical face climbing with a couple of aid climbing routes.
(*Yeonsan-am*) - Yeonsan-am 내연암 is located over the suspension bridge. It offers good face climbing. The rest of the crags are spaced out gradually along the stream to the temple.
(*Sinseondae*) - This crag has two 5.9 routes and is 80m high. It is not climbed very often because of the bad access and the poor quality of rock. However, the multi-pitches offer a great view.
(*Guimyeon-am*) - The routes here are moderate and range from vertical, crack, and overhung climbing.
(*Arirang Boulder*) - This crag is relatively short and small. It offers steep, overhung routes.
(*Seoun-am*) - Seoun-am 서운암 was developed with easy routes for beginners.

Directions
(*Gwaneum-am*) - 36.260262N 129.301486E
(*Yeonsan-am*) - 36.260418N 129.301314E
(*Sinseondae*) - 36.260487N 129.301357E
(*Guimyeon-am*) - 36.258177N 129.306335E
(*Arirang Boulder*) - 36.255192N 129.308052E
(*Seoun-am*) - 36.252839N 129.315616E
Jungsan-ri, Songra-myeon, Buk-gu, Pohang-si 포항시 북구 송라면 중산리

(*Gwaneum-am*) - Buses run from Phohang 포항 to Bogyeong-sa 보경사 every hour. It takes forty minutes to reach Bogyeong-sa 보경사. From the parking lot, follow the main trail to Yeonsan Waterfall 연산폭포. You will pass a couple of waterfalls before reaching Yeonsan Waterfall 연산폭포. You can't miss the crag though because it is next to the waterfall by the suspension bridges. The approach time will be forty minutes from the parking lot.
(*Yeonsan-am*) - This crag is located over the bridge by Gwaneum-am 관음암. It will be to your right.
(*Sinseondae*) - This crag is five minutes down the trail from Gwaneum-am 관음암. It will be to your left.
(*Guimyeon-am*) - Guimyeon-am 귀면암 sits below Samyong Waterfall 삼영폭. It will be on your right on the main trail towards the temple.
(*Arirang Boulder*) - This crag is located below Ssangsang Waterfall 쌍생폭. Facing the temple, it will be on your right.
(*Seoun-am*) - This crag is located in the woods, across from a snack bar. It's only five minutes past the first temple.

Gear
13 draws and a 60m rope. For the multi-pitch, bring 12 draws and two 50m ropes.

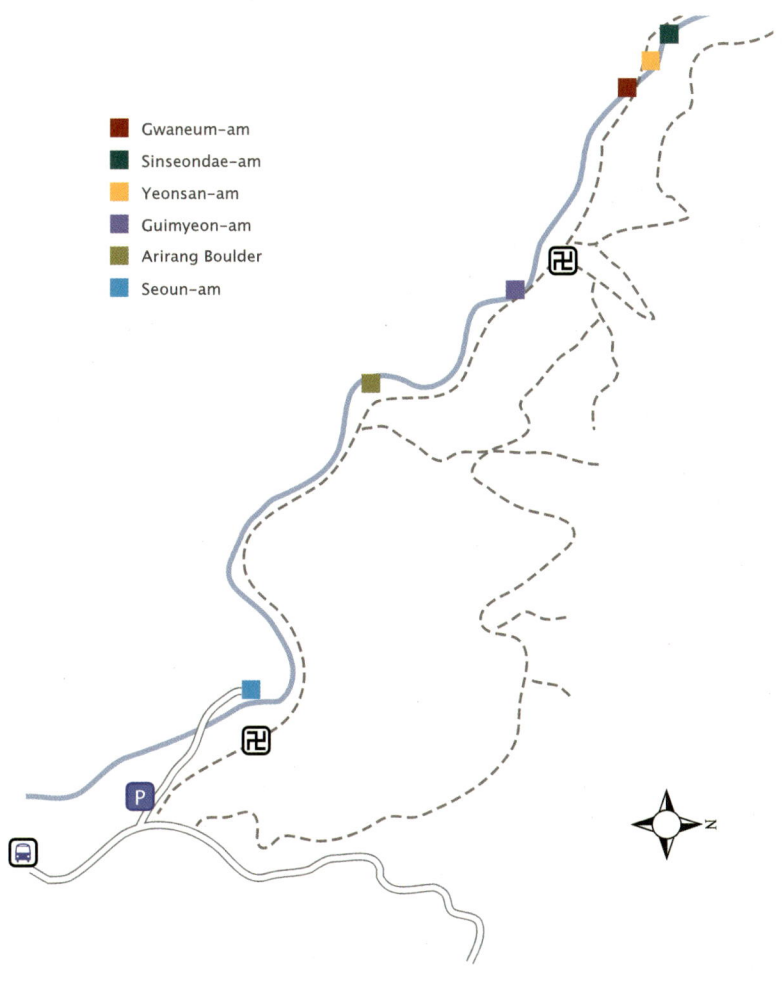

Safety
Aside from the main crag, Gwaneum-am 관음암, a few of the bolts and anchors on the rest of the crags are rusty. Also, some of the rock is a little rotten so be cautious. A helmet is recommended.

Additional Comments
The setting around the main crag is spectacular and so is the hiking trail to the crag. There are min-baks 민박 and camping sites on the left side of the entrance.

Gwaneum-am 관음암

Route Name	Grade	Height
Owl 부엉이	5.9	36
Crack Route 크랙길	5.10c	50
Goryong Route 고룡 A	5.12c	20
Goryong Route 고룡 B	5.11b	20
Older Brother Route 형님길	5.12a	30
Younger Brother Route 아우길	5.10d	35
Bear Route 곰길	5.10d	30
Sisyphus 시지프스	5.11c	30
Alley Route 골목길	5.10c	30
Last Road 마지막길	5.10b	38
Bat 박쥐	5.10c	20
Direct 다이렉트	5.12b	12

Seoun-am 서운암

Route Name	Grade	Height
Tap 꼭지	5.10a	10
Leaving The Office 퇴근	5.10b	10
Baduki 바둑이	5.10b	10
Hyeondu 현두	5.10c	10
Hawaii 하와이	5.10d	10

Arirang Boulder 아리랑볼더

Route Name	Grade	Height
Spirit 혼	5.12a	8
My Love, Stand By Me 내사랑내곁에	5.10a	8
The End Of Goodbye 이별의끝	5.9	10
For One Lady 한여인을위하여	5.11a	10
Goblin 도깨비	5.10c	10
New Challenge 새로운도전	5.10a	7
Seonyouhwa 선유화	5.10b	15
Arirang Express 아리랑특급	5.10d	15
Arirang Alone 홀로아리랑	5.10d	10

Guimyeon-am 귀면암

Route Name	Grade	Height
Heaven 천상	5.10b	20
Earth 천하	5.10a	20
Youa 유아	5.10b	20
Dokjon Bat	5.11a	20

Yeonsan-am 내연암

Route Name	Grade	Height
Apple Box 애플박스	5.10b	25
Loneliness 고독	5.10a/b	25
South Gate 남문	5.10b	25
Sky 하늘	5.11b	25

Sinseondae-am 신선대암

Route Name	Grade	Height
Incense Burner 향로	5.9	80*
Grandmother 할매	5.9	80*

*Multi-pitch info is unavailable at this time

Seoksan-am 석산암

Route Name	Grade	Height
Number 1	5.10a	32
Number 2	5.10b	39
Number 3	5.10b	54 (2p)
1p (5.10a|34m) 2p (5.10b|20m)		
Number 4	5.10c	56 (2p)
1p (5.10a|29m) 2p (5.10c|27m)		
Number 5	5.10a/A0	51 (3p)
1p (5.8|19m) 2p (A0|16m) 3p (5.10a|16m)		
Number 6	5.11c	40 (2p)
1p (5.10c|22m) 2p (5.11c|18m)		
Number 7	5.10a	44 (2p)
1p (5.10a|27m) 2p (5.9|17m)		
Number 8	5.10a	21
Number 9	5.9	26
Last Road 마지막길	5.10b	38
Bat 박쥐	5.10c	20
Direct 다이렉트	5.12b	12

Ami-san, Seoksan-am 아미산 석산암

Description
Seoksan-am is located on a mountain called Ami-san 아미산. It has great views and trails for hikers. This crag was opened to the public in 2007 with nine routes. It is made of rhyolite rock, which is the volcanic equivalent of granite. Most of the routes are slab and face climbing. Seoksan-am faces south.

Directions
36.16855N 128.844824E
Seoksan-ri, Goro-myeon, Gunwi-gun 군위군 고로면 석산리

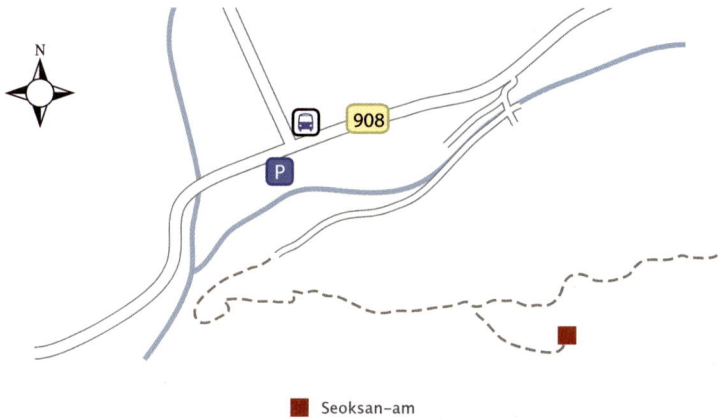

Seoksan-am

From Daegu 대구, take a bus to Gunwi 군위 and transfer to a local bus heading to Seoksan-ri 석산리. Get off at Gaamsamgeo-ri 가암삼거리. The mountain can be seen from across the road. There are three protruding rocks on the mountain. The crag is located on the south-side of the biggest rock. At the trailhead there is a hiking map. Follow the trail in the valley for ten minutes. Then, take the trail that branches off to the right and continue up another five minutes to reach the crag.

Gear
12 draws and a 60m rope.

Safety
The rocks are loose and sharp so a helmet is recommended. The first two routes are a bit longer than the others to top-rope and the belay for the second climber should be done at the anchors on the top of the routes. The belay station on the east side of the wall is unstable.

Additional Comments
Ami-san offers good ridge climbing and there are campsites available around the crag. The routes here don't have names, but they have been numbered, which is shown on the page left.

Hakga-san, Sangsa-bawi 학가산 상사바위

Description
Sangsa-bawi is located on the south foot of Hakga-san, between Andong-gun, Bukhu-myeon 안동군북후면 and Yeocheon-gun, Bomoon-myeon 예천군보문면. It is granite rock. Most of the routes are slab and face climbing. There are some nice multi-pitch lines that can be climbed traditionally. However, most of the routes are usually being climbed only single-pitch sport climbing.

Dong-il Ryou, the author, climbing Wing 날개/5.11a.

Directions
36.662119N 128.603125E
Sanseong-ri, Bomun-myeon, Yecheon-gun 애천군 보문면 산성리

From Yeocheon Intercity Bus Terminal 예천, take a bus bound for Sanseong-ri 산성리. Get off at the last stop and walk to Neureuch Village 느르치 which will take twenty minutes. At the village, hike up the trail on the northside, in the middle of the remote village. The trailhead is hard to find. However, continue making your way through the woods and hike up straight towards the crag, which is visible from the village. The trails behind the village end up converging into a single trail half way up. It will take approximately thirty minutes to reach the crag from the village.

Gear
10 draws, two 50m ropes, and a set of mid-sized cams.

Safety
The top anchor used for rappelling is weathered and sun-bleached so bring extra webbing.

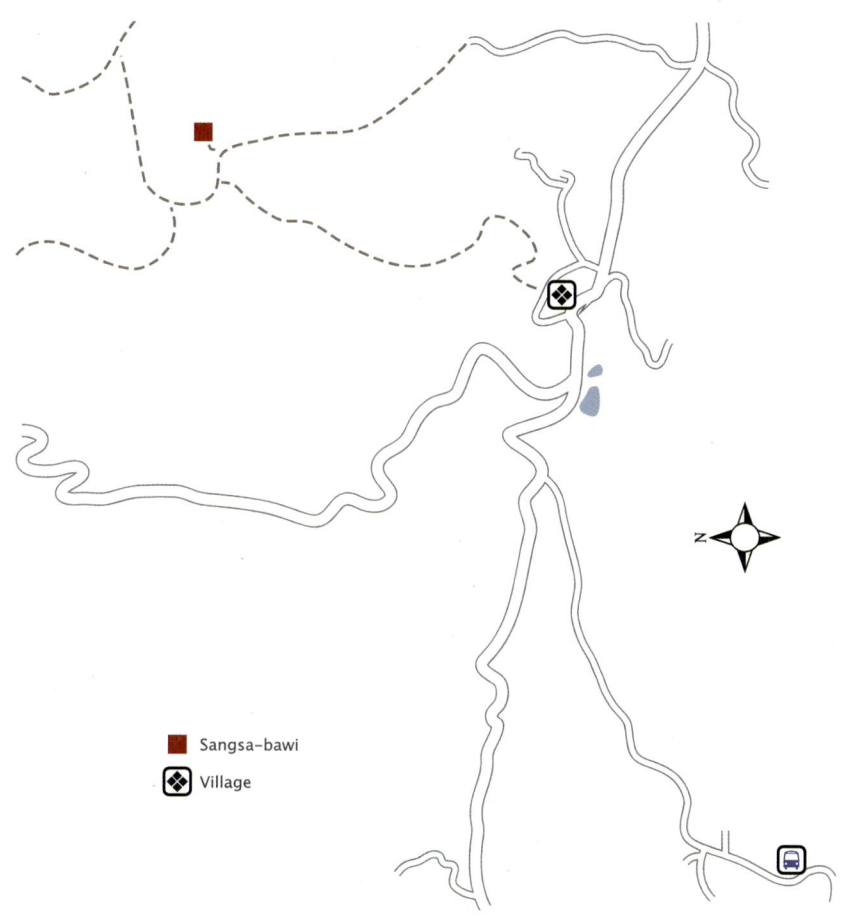

■ Sangsa-bawi
❖ Village

SANGSA-BAWI 상사바위

Route Name	Grade	Height
Ribbon 댕기	5.11a	100*
Sky 하늘 **1p** (5.10a|25m) **2p** (5.10b|30m) **3p** (5.11*|25m) **4p** (5.10a|20m)	5.11*	100 (4p)
Wing 날개	5.11a	100*
Lord 천주	5.10*	100*
Initiation 입문	5.10c	100*

*Multi-pitch info is unavailable at this time

Chungcheongnam-do

충청남도

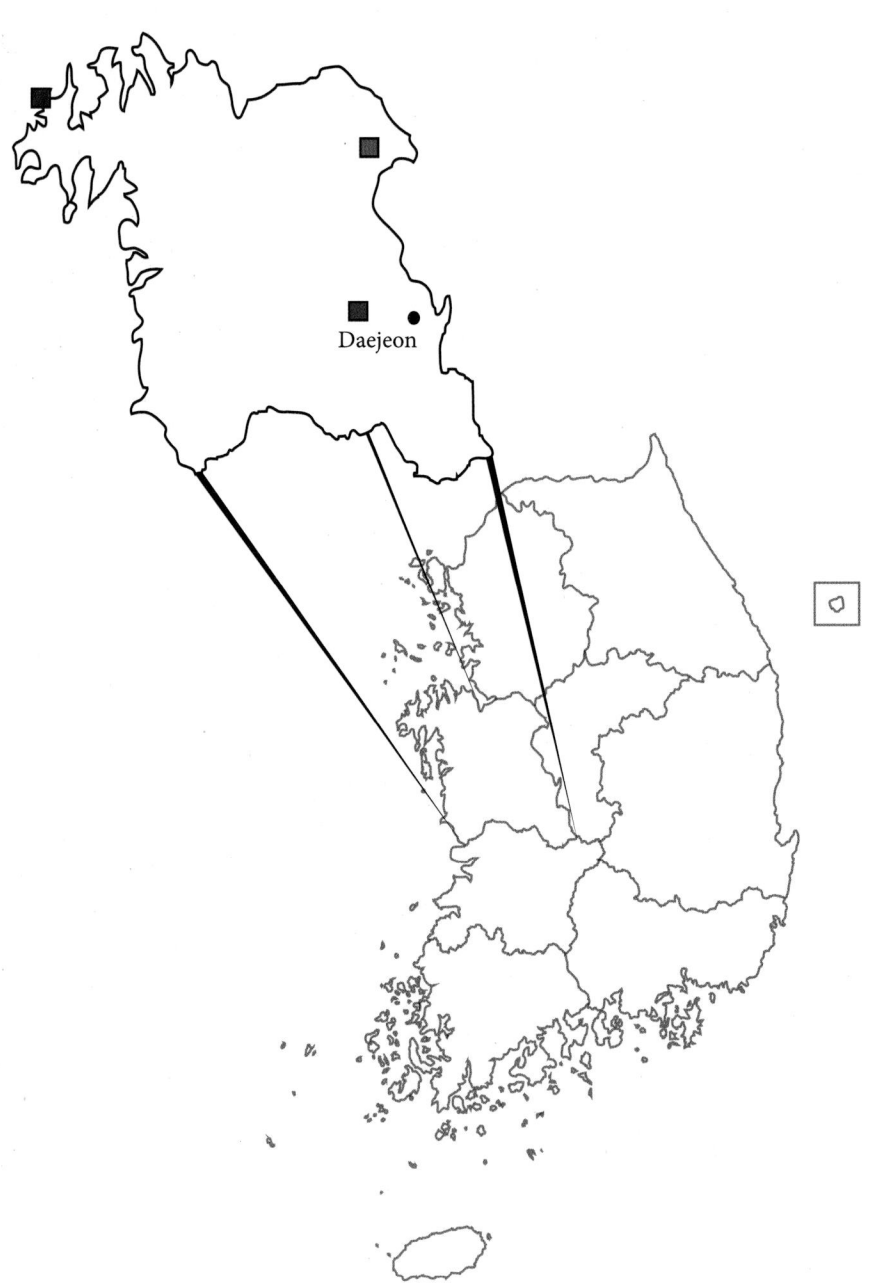

CHUNGCHEONGNAM-DO PROVINCE 충청남도

- Seonbul-am, Gyeoryong-san
- Hwangjeok-bong OB Slab, Gyeoryong-san
- Bagaji-bawi, Gyeoryong-san
- Byeongcheon-am
- Hagampo-amjang

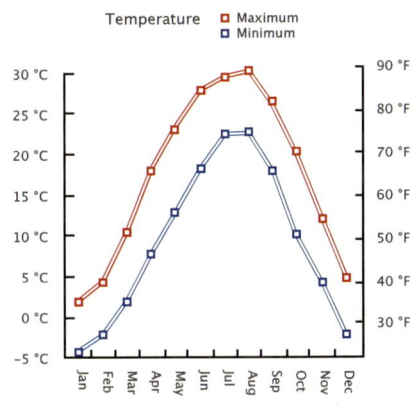

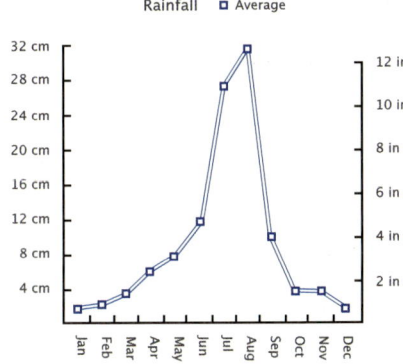

Gyeoryong-san 계룡산

Description
(*Seonbul-am*) - As the premier crag of Chungcheongnam-do 충청남도, Seonbul-am boasts of great slab, crack, and high-angle face climbing on excellent, highly featured granite rock. It is located at Gyeoryong-san National Park. Most of the routes are multi-pitch climbs that face southwest.
(*Bagaji-bawi*) - Bagaji-bawi is a granite wall with slab, overhanging, and face climbing.
(*Hwangjeok-bong OB*) - Development began in 1974 with two routes. Since then, six more routes have been added. This crag is 40m high and 40m wide. It is a granite wall of good quality slab climbing with routes that are relatively easy. Also, a superb panorama of the mountains awaits from the belay perch.

Directions
(*Seonbul-am*) - 36.354917N 127.207539E
(*Bagaji-bawi*) - 36.349179N 127.243094E
(*Hwangjeok-bong*) - 36.353016N 127.23876E
Hakbong-ri, Banpho-myeon, Gongju-si, Chungcheongnam-do
충남 공주시 반포면 학봉리

(*Seonbul-am*) - From Daejeon 대전, take a bus to Donghak-sa 동학사. At the final bus stop, Donghak-sa 동학사, walk past the ticket counter and continue hiking up the main trail for twenty minutes until you reach the Rescue Mark 5-5. Walk past the Rescue Mark 5-5 for 70m and then take the trail to your right. A tiny valley will be on your left as you follow the trail. Continue up for fifteen minutes.
(*Bagaji-bawi*) - From the parking lot at Gyeorong-san National Park (following the same direction as Seonbul-am to get to the park), walk towards the campsite. Continue to the back of the campgrounds and walk past the blue water tank. Continue past the fence by the tank. Hike straight up the main trail and follow the sign that leads you to the crag. The hike will take thirty minutes.
(*Hwangjeok-bong OB*) - This crag can be approached by either taking the trail to Bagaji-bawi or by taking the trail around the solitary house that is by the campsite. When taking the Bagaji-bawi trail, take the right trail at the fork by the first trail guide sign. Continue on the trail for ten minutes and cross over the dry streambed. Don't stay on the prominent ridge before the streambed. Make your way up the main trail with the valley on your left for twenty minutes until you reach the crag. When taking the trail by the solitary house, go to the right side of the house and follow the "no trail" sign at the start of the streambed. Follow the trail for thirty minutes to reach the crag.

Gear
(*Seonbul-am*) - 10 draws and a 60m rope. There is an opportunity for aid–climbing equipment as well.
(*Bagaji-bawi*) - 12 draws and a 60m rope.
(*Hwangjeok-bong OB*) - 10 draws, a 60m rope, and a set of small to mid-sized cams.

Additional Comments
To climb here, you need a permit from the ranger office. The process is simple. Step into the ranger office and show your identity card.

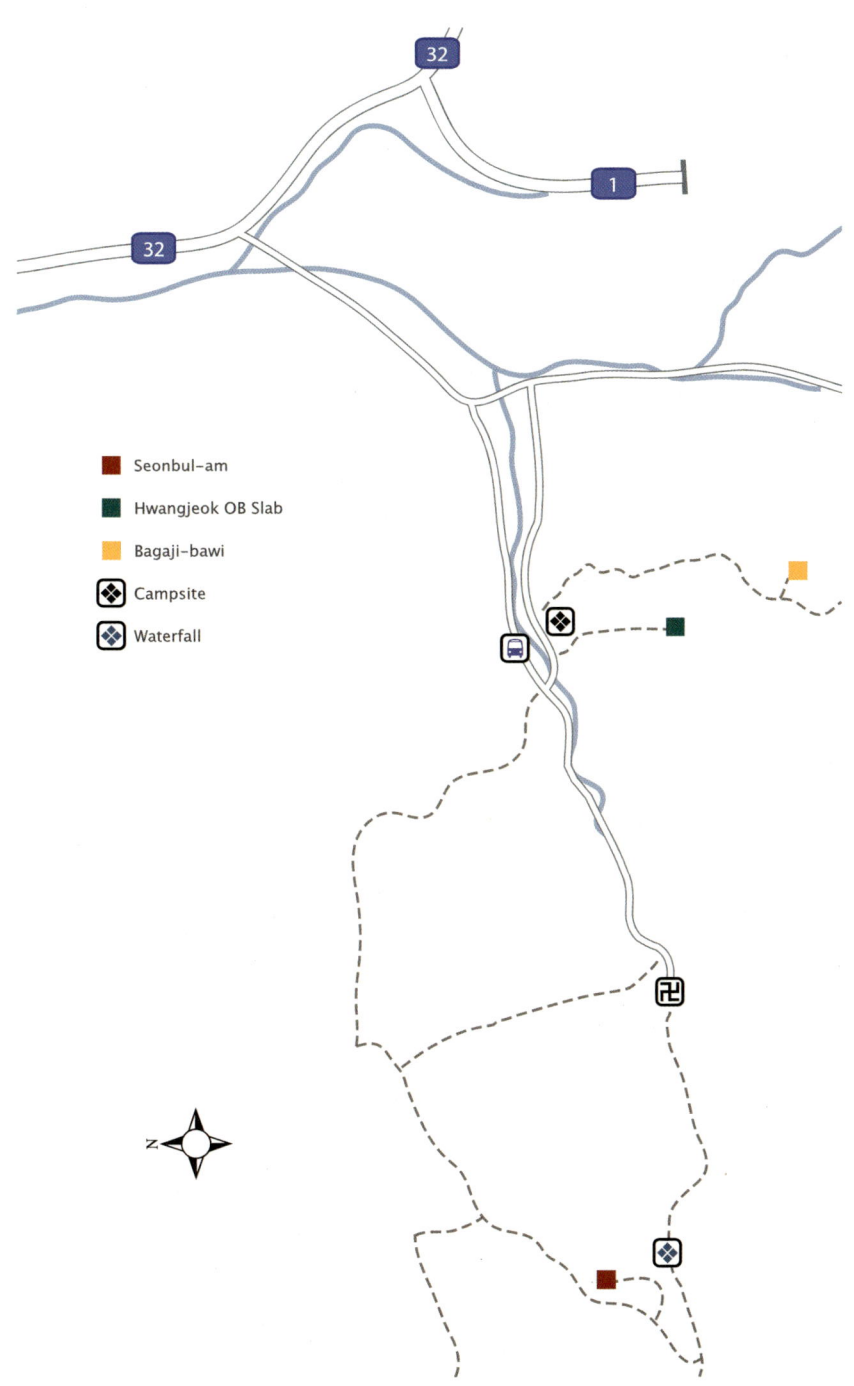

SEONBUL-AM 선불암

Route Name	Grade	Height
Agricultural Academy 농대 C	*	36
Agricultural Academy 농대 B	*	36
CAC 1p (5.12c|22m) 2p (*|*m) 3p (*|*m)	5.12c	77 (3p)
OK	5.10d	18
Agricultural Academy 농대 A	5.11b	18
DCC 1p (5.11a|20m) 2p (*|18m)	5.11a	38 (2p)
Existing 기존 77 1p (5.11b|22m) 2p (5.9|20m) 3p (5.8|35m)	5.11b	77 (3p)
Water Tank 물통	5.9	17
Sense Mint 쎈스민트	5.11b	16
Euphoria 희열	5.10c	12
Jogong 조공 1p (*|*m) 2p (*|*m)	5.10b	66 (2p)
Seonbul Slab 선불슬랩	5.8	35

BAGAJI-BAWI 바가지바위

Route Name	Grade	Height
Youngrok 영록	5.8	15
Frog 개구리	5.10c	17
Gayageum 가야금	5.11a	17
Gaeseong's Seller In Venice 베니스의개성상인	5.11a	16
Rejuvenation 회춘	5.11d	15
Gu-minator 구미네이터	5.12a	12
Checkmate 만패불청	5.11b	16
Blue Jeans 블루진	5.11c	55
Silk Road 실크로드	5.11c	56
Thalay 탈레이	5.12a	20
Yaagh 아하야	5.10b	15
Red Temptation 빨간유혹	5.11b	30
Yongak 용악 A	5.11a	25
Yongak 용악 B	5.10d	25
Yongak 용악 C	5.11c	25

Hwangjeok-bong OB Slab 황적봉 OB 슬랩

Route Name	Grade	Height
Lightning 번개	5.9	30
Engagement 약혼	5.10*	43
Hwangjeok 황적 D	5.9	35
Hwangjeok 황적 C	5.10*	34
Hwangjeok 황적 B	5.8	32
Hwangjeok 황적 A	5.8	36
Geonwoo 건우	5.8	30
Master 사부	5.10*	10

BYEONGCHEON-AM 은석산병천암

Description
Although this used to be a gravel quarry, it was developed into a climbing crag. There are currently ten routes with many more still being developed. Byeongcheon-am offers overhanging and face climbing. The routes face southeast and range from 8m to 14m high.

Directions
36.771519N 127.290328E
Gajeon-ri, Byeongcheon-ri, Dongnam-gu, Cheonan-si
천안시 동남구 병천면 가전리

From Cheonan Highway Bus Terminal 천안, take Bus 500 or 42. Get off at Tongilgongeupsa 통일공업사, which is one stop before the Korea Technical Education University 한국기술교육대학. The crag can be seen from the gas station by the bus stop. Walk towards the gas station. At the gas station, cross the street and walk up the road by the factory for ten minutes to reach the crag.

Gear
8 draws and a 50m rope.

BYEONGCHEON-AM 은석산병천암

Route Name	Grade	Height
Brother's Residence 아우내	5.11d	8
An Angel Of Belial 타락천사	5.10d	8
Hahoi Mask 하회탈	5.10c	9
Kishke 순대	5.10a	10
CAC	5.10b	10
KGB	5.12*	15
Big Snake 구렁이	5.10b	15
Byeongcheon 병천 1	5.11a	15
Byeongcheon 병천 2	5.11a	14
The Odd One Out 외톨이	5.8	8

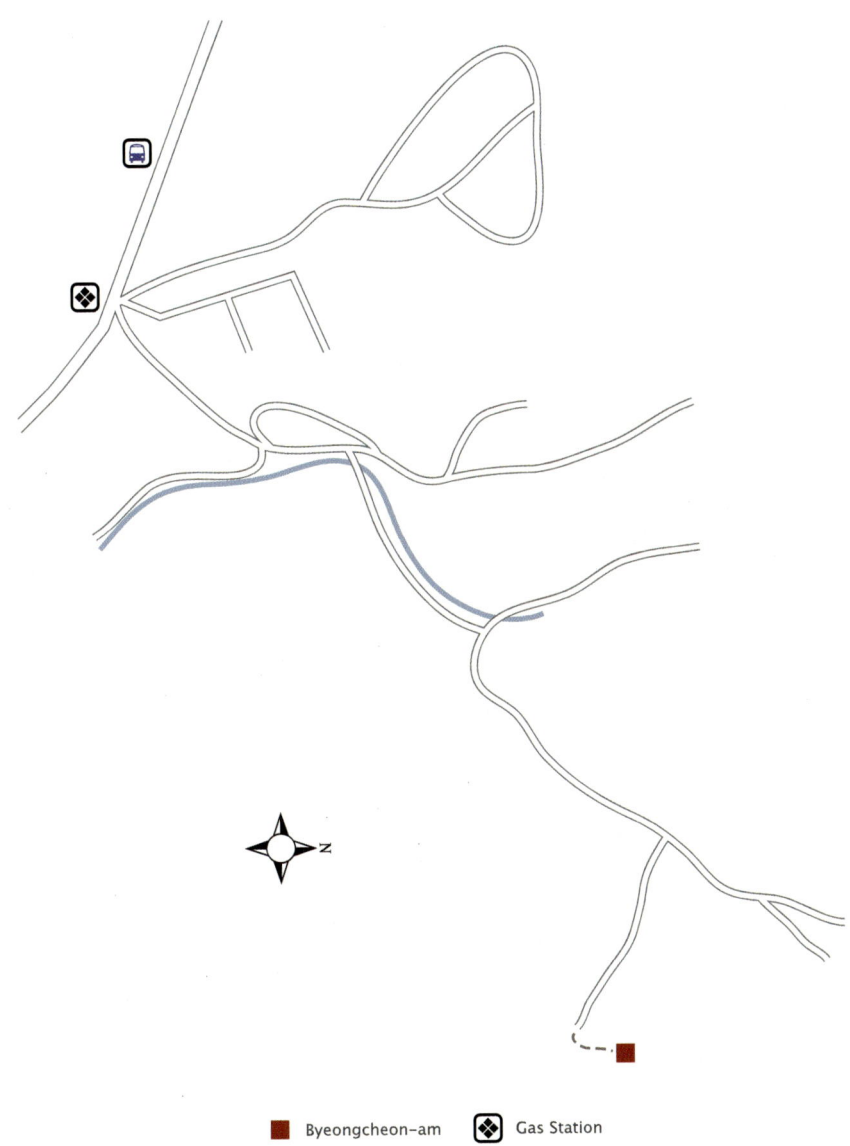

Hagampo-Amjang 학암포암장

Description
This crag, featured on the cover page of Chungcheongnam province, lies on the northwest coast of Korea. Although the crag is short and small, it offers exciting challenges and adventures on the overhanging granite wall with one of the most beautiful seaside settings.

Directions
36.903217N 126.20259E
Banggal-ri, Wonbuk-myeon, Taean-gun
태안군 원북면 방갈리

From Cheonan 천안, take a bus bound for Taean 태안. From there, transfer to Hagampo Beach 학암포. It takes approximately three hours from Cheonan. At Hagampo Beach Bus Stop, walk towards the west end of the beach and continue to the seawall. At the seawall, hike up the trail on the hill to your left. Continue until you reach the top and then walk down the left trail towards the water. Once you reach the water, turn right and make your way along the coast. The approach time will be thirty minutes from the bus stop. When the tide is low, it can be reached by walking along the coast from the seawall.

Gear
11 draws and a 50m rope.

Additional Comments
There are many minbaks 민박 and amenities around the beach. There are also campsites available at the beach south of Hagampo Beach.

■ Hagampo-amjang

Hagampo-amjang 학암포암장

Route Name	Grade	Height
Road To Salt Farm 곰소가는길	5.8	12
Samba's Dream 삼바의꿈	5.9	15
Wand 뽠트 2003	5.10a	15
Blue Sky 푸른하늘	5.10c	15
Twin Rainbow 쌍무지개	5.11b	14
Cumulus 뭉게구름	5.11c	14
Fractus 조각구름	5.12c	12
Hagam's Legend 학암의전설	5.11c	15
Share The Fate With Others 생공사	5.12c	12
Sound Of Wind 바람소리	5.10c	10
Sound Of Wave 파도소리	5.10d	12
Red Light House 빨간등대	5.11b	15

Chungcheongbuk-do

충청북도

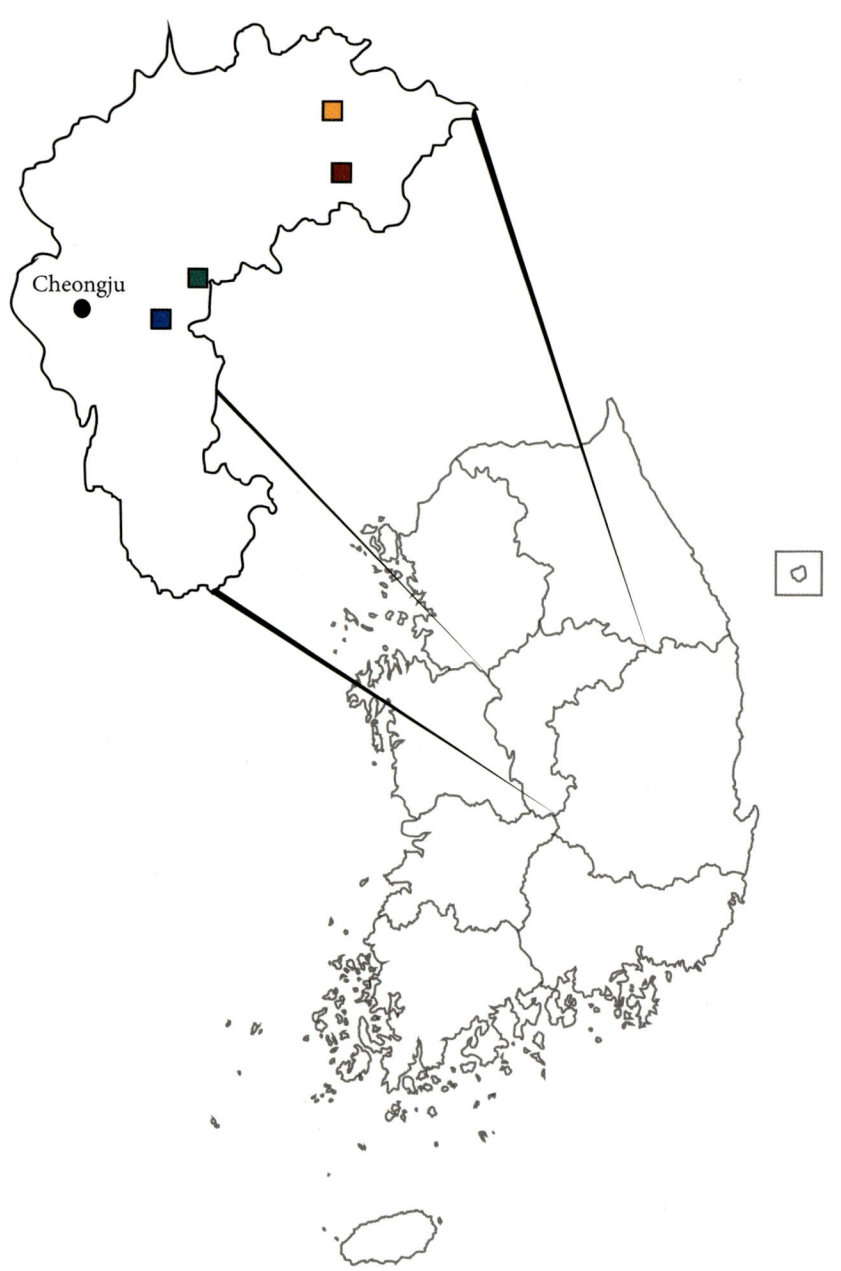

CHUNGCHEONGBUK-DO PROVINCE 충청북도

- Cheongseokgul-amjang
- Baeksuk-amjang
- Sol-bawi, Sokri-san
- Ul-bawi, Sokri-san
- Haksodae, Sokri-san
- Jangwhoinaru-amjang
- Bae-bawi, Jakseong-san
- Woo-bawi, Jakseong-san

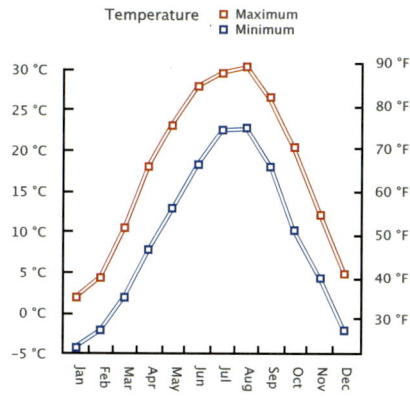

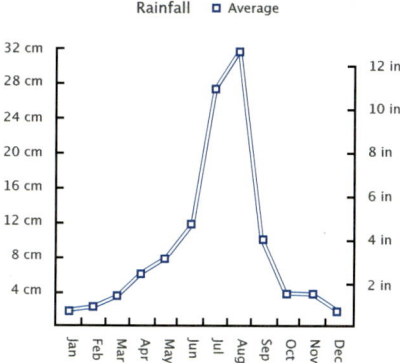

Cheongseokgul-Amjang 청석굴 암장

Description
This is the first limestone crag ever developed in Korea. It was developed in 1992. It has wild features on overhanging pockets that will please you very much as you pull through the crux of the routes. The crag has one 40m long multi-pitch on the far right side.

Directions
36.612875N 127.68685E
Unam-ri, Miwon-myeon, Cheongwon-gun, Chungcheongbuk-do
충북 청원군 미원면 운암리

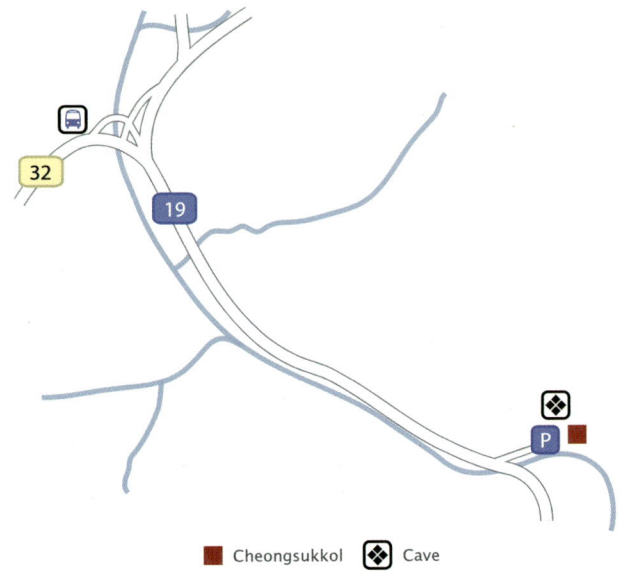

Take a bus from Cheongju 청주 to Miwon 미원. From there, transfer to a bus bound for Boeun 보은 and get off at Cheongseok Maeul 청석마을. Follow the sign that reads "옥화일경" Okhwailgyeong for five minutes. The walk to the crag from the Miwon Bus Stop will take thirty minutes.

Gear
10 draws and a 60m rope.

Safety
The anchor on the multi-pitch is old. A helmet is recommended.

Additional Comments
There is a famous cave next to the crag where a lot of tourists go to picnic by the gazebo.

Cheongseokgul-amjang 청석굴암장

Route Name	Grade	Height
Novice 새내기	5.10d	13
Festival Of Alien 이방인들의축제	5.11a	13
The Great Bear 북두칠성	5.11b	15
Blackhole 블랙홀	5.11c	15
Mona Lisa 모나리자	5.12a	15
Shooting Star 별똥	5.12a	10
Sunshine 햇살	5.10*	20
Rising Light 빛오름	5.10b	40 (2p)*

*Multi-pitch info is unavailable at this time

BAEKSUK-AMJANG 백석암장

Description
Developed from 1993 to 2001, this crag consists of three walls. Most of the routes are slab and face climbs. It seems that this crag hasn't been climbed for a long time and all the walls deserve a good overhaul.

Directions
36.560394N 127.782691E
Baekseok-ri, Sanwoi-myeon Boeun-gun 보은군 산외면 백석리

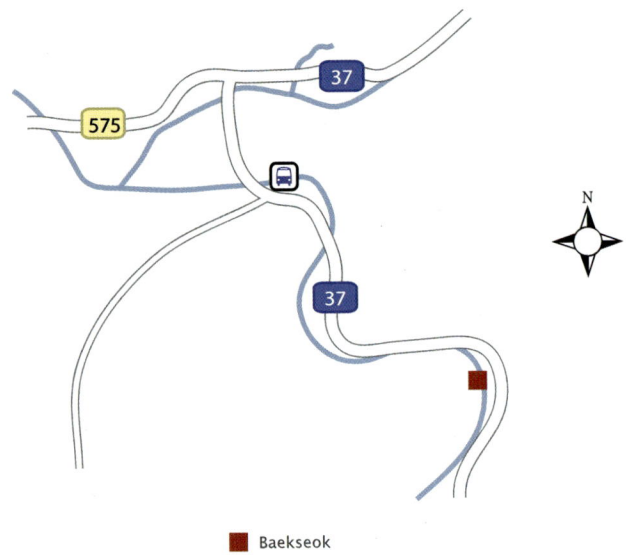

■ Baekseok

From Cheongseokgul-amjang 청석굴암장, take the bus bound for Sanoe-myeon Baekseok 산외면 백석 and get off at Baekseok 1 Bridge 백석 1 교. Walk five minutes along the river towards the crag.

Gear
12 draws and a 60m rope.

Additional Comments
This crag is located right by the river. It would be a great place during the summer if the surroundings were cleaned up.

Baeksuk-Amjang 백석암장

Route Name	Grade	Height
Smile 미소	5.8	20
Belong To The Mountain 산소속 3	5.12b	18
Hairy-faced Person 털보	5.11c	15
Discovery 디스커버리	5.11b	16
Belong To The Mountain 산소속 1	5.11c/d	16
Belong To The Mountain 산소속 2	5.12a	15
Gem 보석	*	15
Baekseok 백석	5.10a	20
Three Brothers 삼형제 1	5.9	15
Three Brothers 삼형제 2	5.8	15
Three Brothers 삼형제 3	5.8	15

Hwayang Gugok - Amjang 화양구곡암장

Description
(*Ul-bawi*) - This crag was developed in 1991. Ul-bawi has two walls. The left side of the dihedral crag consists of somewhat easy face climbs and gradually becomes overhung on the right side with some roof and crack climbing. The crag faces south.
(*Sol-bawi*) - This crag is a great place to practice placing nuts and cams. It offers gem cracks on granite rock. Sol-bawi faces south.
(*Haksodae*) - Haksodae was deveoleped in the late 1980s. It has four small and short routes that offer face and crack climbs.

Directions
(*Ul-bawi*) - 36.664744N 127.837815E
(*Sol-bawi*) - 36.666758N 127.847155E
(*Haksodae*) - 36.662816N 127.825391E
Songmyeon-ri, Cheongcheon-myeon, Goesan-gun 괴산군 청천면 송면리

(*Ul-bawi*) - From Cheongju Intercity Bus Terminal 청주, take a bus heading to Hwayang-dong Hwabuk 화양동 화북. Get off at Hwayang-dong Jayeonhakseupwon 화양동자연학습원. From the bus stop, the crag is 5m to your left by the road.
(*Sol-bawi*) - From the ticket counter, in front of the parking area, walk down the road with the stream on your left for five minutes. The crag will be on your right in the woods.
(*Haksodae*) - The crag is located at the main entrance of Hwayanggugok 화양구곡, and can be reached either by walking along the stream for fifteen minutes from the entrance. Haksodae is across the stream by a steel bridge and can easily be found by the map at the entrance.

Gear
(*Ul-bawi*) - 8 draws and a 50m rope.
(*Sol-bawi*) - 10 draws and a 50m rope, and a set of small to mid-sized cams.
(*Haksodae*) - 5 draws and a 50m rope.

Safety
Some of the anchors are worn out so extra webbing is recommended.

Additional Comments
There are official campsites and facilities available along the clean and beautiful valley. Heaps of boulders are dotted within the valley.
(*Sol-bawi*) - Many bolts have been removed at the beginning of the routes, but there are many micro-lead-nuts placed in the crack which will act as protection.

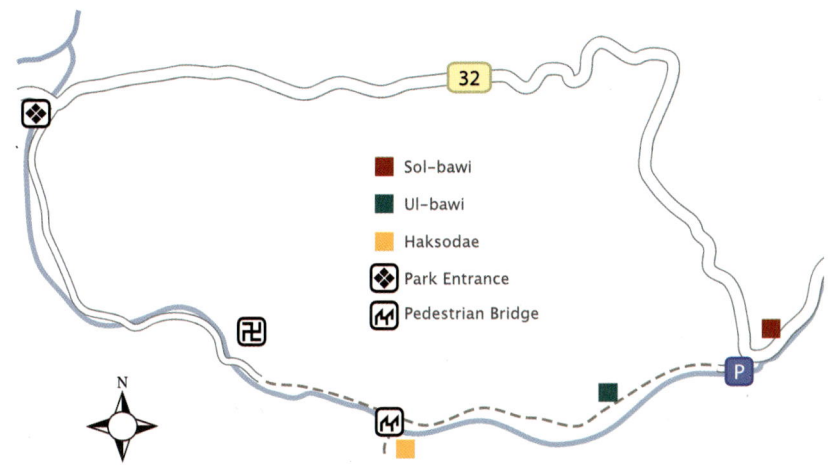

Ul-bawi 울바위 (1 of 2)

Route Name	Grade	Height
Morning Sunshine 아침햇살	5.11d	9
Stretch 기지개	5.11c	9
Birth 탄생	5.10d	11
Long Trip 긴여행	5.11b	11
Reincarnation 환생	5.10a	11
Correction 정정	5.10c	12
Triumphant General 개선장군	5.8	12
Jewel Case 보석상자	5.10b	12
Sunset 노을	5.11a	12
Naughty Kid 장난꾸러기	5.8	12
Cosmos 코스모스	5.11b	11
November 11 월	5.12a	16
Blue Crane 청학	5.11b	9

Ul-bawi 울바위 (2 of 2)

Route Name	Grade	Height
When Autumn Arrives 가을이오면	5.12a	14
Sun 태양	5.12a	13
Wave 파도	5.11c	13
Scent Of Memory 향기로운추억	5.11d	12
Run Away 런웨이	5.12a	14
Osa 오사	5.11a	14
Delight 환희	5.10d	12

Haksodae 학소대

Route Name	Grade	Height
Melody 멜로디	5.9	10
Fantasy 환상	5.10a	13
Fighting Spirit 투혼	5.10a	15
Existing 기존	5.9	10

NOTE: At this time, the route information for Sol-bawi is not available.

JAKSEONG-SAN 배바위작성산

Description
(***Bae-bawi***) - Bae-bawi was developed in the early 1980s. It is mainly vertical climbing on granite rock. The longest climb is 162m long.
(***Sol-bawi***) - This crag is located near the trailhead of Bae-bawi Valley and has short sport climbing routes. It faces southeast and is in the shade all day.

Directions
(***Bae-bawi***) - 37.031816N 128.200343E
(***Sol-bawi***) - 37.029495N 128.198937E
Seongnae-ri, Geumseong-myeon, Jecheon-si 제천시 금성면 성내리

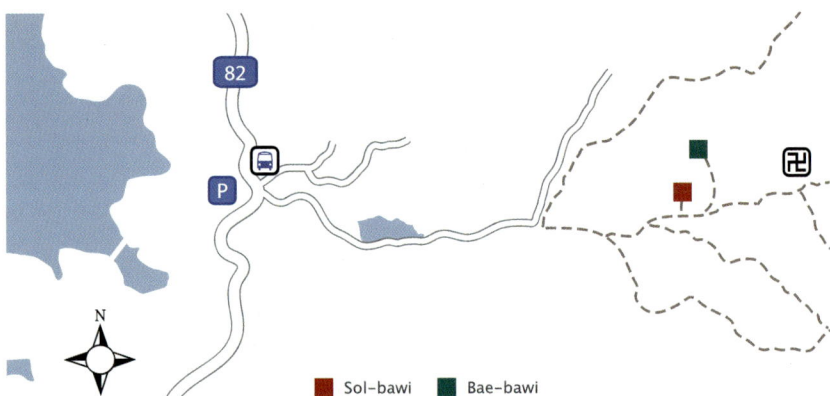

(***Bae-bawi***) - From Jecheon Intercity Bus Terminal 제천, get on a bus bound for Seongnae-ri 성내리 and get off at Seongnae-ri 성내리. Walk through the village for ten minutes and past Muam Reservoir 무암. Around this area is the only official campsite for Jakseong-san. Follow the trail for ten minutes and you will encounter an old film set. Contine past the set and stay on the main trail until you see a big sign on your left that has the crag information. At the sign, cross the stream and hike up for fifteen minutes to reach the crag. It faces southeast.
(***Sol-bawi***) - To access this crag, use the same directions of Bae-bawi, until the crag information sign. At the sign, take the left path that follows the valley for five minutes.

Gear
(***Bae-bawi***) - 10 draws, two 60m ropes, and a full set of cams.
(***Sol-bawi***) - 10 draws and a 50m rope.

Safety
(***Bae-bawi***) - Most of the anchors are solid, but a helmet is still recommended.

Additional Comments
(***Bae-bawi***) - There is an awesome view of Cheongpung Lake 청풍호 and Worak-san 월악산 from the crag. Within the mountains of Mu-am Valley, there are lots of boulders with potential and scattered, short sport climbing routes.

BAE-BAWI 배바위

Route Name	Grade	Height
Number 번 1	5.9	50
Number 번 2	5.6	35
Number 번 3	5.11a	80 (3p)
1p (5.11a|30m) **2p** (5.10d|15m) **3p** (5.10d|35m)		
Number 번 4	5.10a	42 (2p)
1p (5.10a|20m) **2p** (*|22m)		
Number 번 5	5.9	85 (3p)
1p (*|20m) **2p** (*|35m) **3p** (5.9|30m)		
Number 번 6	5.10d	55 (2p)
1p (5.10d|40m) **2p** (*|15m)		
Number 번 7	5.8	65 (3p)
1p (5.8|25m) **2p** (*|20m) **3p** (*|20m)		
Salty Route 소태길	5.11a	65 (3p)
1p (5.11a|20m) **2p** (*|20m) **3p** (*|20m)		
Number 번 8	5.10a	162 (4p)
1p (5.10a|40m) **2p** (5.10a|40m) **3p** (5.9|42m) **4p** (*|40m)		
Number 번 9	5.10b	162 (4p)
1p (*|40m) **2p** (5.10a|40m) **3p** (5.10b|42m) **4p** (*|40m)		
Number 번 10	5.10c/A0	40 (2p)
1p (A0|20m) **2p** (5.10c|20m)		
Number Right 번우측 10	*	45 (2p)*
1p (*|20m) **2p** (*|25m)		
Number Right 번우측 4	*	45 (2p)*
1p (*|20m) **2p** (*|25m)		

*Multi-pitch info is unavailable at this time

SOL-BAWI 솔바위

Glorious Going Out 화려한외출	5.9	*
Reunion 재회	5.10a	*
Fine Tree Field 솔밭	5.10a	*
Humpback 꼽추	5.10b	*
From Bare Feet To Benz 맨발에서 벤츠까지	5.8	*
Road Of Ravine 계곡길	5.10a	*
Too Short 너무짧아요	5.11b	*

*Routes are under 20m high

JANGWHOE-AMJANG 장회나루 암장

Description
This crag has fourteen routes and faces southeast. It is located near Jangwhoinaru Wharf 장회나루 선착장 at Lake Chungju 충주호. Most of the routes are face and crack climbing, with aid climbing on a few of the multi-pitches. There are routes next to the bridge called "설마교" Seolma, but most of them look mossy and are covered with ivy. Some of the bolts and anchors look suspicious. The main crag, further down the road, is in good shape. This crag is a hidden gem with lots of climbs on cracks and overhangs with potential for many more.

Directions
36.928076N 128.251433E
Janghoe-ri, Danseong-myeon, Danyang-gun 단양군 단성면 장회리

From Chungju 충주 or Suanbo 수안보, take the bus bound for Jangwhoinaru Wharf 장회나루 선착장. Get off at the wharf and walk for five minutes towards the bridge called "설마교" Seolma, which will be to your left with the lake on your right. Don't cross the big bridge called "장회교" Jangwhoigyo. From the bridge, the main crag is 300m south. To access the crag, walk down the road for ten minutes with your back to the bridge and the stream to your left. Look for the trail on the right. This crag is visible from the road. It takes less than ten minutes from the bridge.

Gear
12 draws, a 60m rope, and a full set of cams.

Safety
A few of the routes on the main crag are mossy and covered with ivy.

Additional Comments
There are many restaurants and shops at the wharf so you can get anything you need from there. There are tons of boulders around the crags and awesome surroundings.

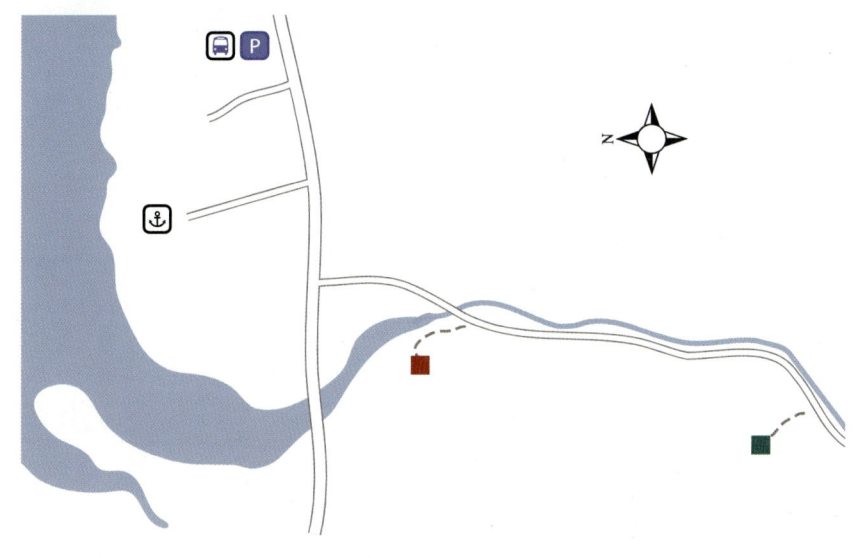

■ Jangwhoinaru-amjang   ■ Jangwhoe-amjang

JANGWHOE-AMJANG 장회나루암장

Route Name	Grade	Height
Road With Path 길있는길	5.11c	7
Road Without Path 길없는길	*	17
Fairy & Lumberjack 선녀와나무꾼 1,2 1p (A*|21m) 2p (5.10d|22m)	5.10d	43 (2p)
Hwangpo Sailer 황포돛단배	5.10c	21
Senior Preference 경로우대길 1p (5.9|22m) 2p (5.10*|20m)	5.10*	42 (2p)
Green Scent 초록향기	5.9	13
Mountain Friend 뫼벗 1p (5.10b|22m) 2p (5.8|18m)	5.10b	40 (2p)
Evening Primrose 달맞이꽃 1p (5.10a|21m) 2p (5.10d|15m)	5.11d	36 (2p)
Landscape Of Hanwoo 한우의풍경	5.10d	21
Route For Two Become One 둘이서하나되는길	5.10a	21
Geum Route 금우길	*	19
A Pillar Of Strength 천하대장군 1p (*|13m) 2p (*|22m)	5.12a	35 (2p)
In The Passage Of Time 세월의흐름속에서	5.11b	25
Brother Route 형제길	*	27

GANGWON-DO

강원도

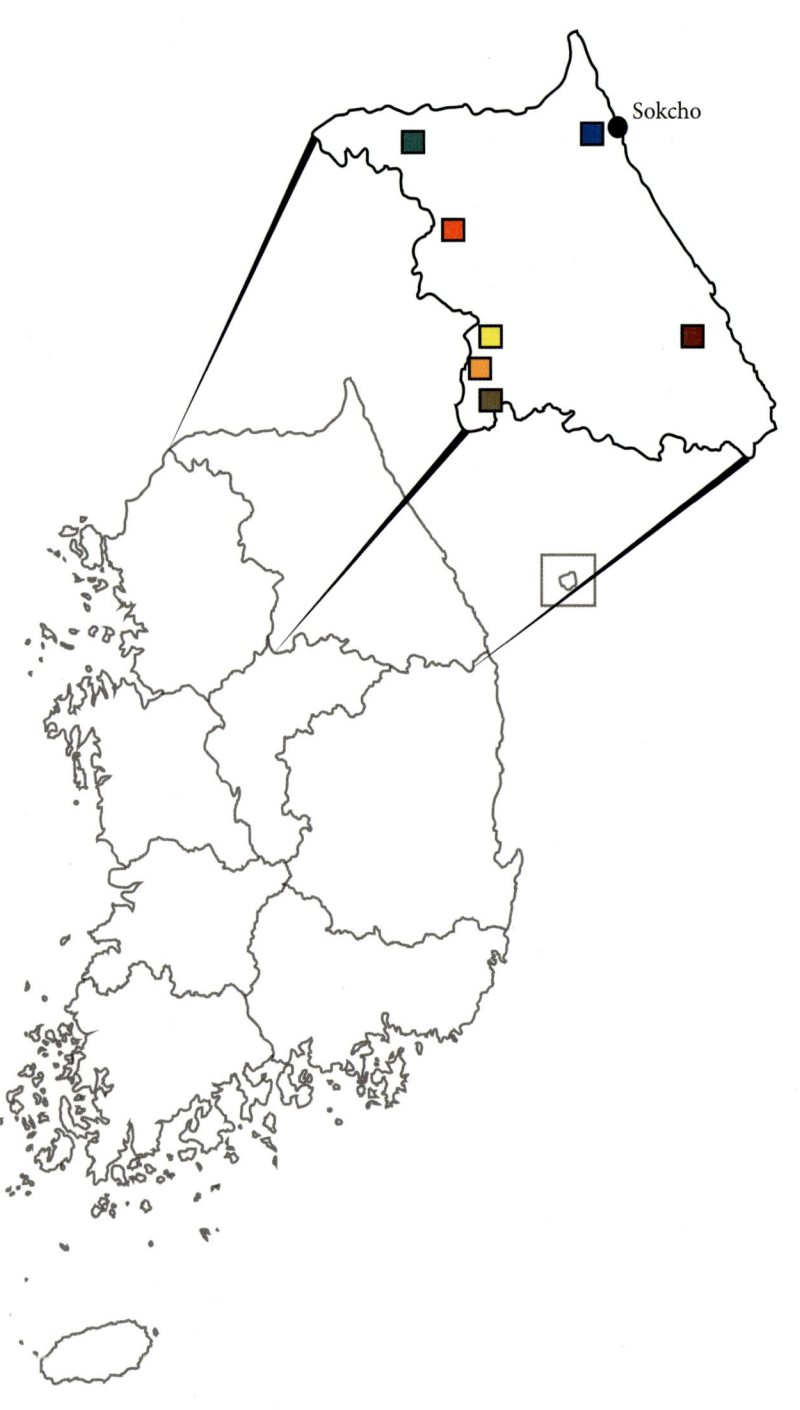

Gangwon-do Province 강원도

- ■ Buchae-bawi
- ■ Daeryuk-bong
- ■ Mumyeong-bawi/Seil Gelande
- ■ Eun-byeok
- ■ Geokbuk-am
- ■ Sangeo-am
- ■ Gorae-am
- ■ Samagui-bawi
- ■ Gadeok-do
- ■ Beom-bawi
- ■ Tanggeon-bawi
- ■ Janggun-byeok
- ■ Jeok-byeok
- ■ Gaya-byeok
- ■ Sumeun-byeok

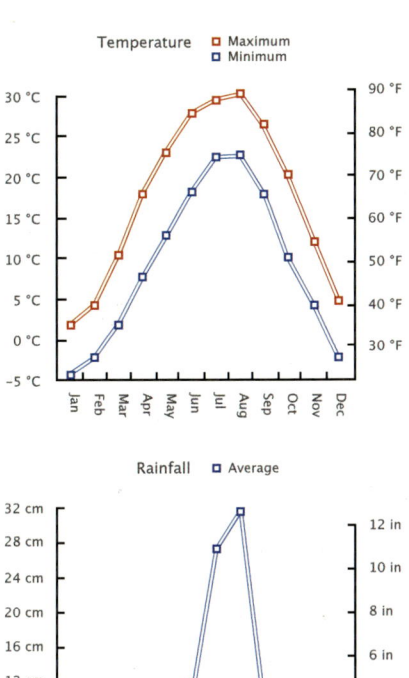

DUTA-SAN, BYEONGPUNG-AM 두타산 병풍암

Description
This crag sits in the stunning Mureung Valley 무릉계곡, which means "A Valley Of Paradise". The climbs here offer fun jamming on different sized cracks. A few of the routes are well bolted, but many of the routes can be easily protected by cams. When you get to the top belay anchors, you can tell why this valley is called Paradise. The wall faces southeast on basalt rock with vertical cracks and overhangs.

Directions
37.458372N 129.000456E
Samhwa-dong, Donghae-si 동해시 삼화동

From Donghae Bus Terminal 동해, which can be accessed from all the major cities, take a bus bound for Mureung 무릉. Get off at the end of the bus line and walk towards the end of the road to the ticket counter. Begin hiking on the main trail of Mureung Valley 무릉계곡. As you hike up, check for the sign that says "쌍폭" Ssangpok. It will take fifty minutes to reach Ssangpok 쌍폭. Past the iron bridge and close to Ssangpok, the crag can be viewed above the trees to your right. Look for the tiny path that ascends steeply to reach the crag. Scramble up the trail for five minutes.

Gear
12 draws, a 60m rope, and a full set of cams.

Safety
A helmet and extra webbing is recommended.

Additional Comments
Each route has its own number at the start that shows the grade. The crag is divided by a cave that sits in the middle of the wall. The cave can be bivouacked. There are also many campsites around the crag. Water can be found by Yongchu Falls 용추폭포. There are many minbaks 민박 and great campsites at the entrance of the mountain.

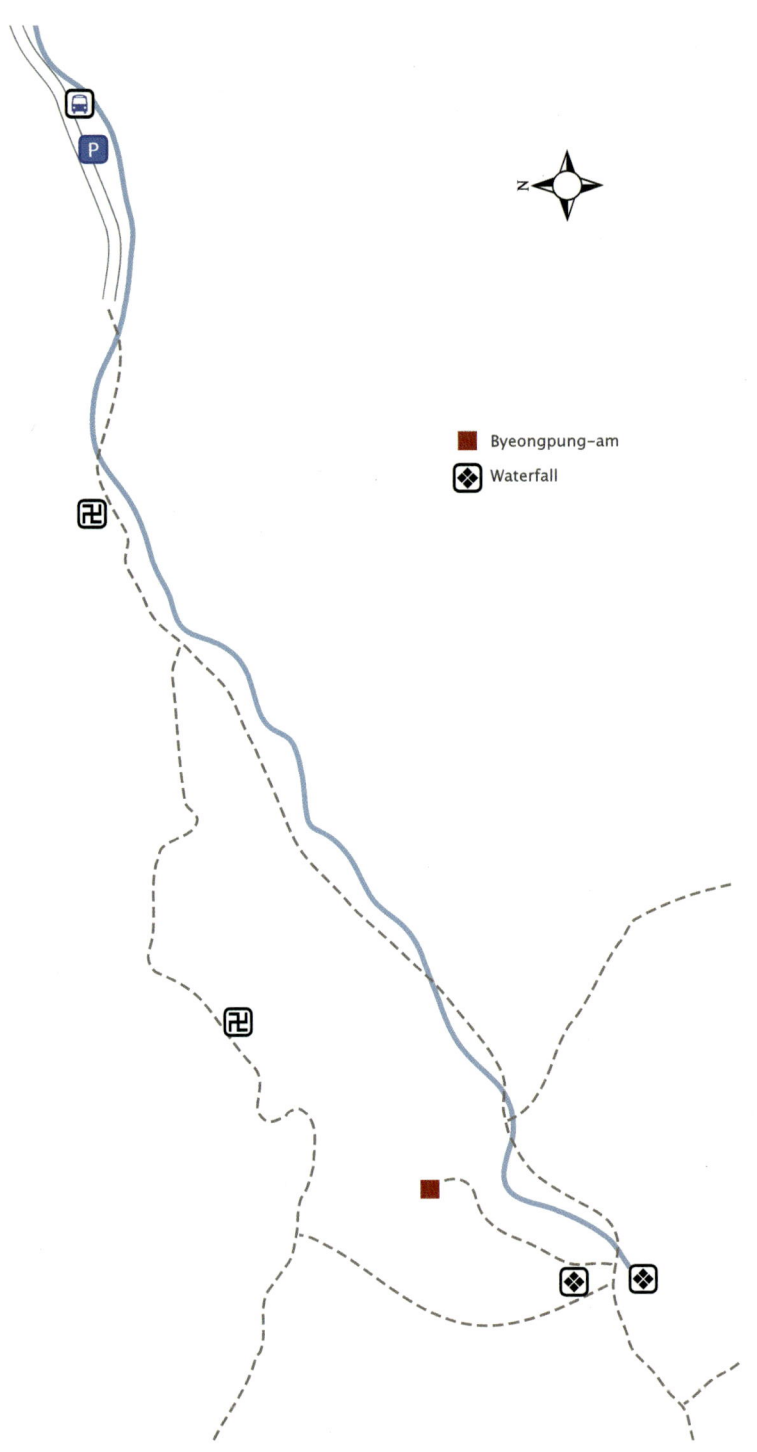

Byeongpung-am 병풍암

Route Name	Grade	Height
Cheongjukil 청죽일	5.10a	30
Rainy Or Snowy, Whatever 비가오나눈이오나 **1p** (5.9|22m) **2p** (5.9|18m)	5.9	40 (2p)
Fine Tree Wind 솔바람 **1p** (5.9|22m) **2p** (5.9|18m)	5.9	40 (2p)
Memory Of The Past 지난날의추억 **1p** (5.10a|30m) **2p** (5.9|20m)	5.10a	50 (2p)
White Wild Rose 찔레꽃 **1p** (5.9|30m) **2p** (5.9|23m)	5.9	53 (2p)
Road To Gooseberry Vine 다래덩쿨길	5.13*	30
La Novia 라노비아	5.11b	22
In The Air 미정	5.13*	25
Writing A Letter At The First Night 첫날밤에쓰는편지 **1p** (5.12b/c|30m) **2p** (*|12m)	5.12b/c	47 (2p)
Beautiful World 아름다운세상	5.11b	27
Hungry Road Amitabul 배고픈길 아미타불 **1p** (5.10b|27m) **2p** (5.9|26m)	5.10b	53 (2p)
Road Between Sleep & Wake 비몽사몽길 **1p** (5.11c/d|30m) **2p** (5.9|22m)	5.11c/d	52 (2p)
Hot Pepper Road 땡초길 **1p** (5.9|30m) **2p** (5.9|22m)	5.9	52 (2p)
Sheriff Road 포돌이길	5.9	27
Tears Of Undutiful Son 불효자의눈물 **1p** (5.9|27m) **2p** (5.9|30m) **3p** (5.9|23m)	5.9	80 (3p)
Wind Sound, Water Sound 바람소리물소리 **1p** (5.10a|27m) **2p** (5.9|30m) **3p** (5.8|23m)	5.10a	80 (3p)
Road Of The Paradise 무릉도원길 **1p** (5.10c/d|30m) **2p** (5.9|33m)	5.10c/d	63 (2p)
Road Of A Friend 친구길 **1p** (5.8|27m) **2p** (5.8|25m)	5.8	52 (2p)

SEORAK-SAN 설악산

Description
(***Janggun-bong***) - Seorak-san National Park is Korea's most famous park and is often considered the most beautiful. It is nestled within the northeast coast of the peninsula. In the park there is a twenty minute hike on primarily flat, paved ground that leads to Biseondae Shelter 비선대, that is frequented by climbers. There is a restaurant attached to the shelter. From the shelter, as you walk towards the crag, you'll come across Geumgang Cave 금강굴, which means "Solidity that can blow human anguish away" and "So solid that it never be broken". This granite crag is divided into two walls: Front Wall and Southwest Wall.

(***Jeok-byeok***) - Its red rock wall may hold some of the most adventurous rock climbing in South Korea. Each route features steep cracks and overhangs from start to finish. Even though this crag is a bit shorter than its neighbor, Janggun-bong, the high view from these routes may give you some shakes. Most of the routes require advanced skill in aid-climbing. Climbs start after an easy 5.7 single pitch. It faces west.

(***Youseon-dae***) - This crag boasts of interesting slab, crack, and chimney climbing. The climbing is primarily trad on granite rock that faces southwest. Beware of several badly placed bolts. New routes have recently been added to this crag. Climbers visit to climb the famous ridge route Geuriumdul 그리움둘.

(***Ulsan-bawi***) - Dubbed as the biggest crag in South Korea, Ulsan-bawi 울산바위 teems with mostly trad routes. This crag has been climbed since the 1960s and roughly thirty routes have been established since then. Abseiling can be done by walking down the main trail, with stone steps, from the observation platform. Because of the popularity of Janggun-bong 장군봉 and Jeok-byeok 적벽, this crag gets fewer climbers all year around. Some of the anchors and bolts are old and sketchy so be aware of the hazards.

(***Sotowanggol-amjang***) - Many climbers travel to this crag because of its relatively shorter approach compared to the other crags on the east side of Seorak Mountain. The climbs vary from cracks, slabs, and steep vertical face climbing with various holds and flakes. The bolts and anchors are pretty good. It faces southwest and there is a beautiful stream that runs past it.

Directions
(***Janggun-bong***) - 38.164331N 128.46424E
(***Jeok-byeok***) - 38.164517N 128.465495E
(***Youseon-dae***) - 38.164821N 128.461525E
(***Ulsan-bawi***) - 38.193048N 128.473799E
(***Sotowanggol-amjang***) - 38.164677N 128.495171E
Seorak-dong, Sokcho-si 속초시 설악동

(***Janggun-bong***) - From any major city, take a bus bound for Sokcho 속초. Get off at the entrance of Seorak-dong 설악동입구. From there, transfer to a local bus heading to Seorak-dong, which is a different bus stop then the stop at the entrance of Seorak-dong. Get off at the end of the line. Hike on the main trail until you reach the bridge right before Biseondae Shelter 비선대. To access the Front Wall, don't cross the bridge to the shelter. At the bridge, take the trail on your right that is by a warning sign and hike up until you reach a fork. Follow the trail that branches off to the left. Continue on the path for ten minutes to get to Front Wall. The approach time will be fifty minutes from the bus stop. To access the Southwest Wall, use the same directions as Front Wall until you reach the shelter. Cross the bridge to get to the shelter, continue past it and cross the suspension bridge to hike up to Geumgang Cave 금강굴. Look for a trail on your left just before the cave. Take it and scramble up for five minutes to get to the start of Southwest Wall.

(*Jeok-byeok*) - The approach for this crag is similar to Janggun-bong. Before the bridge, look for a trail on your right by a warning sign. Follow it and hike up until you reach a fork. Take the right trail and follow this path for five minutes to reach the base of Jeok-byeok. The approach time will be fifty minutes from the bus stop.

(*Youseon-dae*) - The directions are similar to the Janggun-bong Southwest Wall. Continue past the shelter and across the suspension bridge towards Geumgang Cave 금강굴. Stay on the main trail to Madeung 마등. Do not follow the trail to the cave. Hike up for five minutes past the start of the far left route on the Southwest Wall of Janggun-bong. Look for a faint trail located between Rescue Mark 02-01 and 02-02 (don't hike past 02-02). Follow the trail, by a big flat rock to your left, into the woods. Scramble up for a couple of minutes, following signs and arrow marks, to the start of the routes. The approach time will be an hour from the bus stop.

(*Ulsan-bawi*) - From the park entrance, walk on the main trail until you reach a bridge. The trail forks before the bridge. Don't cross the bridge. Take the trail to the right before the bridge and follow the signs for Ulsan-bawi 울산바위. The path passes a temple, Sinheung-sa 신흥사, and a few restaurants. It will take you twenty minutes from the temple to reach the crag.

(*Sotowanggol-amjang*) - Walk towards the cable car station and cross the bridge, Biryonggyo 비룡교, by the ranger station. 150m past the bridge, there is a sign that says "No Trail". Walk up the trail that passes under the sign and continue on for twenty minutes. You will have to cross the stream to get to the crag.

Gear
(*Janggun-bong*) - 10 draws, a 60m rope, and a full set of cams.
(*Jeok-byeok*) - 15 draws, two 50m ropes, and a full set of cams and nuts. Extra small to mid-sized cams with foot aiders are required.
(*Youseon-dae*) - 10 draws, two 60m ropes, and a full set of cams and nuts.
(*Ulsan-bawi*) - 15 draws, two 60m ropes, a full set of cams and nuts. Aid-climbing equipment is recommended.
(*Sotowanggol-amjang*) - 12 draws, two 60m ropes, a full set of cams. There is also one aid-climbing route available.

Safety
A helmet and extra webbing is recommended for the climbing in Seorak-san.
(*Ulsan-bawi*) - Many of the bolts and anchors are old and outdated. Practice extreme caution when using them and back up the anchors with your own gear. Rock fall is common, especially in the couloir.

Additional Comments
Climbing at Seorak-san requires a permit, available at http://www.knps.or.kr. Water and food is available at the shelter and the park entrance. Camping and cooking is not allowed in the park except in designated areas.

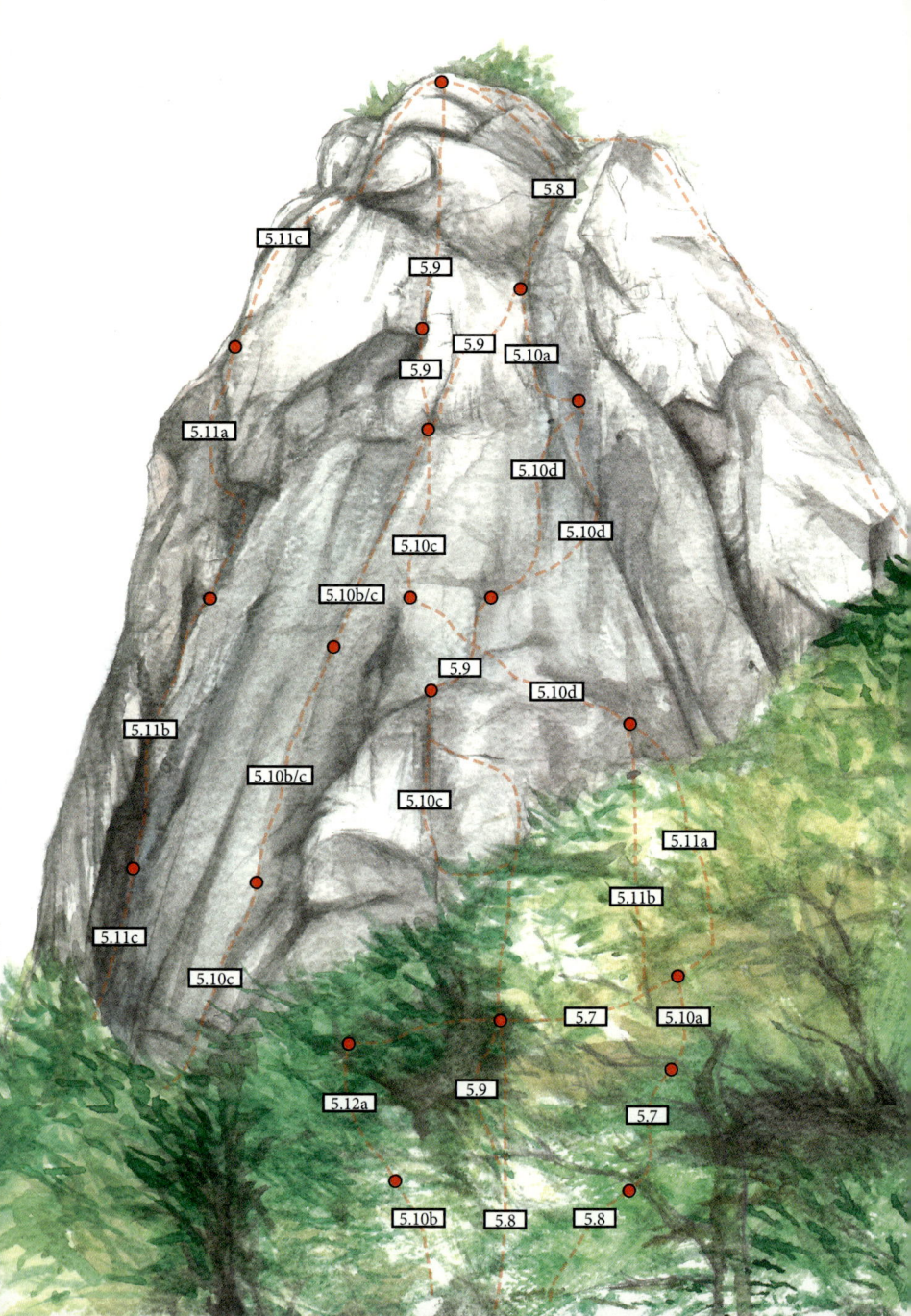

Janggun-bong

JANGGUN-BONG, FRONT WALL 장군봉 정면벽

Route Name	Grade	Height
Gijeong Route 기정길	5.11c	148 (7p)

1p (5.8|45m) **2p** (5.7|25m) **3p** (5.10c|33m) **4p** (5.9|23m)
5p (5.10d|22m) **6p** (5.9|20m) **7p** (5.8|40m)

Gugong-Gil 구공길	5.10c	155 (5p)

1p (5.10c|35m) **2p** (5.10b/c|30m) **3p** (5.10b/c|30m) **4p** (5.9|20m)
5p (5.9|40m)

My Beloved One Born In October First 나의소중한사랑 10 월 1 일생	5.12a	210 (7p)

1p (5.10b|40m) **2p** (5.12a|35m) **3p** (5.7|35m) **4p** (5.11b|35m)
5p (5.10d|30m) **6p** (5.10c|25m) **7p** (5.9|20m)

Existing Route 기존길	5.10d	252 (7p)

1p (5.8|45m) **2p** (5.7|25m) **3p** (5.10c|33m) **4p** (5.9|23m)
5p (5.10d|22m) **6p** (5.9|20m) **7p** (5.8|40m)

General 장군 97	5.11a	125 (4p)

1p (5.8|40m) **2p** (5.7|25m) **3p** (5.10a|30m) **4p** (5.11a|30m)

JANGGUN-BONG, SOUTHWEST WALL 장군봉 남서벽

Route Name	Grade	Height
Geumgang 금강	5.10b	70 (2p)

1p (5.10a|30m) **2p** (5.10b|40m)

Alpine Clutch 알파인클러치	5.11d	168 (7p)

1p (5.9|32m) **2p** (5.10a|23m) **3p** (5.9|20m) **4p** (5.10a|18m)
5p (5.10c|20m) **6p** (5.11a|30m) **7p** (5.11a|20m)

Seoki's Farm 석이농장	5.10d	180 (8p)

1p (5.4|20m) **2p** (5.10a|27m) **3p** (5.10b|29m) **4p** (5.10b|30m)
5p (5.10a|20m) **6p** (5.10b|20m) **7p** (5.10c|20m) **8p** (5.10a|8m)

Corder 꼬르데	5.10b	168 (7p)

1p (5.4|20m) **2p** (5.11a|30m) **3p** (5.11a|28m) **4p** (5.10b|35m)
5p (5.10a|15m) **6p** (5.10a|18m) **7p** (5.10b|22m)

Alpine Kolon 알파인코오롱	5.11b	160 (5p)

1p (5.8|35m) **2p** (5.10b|40m) **3p** (5.10a|30m) **4p** (5.11b|23m)
5p (5.10b|32m)

A2O	5.10a	183 (7p)

1p (5.10a|30m) **2p** (5.9|40m) **3p** (5.2|20m) **4p** (5.6|20m)
5p (5.8|25m) **6p** (5.9|28m) **7p** (5.10a|20m)

JEOK-BYEOK 적벽

Route Name	Grade	Height
College Of Education Route 교대길	5.12b/A0	70 (3p)
1p (5.12b|25m) **2p** (A0|20m) **3p** (A0|25m)		
Croni-Gil 크로니길	A1	75 (3p)
1p (*|30m) **2p** (A1|20m) **3p** (A0|25m)		
Being The Sole Lead 독주길	5.8/A1	75 (3p)
1p (A0|30m) **2p** (A1|20m) **3p** (5.8|25m)		
Echo-Gil 에코길	5.11c/A2	98 (4p)
1p (5.11c|18m) **2p** (A1|40m) **3p** (A2|20m) **4p** (5.8|25m)		
Mura-Gil 무라길	5.9/A4	100 (4p)
1p (5.9|20m) **2p** (A1|25m) **3p** (A4|25m) **4p** (5.8|30m)		
(No Name) 무명	5.9/A1	65 (2p)
1p (5.8|40m) **2p** (5.7|25m)		

YOUSEON-DAE 유선대

Route Name	Grade	Height
Yonghwa 용화 A	5.10c	120*
Yonghwa 용화 B	5.10c	125*
Insugil 인수길	5.11a	130*
Gyodaegil 교대길	5.10	165*
Youseon 유선 D	5.10	150*
Youseon 유선 C	5.10	195*
Youseon 유선 B	5.10	165*
Iryukgongcheon 이륙공천	5.10d	186*
Youseon D Variation 유선 D 변형	5.9/5.10a	165*

*Multi-pitch info is unavailable at this time

ULSAN-BAWI 울산바위 (1 OF 2)

Route Name	Grade	Height
(No Name) 미상 1	5.10b	180 (7p)

1p (*|30m) **2p** (5.10b|30m) **3p** (*|40m) **4p** (5.9|20m) **5p** (*|*m)
6p (*|*m) **7p** (*|*m)

(No Name) 미상 2	5.10b	230 (5p)

1p (5.10a|25m) **2p** (5.8|40m) **3p** (5.9|20m) **4p** (5.10b|45m) **5p** (*|30m)

(No Name) 미상 3	5.10b/A0	185 (5p)

1p (5.9|45m) **2p** (A0|45m) **3p** (5.9|20m) **4p** (5.10b|45m) **5p** (*|30m)

(No Name) 미상 4	5.9/A0	130 (4p)

1p (5.9|30m) **2p** (*|30m) **3p** (A0|30m) **4p** (*|40m)

Yoban Route 요반길	5.9	225 (7p)

1p (5.9|35m) **2p** (5.9|40m) **3p** (*|40m) **4p** (*|20m) **5p** (*|60m)
6p (*|40m) **7p** (*|45m)

Digno 사선크랙	5.9	234 (7p)

1p (5.9|30m) **2p** (5.8|38m) **3p** (*|25m) **4p** (*|25m) **5p** (*|38m)
6p (*|38m) **7p** (*|40m)

64 Bolt Route 64 볼트길	5.9/A0	180 (5p)

1p (5.9|25m) **2p** (A0|25m) **3p** (*|35m) **4p** (A0|35m) **5p** (*|35m)

Bat Route 박쥐길	5.9/A1	135 (5p)

1p (5.9|25m) **2p** (5.9|25m) **3p** (A1|20m) **4p** (A0|35m) **5p** (*|35m)

Munridae #2 문리대 2 번	5.9	132 (5p)

1p (5.8|32m) **2p** (5.9|30m) **3p** (5.9|25m) **4p** (*|20m) **5p** (*|*m)

Lightning Route 번개길	5.9/A0	123(4p)

1p (5.9|33m) **2p** (*|25m) **3p** (A0|25m) **4p** (*|40m)

Munridae #1 문리대 1 번	*	100 (4p)

1p (*|*m) **2p** (*|*m) **3p** (*|*m) **4p** (*|*m)

Munridae Route 문리대길	5.9/A0	201 (7p)

1p (5.9|40m) **2p** (5.8|40m) **3p** (5.8|30m) **4p** (A0|28m) **5p** (*|20m)
6p (5.7|28m) **7p** (5.7|15m)

(No Name) 미상 5	*	100 (3p)

1p (*|20m) **2p** (*|20m) **3p** (*|40m)

Silver Route 은벽길	5.11b/A0	45 (2p)

1p (5.11b|25m) **2p** (A0|20m)

ULSAN-BAWI 울산바위 (2 OF 2)

Route Name	Grade	Height
No Name 미상	*	70 (2p)

1p (*|25m) **2p** (*|45m)

Venus Route 비너스길	5.10c	200 (6p)

1p (5.9|30m) **2p** (5.10a|30m) **3p** (5.10c|25m) **4p** (5.10|50m) **5p** (*|30m) **6p** (*|35m)

Red Route 붉은벽길	*	190 (5p)

1p (*|20m) **2p** (*|20m) **3p** (*|20m) **4p** (*|20m) **5p** (*|40m)

Bolt Route 볼트길	*	55 (2p)

1p (*|30m) **2p** (*|25m)

Red Wall 붉은벽 C	5.9/A0	250 (5p)

1p (*|60m) **2p** (*|30m) **3p** (5.9|20m) **4p** (5.8|25m) **5p** (A0|20m)

Step Slab Route 계단슬랩길	5.9/A0	230 (5p)

1p (5.9|20m) **2p** (5.7|30m) **3p** (*|20m) **4p** (5.8|25m) **5p** (A0|20m)

Mountain Friend Route 악우길	A0	230 (6p)

1p (*|52m) **2p** (*|41m) **3p** (*|32m) **4p** (*|31m) **5p** (A0|45m) **6p** (*|40m)

Mak Crack 막크랙	*	190 (7p)

1p (*|30m) **2p** (*|35m) **3p** (*|35m) **4p** (*|30m) **5p** (*|25m) **6p** (*|25m) **7p** (*|20m)

Letter "兵" 兵 자있는곳	*	207 (7p)

1p (*|17m) **2p** (*|28m) **3p** (*|18m) **4p** (*|31m) **5p** (*|36m) **6p** (*|27m) **7p** (*|40m)

Letter E marked Route E 자표시루트	*	202 (7p)

1p (*|27m) **2p** (*|18m) **3p** (*|36m) **4p** (*|17m) **5p** (*|34m) **6p** (*|32m) **7p** (*|38m)

Right Crack 우측크랙	*	134 (5p)

1p (*|29m) **2p** (*|35m) **3p** (*|35m) **4p** (*|30m) **5p** (*|15m)

Northeast Wall 1 Course 북동벽 1 코스	*	130 (6p)

1p (*|20m) **2p** (*|20m) **3p** (*|40m) **4p** (*|40m) **5p** (*|40m) **6p** (*|20m)

Sotowanggol-amjang 소토왕골암장 (1 of 2)

Route Name	Grade	Height
Broomstick 빗자루	5.10a	30
Hoe 호미	5.10c	30
Viper 독사	5.10b	34
Beehive 벌집 **1p** (5.11a|30m) **2p** (5.11b|28m)	5.11b	58 (2p)
Companion Route 벗길 **1p** (5.10a|30m) **2p** (5.10b|40m)	5.10b	70 (2p)
Hole 구멍 **1p** (5.10a|33m) **2p** (5.11b|42m)	5.11b	75 (2p)
Water Route 물길 **1p** (5.10a|41m) **2p** (5.11b|40m)	5.11b	81 (2p)
Fallen Blossoms On A Stream 낙화유수 **1p** (5.10b|40m) **2p** (5.10b|45m) **3p** (5.10c|20m) **4p** (5.9|10m) **5p** (5.10c|45m)	5.10c	160 (5p)

Sotowanggol-amjang 소토왕골암장 (2 of 2)

Route Name	Grade	Height
Dream Palace 꿈의 궁전	5.11*/A0	130 (5p)

1p (5.8|10m) **2p** (5.10c|28m) **3p** (5.10*|30m) **4p** (5.11*/A0|22m) **5p** (5.10c|40m)

Some Of The Dream 어떤이의 꿈	5.11a	206 (6p)

1p (5.9|30m) **2p** (5.10a|32m) **3p** (5.11a|42m) **4p** (5.10b|37m) **5p** (5.10c|40m) **6p** (5.6|25m)

Bridge Over Troubled Water 험한세상의 다리가 되어	5.11b	147 (7p)

1p (5.7|17m) **2p** (5.10a|23m) **3p** (5.10a|10m) **4p** (5.11b|26m) **5p** (5.10c|22m) **6p** (5.8|29m) **7p** (5.10b|20m)

Mountain Light 산빛 J.K	5.8/A4	146 (3p)

1p (*|48m) **2p** (*|53m) **3p** (*|45m)

SEORAK-SAN 2 설악산

Description
(*Agal-bawi*) - Agal-bawi was opened to the public in 2000. This crag is located next to Okyeotang Rest Area 옥녀탕휴게소, 3km west of Jangsudae Ranger Office 장수대 on Hangyeoryeong 한계령 from Yangyang 양양. Agal-bawi is named after a mouth because of the strange shape at the top of the rock. Although it faces south, the trees around the crag offer pleasant shade.
(*Mireukjanggun-bong*) - This crag rests on the west part of Seorak Mountain. It is solid granite rock with sweet lines of cracks, face, slab, and some bolted routes for your pleasure. The north part is shorter than the south, but it has some challenging routes on the multi-pitches. It faces west. Routes start from the left by the chart. Spectacular summit views await you at the top.
(*Sinseondae*) - Sinseondae was developed in 2004. It faces southeast. It gets sun for a couple of hours in the morning, but it will be in the shade all afternoon. This crag offers a steep vertical face and partially overhanging climbs on granite rock that faces the gigantic Mireukjanggun-bong. Scenic views from each anchor provide climbers with an enjoyable finish.

Directions
(*Agal-bawi*) - 38.120386N 128.318242E
(*Mireukjanggun-bong*) - 38.125847N 128.338079E
(*Sinseondae*) - 38.125172N 128.33559E
Hangye-ri, Buk-myeon, Inje-gun 인제군 북면 한계리

(*Agal-bawi*) - This crag can be reached by bus from Yangyang 양양, Osaek 오색, or Wontong 원통. Take a bus to Jangsudae 장수대. To save time, you can ask the bus driver to drop you off at Okryeotang Rest Area, before the Jangsudae Ranger Office. At Jangsudae, you can approach the crag by walking east to Okryeotang Rest Area 옥녀탕. Agal-bawi is located directly behind the rest area.
(*Mireukjanggun-bong*) - From Jangsudae 장수대, walk west towards the bridge Jangsu #3 장수 3 교. You will see a sign that says "Trail is off limits". Walk past the sign and follow the trail up into the forest. Continue on the trail to the crag for twenty minutes until you reach a stream. The crag will be on your right.
(*Sinseondae*) - This crag is across the stream from Mireukjanggun-bong 미륵장군봉.

Gear
(*Agal-bawi*) - 10 draws and a 50m rope.
(*Mireukjanggun-bong*) - 12 draws, two 60m ropes, a set of mid-sized cams.
(*Sinseondae*) - 10 draws and a 60m rope. A full set of cams is needed for the route "Until Sun Goes Down 노을이질때까지".

Safety
(*Mireukjanggun-bong*) - A few of the routes are run out. A helmet and extra webbing is recommended.
(*Sinseondae*) - The quality of the rock is a bit crumbly and rockfall is common so a helmet is recommended. It will be faster to walk down, rather than abseiling, by following the ridge behind the routes.

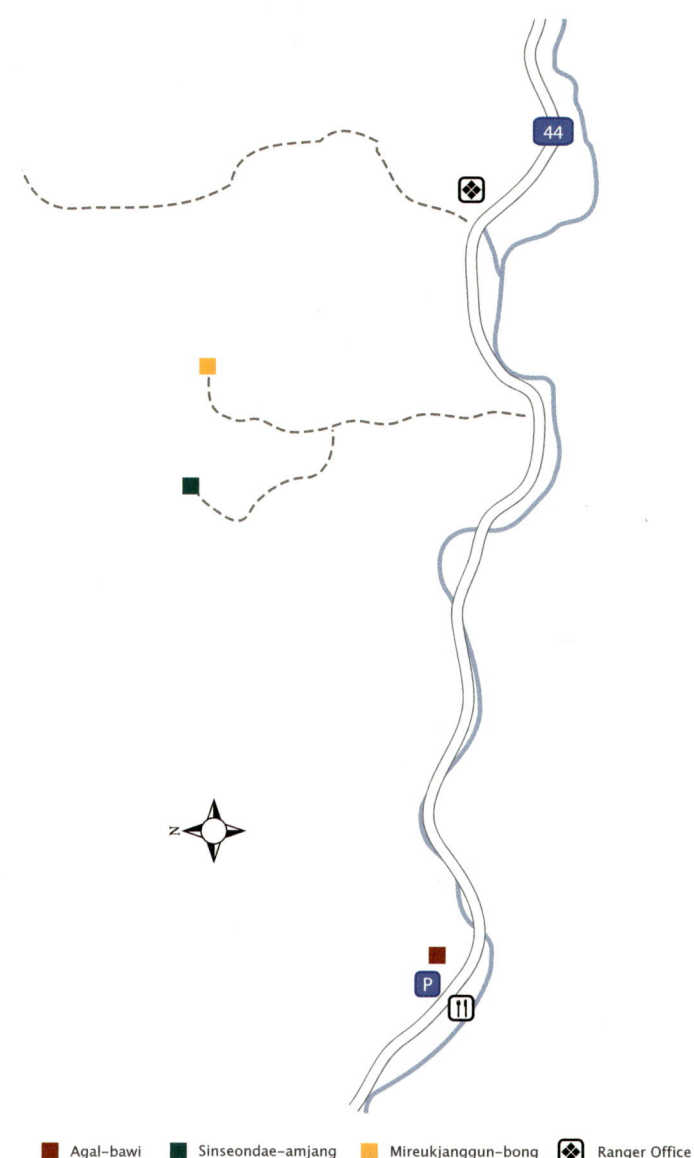

■ Agal-bawi   ■ Sinseondae-amjang   ■ Mireukjanggun-bong   ◈ Ranger Office

Additional Comments
Climbing at Seorak-san requires a permit, available at http://www.knps.or.kr. Water and food is available at Jangsudae Rest Area 장수대.
(*Agal-bawi*) - There is a great restaurant and store at the Jangsudae Rest Area 장수대. You can get great meals and snacks at the restaurant before heading down to the crag.
(*Sinseondae*) - There is a variation route between the third and fourth route from the left.

Agal-bawi 아갈바위

Route Name	Grade	Height
Amitostigma Gracilis 병아리난초	5.9	10
Bistorta Manshuriensis 범꼬리	5.10a	10
Hanabusaya Asiatica 금강	5.10c	10
Hanabusaya Asiatica 초롱 2	5.10c	11
Valerianaceae Plant 마타리	5.12b	18
Leontopodium 솜다리	5.10a	18
Taxus Cuspidata 주목	5.10b	18
Thyme 백리향	5.11a	20
Lycocionum Pseudo 진교	5.10b	20
Lightyellow Sophora 도둑놈의지팡이	5.11a	15
Thalictrum Filamentosum Maxim 산꿩의다리	5.10d	30

Mireukjanggun-bong 미륵장군봉 (1 of 2)

Korak Route 코락길	5.10	312 (12p)

1p (5.7|44m) **2p** (5.7|35m) **3p** (5.7|30m) **4p** (5.8|20m) **5p** (5.9|16m) **6p** (5.10*|17m) **7p** (5.9|20m) **8p** (5.10*|20m) **9p** (5.9|20m) **10p** (5.6|20m) **11p** (5.7|35m) **12p** (5.7|35m)

Titan Route 타이탄길	*	210 (6p)

1p (*|40m) **2p** (*|30m) **3p** (*|45m) **4p** (*|25m) **5p** (*|30m) **6p** (*|35m)

Kamp	5.10b	180 (5p)

1p (*|40m) **2p** (*|45m) **3p** (*|35m) **4p** (*|40m) **5p** (*|20m)

Photo Courtesy of Lea Gang, 강레아

Mireukjanggun-bong 미륵장군봉 (2 of 2)

Route Name	Grade	Height
Hangawi 한가윗길	5.11a/b	150 (6p)

1p (*|35m) **2p** (*|43m) **3p** (*|50m) **4p** (*|25m) **5p** (*|30m) **6p** (*|30m)

Route For Old Bachelor 노총각길	5.11b	175 (5p)

1p (5.9|35m) **2p** (5.11a|30m) **3p** (5.11b|40m) **4p** (*|45m) **5p** (5.10a|25m)

Sinseondae-amjang 신선대암장

Route Name	Grade	Height
Road To Baritagi 바리타기가는길	5.12a	80 (4p)

1p (5.7|44m) **2p** (5.7|35m) **3p** (5.7|30m) **4p** (5.8|20m)

Until Sun Goes Down 노을이질때까지	5.11a	100 (5p)

1p (*|40m) **2p** (*|30m) **3p** (*|45m) **4p** (*|25m) **5p** (*|30m)

Going Through Summer 여름나기	5.9	100 (4p)

1p (*|40m) **2p** (*|45m) **3p** (*|35m) **4p** (*|40m)

Welcome Route 환영길	5.10a	100 (6p)

1p (*|35m) **2p** (*|43m) **3p** (*|50m) **4p** (*|25m) **5p** (*|30m) **6p** (*|30m)

White Heart 하얀마음	5.10b	100 (4p)

1p (5.9|35m) **2p** (5.11a|30m) **3p** (5.11b|40m) **4p** (*|45m)

Brother First 형님먼저	5.9	100 (4p)

1p (*|35m) **2p** (*|43m) **3p** (*|50m) **4p** (*|25m)

GANHYEON-AM 간현암

Description
Ganhyeon-am is one of the most popular sport climbing crags in South Korea. It features a ton of fun climbing on easy slab, exciting face climbing, overhanging climbing, and a few multi-pitches with enough grade variations to offer something for everyone. On top of that, the setting, encompassed by the clean river, are outstanding. It is a kind of limestone rock that faces southeast. The wall gets sun all summer long.

Directions
37.368639N 127.822849E
Ganhyeon-ri, Jijeong-myeon, Wonju-si 원주시 지정면 간현리

From Downtown Wonju 원주, take the bus bound for Ganhyeon Park 간현. Cross the bridge from the park and then continue on to the smaller one. Walk for five minutes towards the restaurant and minbak 민박 area. The approach time from the Ganhyeon Bus Stop will be fifteen minutes.

Gear
12 draws and a 60m rope.

Safety
Be aware that the longer routes need safety knots at the end of the rope.

Additional Comments
In front of the crag, across the river, there are lots of amenities and excellent camping sites too. During the summer holiday season, you may want to set up your tent as far away from these sites as possible because parties go on all night and the noise can be terrible.

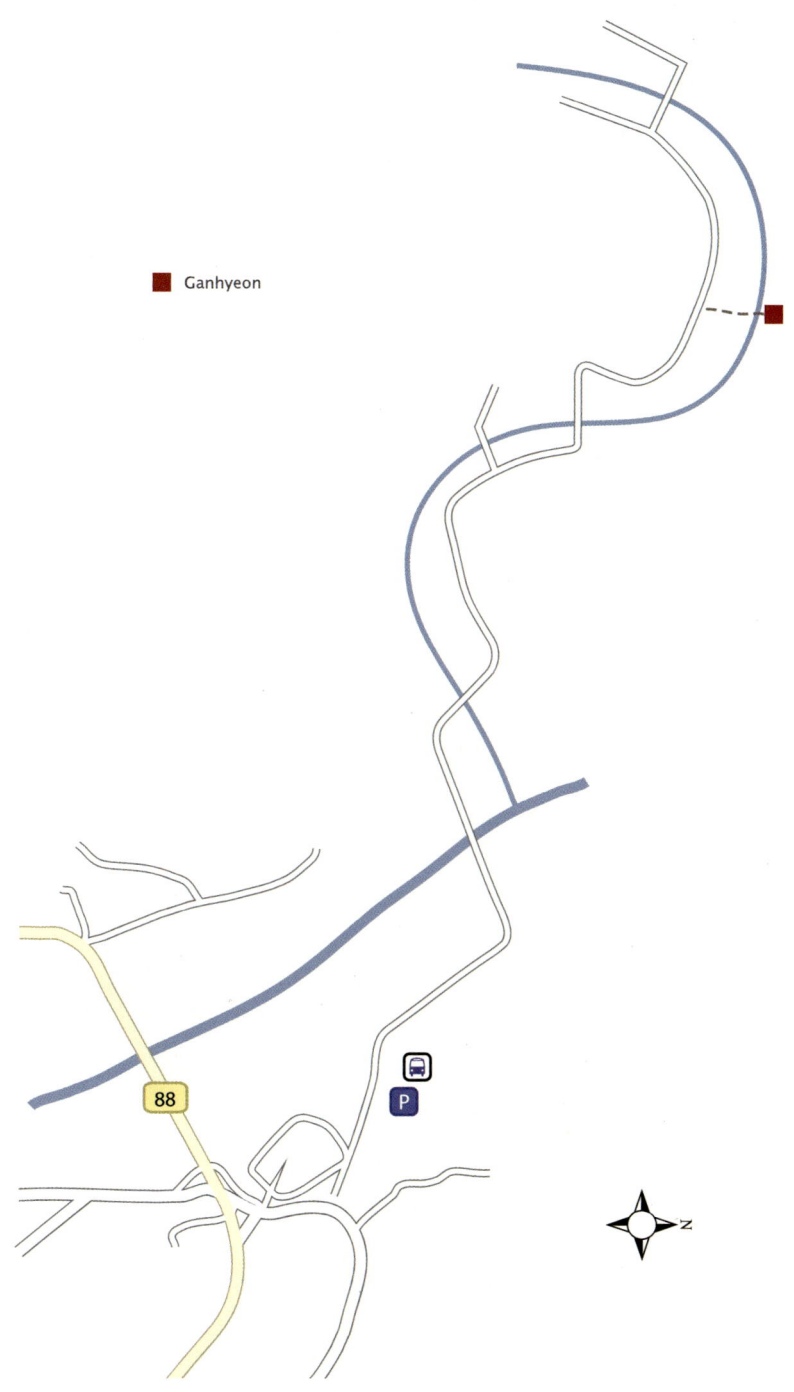

Ganhyeon-am 간현암

Route Name	Grade	Height
Blueprint For The Future 미래도	5.9	21
Meeting 만남	5.10a	19
The Eve Of Joining The Army 입영전야	5.9	18
Bara Master 바라사부	5.10c	10
Sequence Of Errors 실수연발	5.10b	15
Gold Medal 금메달	5.11a	15
A Beautiful Woman 가인	5.9	15
Birth 탄생	5.9	15
White Tiger 백호	5.11a	8
Ira 이라	5.10a	8
Dosaegi 도새기	5.10d	8
Ara 아라	5.10c/d	9
Incompletion 미완성	5.10c	9
Mangeon 만건	5.11a	30
Vastness 만경	5.10b	30
Bee-Sting 벌침	5.10b	18
Ant's Nest Crack 개미둥지크랙	5.11d	35 (3p)

1p (5.8|13m) 2p (5.11d|8m) 3p (5.10c|14m)

Route Name	Grade	Height
Vulcan 발칸	5.10a	12
Around The Corner Of Winter 겨울이오는길목	5.10c	11
VIP	5.10d	10
Hero 영웅	5.9	10
A Monster Serpent 이무기	5.8	10
The Best 지존	5.10c	18
Reopening 신장개업	5.10a	18
Wife 마누라	5.10b	18
Half Asleep & Half Awake 비몽사몽	5.8	15
Tail 꽁지	5.9	38 (3p)

1p (5.8|15m) 2p (5.5|13m) 3p (5.9|10m)

Route Name	Grade	Height
Bluebird 블루버드	5.10c	46 (3p)

1p (5.9|20m) 2p (5.10a|15m) 3p (*|11m)

Route Name	Grade	Height
Better Day Than Yesterday 어제보다좋은날	5.10c	44 (3p)

1p (5.6|20m) 2p (5.10b|15m) 3p (5.10b|20m)

Route Name	Grade	Height
Slot Machine 슬롯머신	5.11a	15
Spring Day When Magnolias Bloom 목련이피는봄날	5.10d	48 (3p)

1p (5.9|14m) 2p (5.10d|14m) 3p (5.10a|20m)

Route Name	Grade	Height
Bullying 돌림빵	5.11b	13
Wonju 원주	5.10d	28 (2p)

1p (5.7|15m) 2p (5.10d|13m)

Route Name	Grade	Height
Rainy Day 비오는날에	5.10d	27 (2p)

1p (5.10*|12m) 2p (5.10d|15m)

Route Name	Grade	Height
A Stone 돌맹이하나	5.12*	28 (2p)

1p (5.9|11m) 2p (5.12*|17m)

Route Name	Grade	Height
Reform 개혁	5.11*	28 (2p)

1p (5.8|10m) 2p (5.11*|18m)

Route Name	Grade	Height
Sister-In-Law 형수	5.11*	28
Ouch 흑	5.10a	18
Elida 엘리다	5.10b	19
Solo Lead 독주	5.10a	17
Star Is Sinking 별이진다네	5.10b	18
Sister-In-Law 형수 2	5.12b/c	15
Sintoburi 신토불이	5.13a	13
Wongol Road 원골길	5.13a/b	16
Green 그린	5.12c	13
1004	5.12d	13
Wave 물결	5.12a	18
Deep Seas 딥시스	5.12d	17
YS	5.12b	18
Deep Seven 딥세븐	5.12a	18
Honeymoon 허니문	5.12d	17
December 5th 12 월 5 일	5.10a	15
Slicker 깍쟁이	5.10b	15
In The Passage Of Time 흐르는시간속에	5.10c	14
Loneliness 고독	5.10a/b	14
A Tenacious Person 독종	5.9	13
Ganhyeon-am Ridge 간현암리지	5.9	30 (2p)

1p (5.9|10m) 2p (5.9|20m)

DAEDAP-BAWI 대답바위

Description
Daedap-bawi is a small crag. It is 15m high and 50m wide. There are twenty-eight routes and the climbs vary from vertical and crack, to overhanging climbing.

Directions
37.430637N 127.896781E
Sanhyeon-ri, Hojeo-myeon, Wonju-si 원주시 호저면 산현리

From Wonju Bus Terminal, 원주 take a bus bound for Sanhyeon 산현. Get off at Sanhyeon Public Health Center 산현보건소. Walk northwest along the road for five minutes. The crag can be seen from the road. Cross the rice field to reach it.

Gear
10 draws and a 50m rope.

Safety
This crag seems to be visited less and less. A lot of the bolts and anchors have become rusty.

Additional Comments
Please respect the farmers during the busy farming season.

DAEDAP-BAWI 대답바위 (1 OF 2)

Route Name	Grade	Height
Can 깡통	5.10b	8
Tadpole 올챙이	5.10b	7
Ggong 꽁	5.10c	6
Sky Dream 하늘꿈	5.10a	8
Don't Fall 떨어지지마	5.10b	8
Moon In Rising Sun 해솟음달	5.10c	9
Another Dream of Road 또하나꿈의길	5.11a	10
In Class 수업중	5.10b	10
Rendezvous 랑데부 3	5.12a	13
Rendezvous 랑데부 2	5.10b/c	10
Rendezvous 랑데부 1	5.12a	10
Quack 엉터리	5.11b	10
Jealousy Moon 시샘달	5.11c	10
Nest 둥지	5.11b	10
Unnamed 미정	5.10b	10

DAEDAP-BAWI 대답바위 (2 OF 2)

Route Name	Grade	Height
Beauty 미	5.12c	8
SEO	5.11c	12
Born on the 27th of October 10월 27일생	*	12
Honey, Bee, Pumpkin, Flower & Beehive 꿀벌과호박꽃그리고벌통	*	12
Two Stones 돌맹이둘	*	12
2002	*	12
Nani 난이	5.11d	12
Welcome 환영	5.11c	10
Blessed Day 축복받은날	5.11b	10
Bat Route 박쥐길	5.9	9
V Crack V 크랙	5.8	10
Where Is The Destination 그곳은어디메뇨	5.11c	8
People Who Open the Daybreak 새벽을여는사람들	5.10a	8

BAEKWOON-SAN, SANG-BAWI 백운산 상바위

Description
This crag was developed in 1992 with seven routes. It faces southwest on granite rock. It offers mostly easy slab multi-pitch climbing, except for the route called "Sangseok". Sang-bawi is usually quiet and is a good place to train beginners.

Directions
37.239246N 127.911243E
Guirae-ri, Guirae-myeon, Wonju-si 원주시 귀래면 귀래리

From Wonju 원주, take the bus heading to Guirae 귀래. Get off at Cheongwon Rest Area 청원휴게소. It will take forty minutes from Wonju to get there. With your back to the rest area, walk left on the forest road that is by a big tomb. The crag can be seen on your right from time to time while walking along the road. Continue on the flat forest road for twenty-five minutes until you see a sign that says "상바위" Sang-bawi. At the sign, look for a trail on your right that starts to ascend steeply. Scramble up for ten minutes to reach the crag.

Gear
10 draws and a 60m rope. The Sangseok 상석 route requires a set of small to mid-sized cams.

Safety
A helmet and extra webbing is recommended. The wall is a bit mossy, but most of the bolts and anchors are in good condition.

Additional Comments
Water and snacks should be available at the shop by the bus stop.

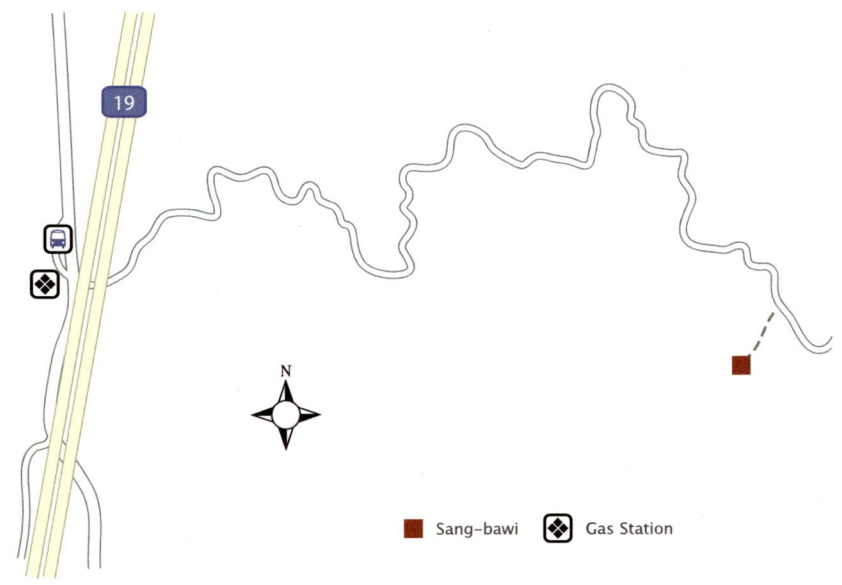

Sang-bawi 백운산

Route Name	Grade	Height
Introduction Route 입문길	5.9	82 (3p)
1p (5.9|25m) **2p** (5.8|17m) **3p** (5.9|40m)		
Discharge 제대	5.11c	76 (3p)
1p (5.10d|23m) **2p** (5.10b|23m) **3p** (5.11c|30m)		
Enlistment 입대	5.11b	67 (3p)
1p (5.11b|32m) **2p** (5.6|14m) **3p** (5.10b|21m)		
Yeong-Ju 영주	5.11a	30
Sangseok Route 상석길	5.9	75 (3p)
1p (5.9|28m) **2p** (5.6|14m) **3p** (5.9|33m)		
China Pink 패랭이	5.10d	64 (2p)
1p (5.10b|37m) **2p** (5.10d|27m)		
Partner 파트너	5.10c	57(2p)
1p (5.9|30m) **2p** (5.10c|27m)		

EUIAM-AMJANG 의암암장

Description
This crag is located by a lake with awesome settings. It offers tons of features, but a lot of the holds and edges are sharp. It is a kind of quartz rock that faces southeast.

Directions
37.840652N 127.677602E
Euiam-ri, Sindong-myeon, Chuncheon-si 춘천시 신동면 의암리

To access the crag, take a bus from downtown Chuncheon 춘천 to Euiam Dam 의암댐.

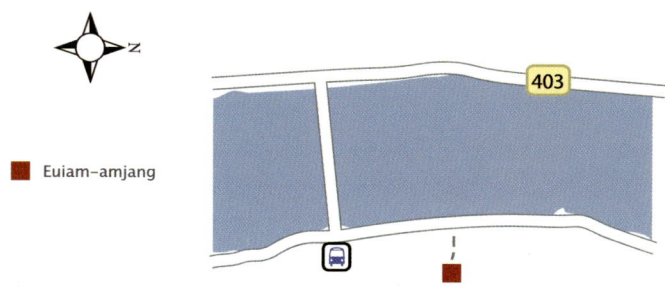

From Euiam Dam Bus Stop, walk down the road with the lake to your left. Walk past the restaurants for 200m until you see a small parking space and hiking map to your right on the road. Past the map, hike up for 20m and when you reach a fork, take the trail that branches off to the right. The approach time to get to the crag from the bus is ten minutes.

Gear
12 draws and a 60m rope.

Safety
The left wall of the crag is a bit loose and mossy.

Additional Comments
I climbed this crag before it was opened to the public. All the bolts and anchors were new. I believe that this crag will draw many visitors. There is a great ridge route near Euiam-amjang. There are also lots of stores and restaurants around the bus stop.

EUIAM-AMJANG 의암암장

Route Name	Grade	Height
Noddang & Dharma 노땅과달마	5.11a	8
Solitude On The Terrace 테라스의고독	5.11b	10
As It Is 그대로	5.10c	14
Beehive 벌집	5.12b	13
Wish 소망	5.12b	13
Bear's Sole 곰발바닥	5.11c	17
Shower 소나기	5.9	15
Legend Of Autumn 가을의전설	5.9	18
December 디셈버	5.10a	20
Ten Dance 텐댄스	5.10a	8
Weekday Class 평일반 1p (5.10a|27m) 2p (5.10b|25m)	5.10b	52 (2p)
Turtle 거북이 1p (5.10a|25m) 2p (5.10d|12m)	5.11a	37 (2p)
Chuncle 춘클 A	5.10b	11
Chuncle 춘클 B	5.10c	12
Chuncle 춘클 C	5.10b	12
Tears In Jerry 제리의눈물	5.10b	16
Dimple 보조개	5.10c	18
Let's Hang Out, Dharma 달마야놀자	5.10b	19
Seoki 석이 1p (5.10a|28m) 2p (5.10c|25m)	5.10c	53 (2p)
Hummingbird 꿀벌새 1p (5.10c|24m) 2p (5.10b|24m)	5.10c	48 (2p)
Balance 발란스	5.11a	11
Lakeside 호반	5.10c	11
Miss 미스	5.10b	8
Ujins 우진스	5.10a	24
Merry-Go-Round 회전목마	5.10c	13

YONGHWA-SAN, SAENAM-BAWI 용화산 새남바위

Description
The name of this granite crag means "Birds are flying". It offers mostly challenging crack climbs with natural trees in the middle of the routes. As this crag is located in a remote region, it is a quiet place to enjoy climbing. Saenam-bawi faces south and is in sun all day.

Directions
38.037681N 127.743917E
Goseong-ri, Sabuk-myeon, Chuncheon-si (춘천시 사북면 고성리)

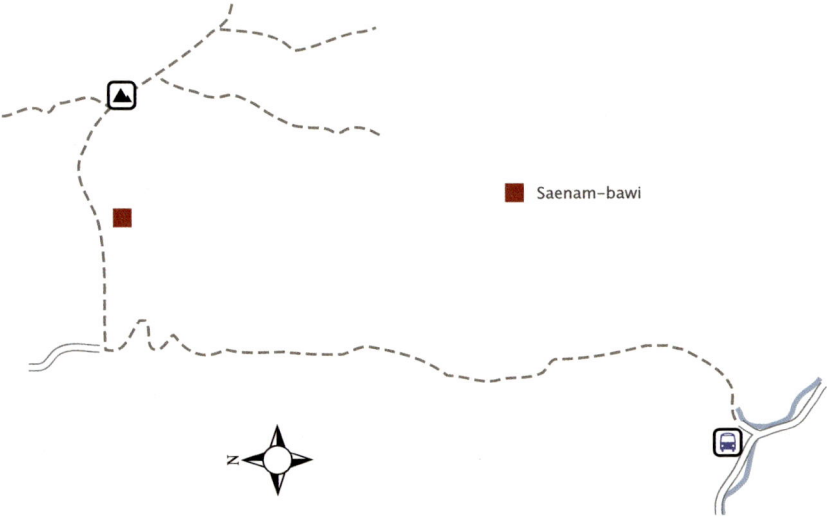

To reach the crag, take a bus from Chuncheon 춘천 bound for Yangtong 양통. It will take an hour. Get off at the end of the line. Walk straight up the road to the north until you reach the bridge Sayeogyo 사여교. At the bridge, stay to the left (don't cross the bridge) and hike up for an hour until you reach an unpaved road on the hill. Go right at the hill and you will reach the crag in fifteen minutes. The crag is visible from the bus stop.

Gear
10 draws, a 50m rope, and a full set of cams.

Safety
A helmet is recommended. Instead of abseiling, you can take the trail at the top of the hill to walk down. A few of the bolts and anchors are not in good condition, so bring a few slings to back up the protection.

Additional Comments
Water and food should be purchased beforehand.

Photo Courtesy of Lea Gang, 강레아

SAENAM-BAWI 새남바위

Route Name	Grade	Height
Saenam 새남 B	5.10*	85 (3p)
1p (*|35m) **2p** (*|35m) **3p** (*|15m)		
Yellow Submarine 노란잠수함	5.11c	30
Head Wall 정면벽	5.10*	60 (2p)
1p (5.10*|25m) **2p** (5.10*|35m)		
Blue Dragon Route 청룡길	5.11d	130 (4p)
1p (5.9|25m) **2p** (5.10d|20m) **3p** (5.11d|40m) **4p** (5.10b|45m)		
Mae Route 매길	5.10a	107 (3p)
1p (*|40m) **2p** (*|40m) **3p** (*|27m)		
Madame Route 마담길	5.10c	110 (3p)
1p (5.10c|35m) **2p** (*|35m) **3p** (5.10c|40m)		
Niche Route 사잇길	5.10*	100 (3p)
1p (*|40m) **2p** (*|35m) **3p** (5.10c|30m)		
Saenam 새남 A	5.10a	127 (4p)
1p (5.8|35m) **2p** (5.10*|37m) **3p** (5.10a|25m) **4p** (*|30m)		
Wand Route 완트길	5.12a	60 (2p)
1p (5.12a|30m) **2p** (*|30m)		
Giant Route 거인길	5.10/A0	135 (4p)
1p (5.8|35m) **2p** (5.8|40m) **3p** (5.10a|30m) **4p** (5.7|30m)		
The Myth Of Yonghwa Mt. 용화산의전설	5.11b	22

BOKGYEO-SAN 복계산

Description
These crags are in the northernmost location near the DMZ, which means this area remains untouched. With a clean stream and fresh air, it is a great place for weekend outings.
(***Deokgu-bawi***) - This crag consists of single-pitch sport climbing on an easy face and the routes become steeper as you move further to the right. It is granite rock and faces southwest.
(***Maewoldae-amjang***) - This place offers slab, cracks, and steep vertical face climbs with multi-pitches. It faces southeast.

Directions
(***Deokgu-bawi***) - 38.198613N 127.481857E
(***Maewoldae-amjang***) - 38.200081N 127.484879E
Jamgok-ri, Geunnam-myeon, Cheolwon-gun 철원군 금남면 잠곡리

(***Deokgu-bawi***) - From Dong-Seoul Bus Terminal 동서울버스터미널, take a bus to Uijeongbu 의정부. From Uijeongbu 의정부, take a bus heading to Wasu-ri 와수리 and transfer to a bus bound for Maewoldae 매월대. There is a small restaurant called "매월산장" Maewolsanjang at the end of the line where you can stay the night. At the restaurant, look for the sign that shows you the direction to Maewoldae-amjang. Hike up the trail by the sign (Don't take the main trail by the stream or cross the bridge) for ten minutes until you arrive at Deokgu-bawi.
(***Maewoldae-amjang***) - From Deokgu-bawi, hike up to the right for five minutes to get to Maewoldae-amjang. It will take roughly two and a half hours to reach the mountain from Seoul.

Gear
(***Deokgu-bawi***) - 7 draws and a 50m rope.
(***Maewoldae-amjang***) - 10 draws, two 60m ropes. The routes are bolted, but you can bring a set of cams if you want to place gear.

Additional Comments
It will be hard to go on a day trip from Seoul so a weekend trip is recommended. Water and snacks can be bought at the restaurant.

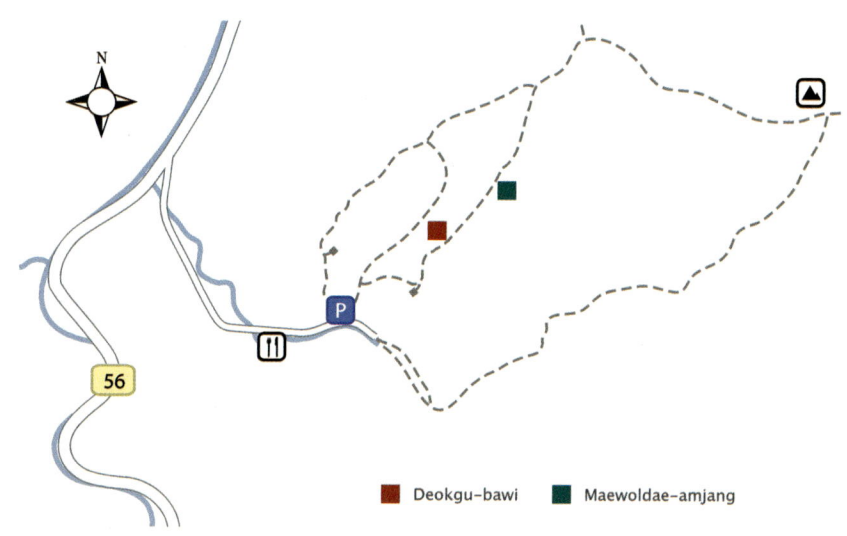

Maewoldae-amjang 매월대암장

Route Name	Grade	Height
Ignorant Man 무식이	5.12b	20
Taeback 태백 1	5.12b	10
Taeback 태백 2	5.12b	10
Regret 후회	5.11a	15
Terrace 테라스	5.12b	23
Ah! So Scary 아! 살떨려	5.10b	* (2p)
1p (5.9|*m) 2p (5.10b|*m)		
Jiseong Route 지성길	5.11b	* (3p)
1p (5.10c|*m) 2p (5.11b|*m) 3p (*|*m)		
The Ring Of Spring 소리샘	5.10a	63 (2p)
1p (5.9|28m) 2p (5.10a|35m)		
Sweetheart 이쁜이	5.10c	56 (3p)
1p (5.9|*m) 2p (5.10c|*m) 3p (5.10b|*m)		
Suni Route 순이길	5.9	* (2p)
1p (5.9|*m) 2p (5.9|*m)		

Deokgu-bawi 덕구바위

Route Name	Grade	Height
Meeting With Teaback 태백과의만남	5.12a	8
Smile Of Duckgoo 덕구의미소	5.11a	10
Youhoo 유후	5.12b	14
Honeypot 꿀단지	5.10c	13
Ggeokjeongi 꺽정이	5.10a	13
Duck-i 덕이	5.10*	17
Ten Fingers 열손가락	5.10a	15
Crossroads 십자로	5.10*	18
Everyone 누구나	5.9	20
Be Strong, Kumsoon 굳세어라금순아	5.8	8
108 Torments Of Mankind 백팔번뇌	5.7	52 (2p)*
Maewoldang 매월당	5.10b	37 (2p)*
Seoyeon 서연	5.10c	11
Lady 여인	A2	12

*Multi-pitch info is unavailable at this time

Gyeonggi-do

경기도

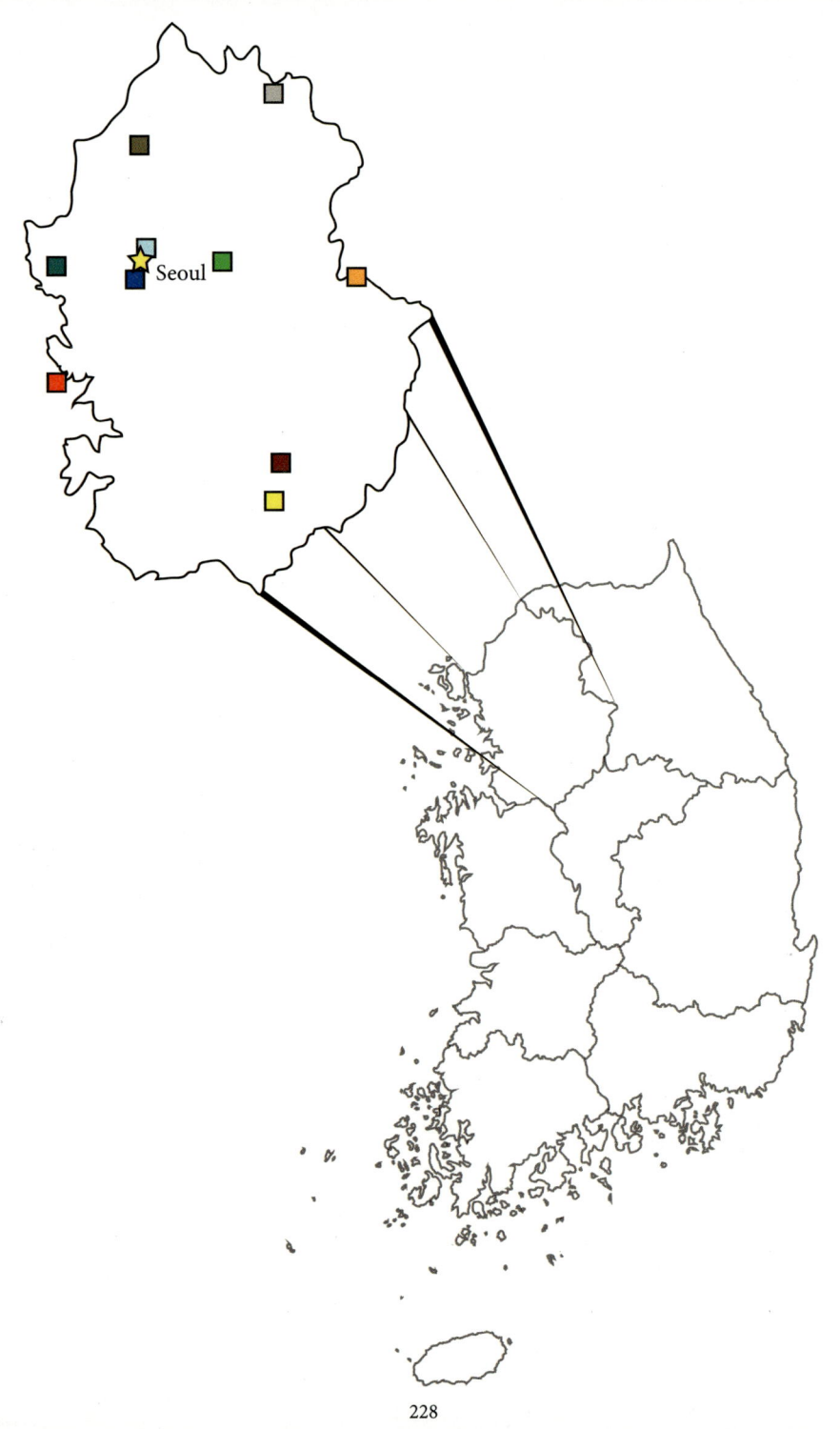

Gyeonggi-do Province 경기도

- Insu-bong, Bukhan-san
- Seonin-bong, Dobong-san
- Daeju-amjang, Surak-san
- Naewon-am, Surak-san
- Muakjae Ansan-amjang
- Byeongpung-am, Obong-san
- Mirae-am, Morak-san
- Mae-bawi, Suri-san
- Byeongpung-Bawi, BAC
- Sumeun-am
- Nocles-amjang
- Gwanack-amjang
- Beomgul-am, Namhansansung
- Hamheudongcheon-amjang
- Hanagae-amjang
- Dwaejigul-amjang, Doderum-san
- Jobi-am, Jobi-san
- Samhyeongjae-bawi, Sori-san
- Seolgwi-am, Gamak-san
- Chak-bawi, Myeongsung-san

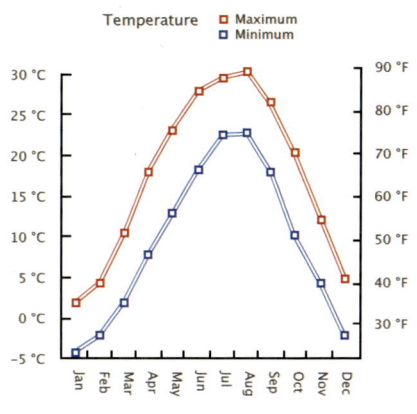

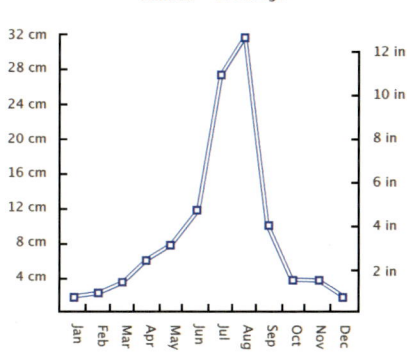

BUKHAN-SAN, INSU-BONG 북한산 인수봉

Description
When Yvonne Chouinard was a soldier in Korea, he could see the potential of climbable rock. He left his legacy in the mountains skirting the north of Seoul, including the omnipresent Insu Peak 인수 in Bukhan-san National Park 북한산. This balding granite zenith can get mighty crowded on the weekend. So if you are up for the ascent, it is best to go on a weekday or at the crack of dawn on a Saturday or Sunday. Rarely will you see a two-man team scaling this giant geological formation. A team of five to eight is a much more common sight and rightly the more laborious and lengthy of an endeavor. The climbing here is stellar and pitch by pitch, the great city of Seoul is unveiled behind you.

Directions
37.659609N 126.980013E
Ui-dong, Gangbuk-gu, Seoul 서울 강북구 우이동

To access the crag, take Exit 3 from Suyu Station 수유 (Line #4) and take a bus bound for Ui-dong 우이동. Get off at the end of the bus line. From the bus stop, walk for twenty minutes to Doseon-sa Parking Lot 도선사. It will save time if you take a taxi at the last bus stop. If you are in a climbing team, grab a cab directly from Suyu Subway Station to the parking lot. Splitting the cost between a few people will be cheaper and definitely faster than the buses. From the parking lot, take the main trail that passes by the ticket office. The trail leads straight up to the trailhead for Insu-bong 인수봉. After Rescue Mark 20-1, the trail goes down slightly and soon after you will see the magnificent face of Insu-bong 인수봉. Hike right for ten minutes past the ranger station to the base of the crag. Don't hike straight up the main trail past the ranger station. The approach time will be thirty minutes from the parking lot.

Gear
10 draws, a 60m rope, and a full set of cams with extra mid-sized cams.

Safety
This crag experiences a lot of traffic so you might encounter rusty corroded ring-bolts and large sections where routes are run-out. Abseiling can be done at the top of the peak facing the neighboring peak Baekundae 백운대. Rappelling from the right station lowers you to a scary overhang. Helmets are recommended.

Additional Comments
For camping, you need to get a permit from the ranger station. Get water and snacks at the parking lot.

There is a route map at the base of Insu-bong. Detailed beta is also available at:
http://www.nepa.co.kr/Academy/RockNavigation.aspx?mtcode=Mt2&pocode=PO707

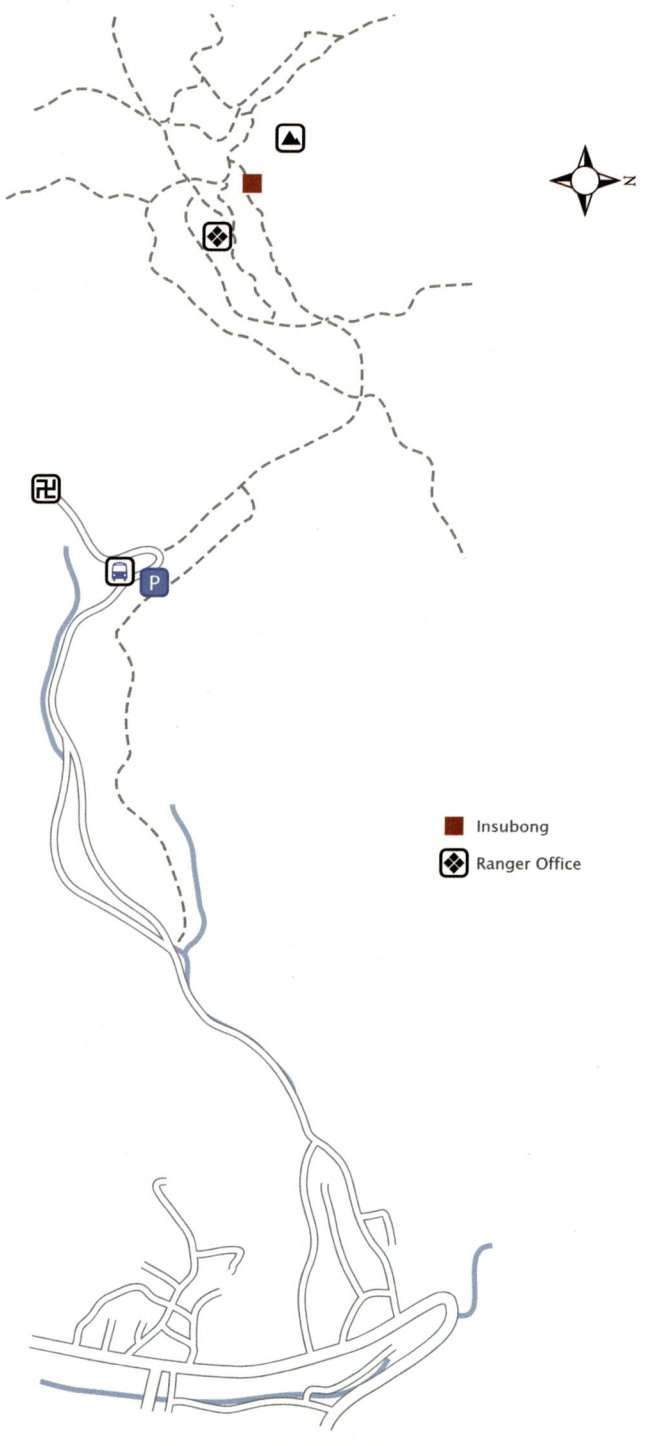

Insu-Bong

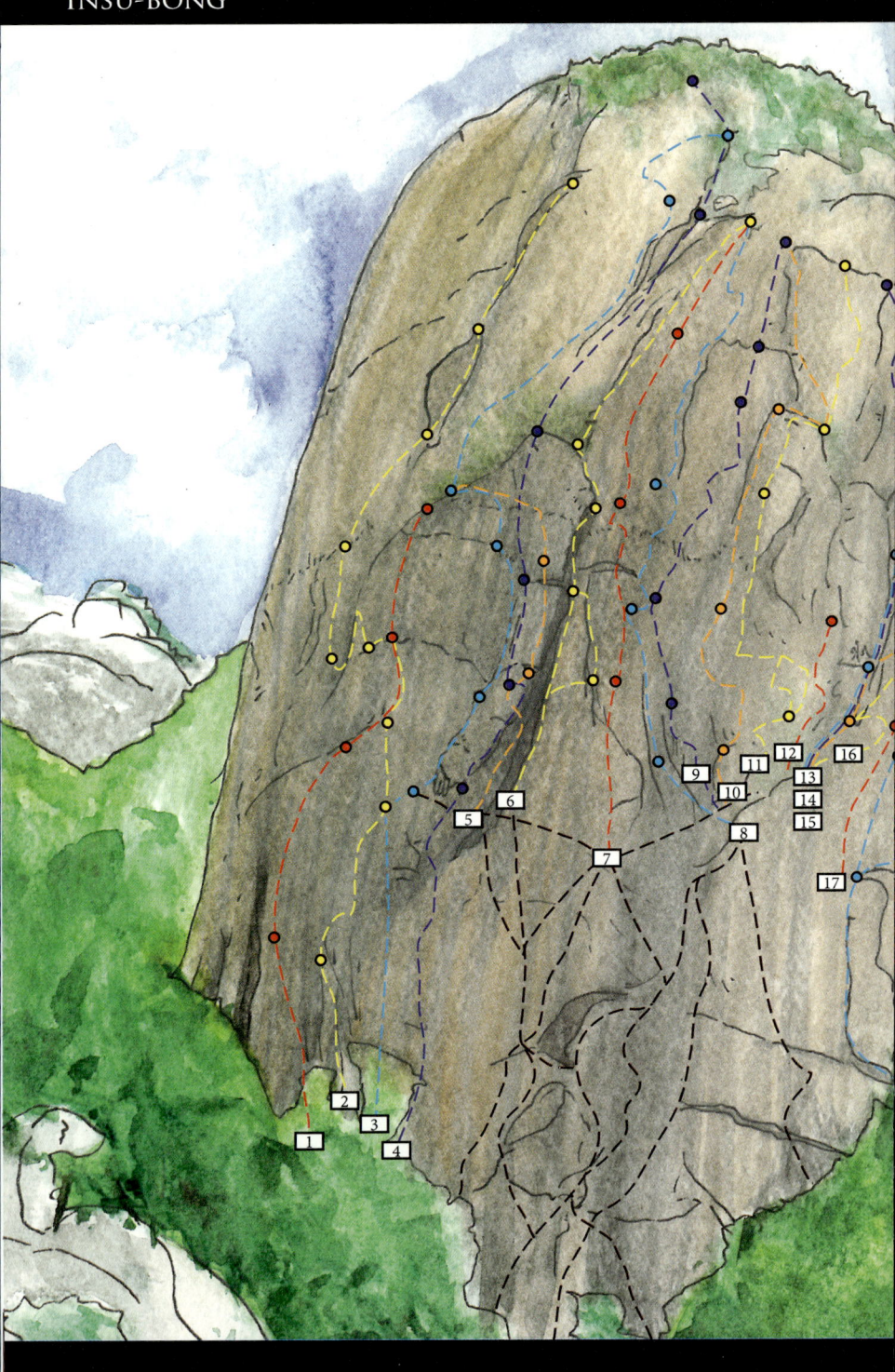

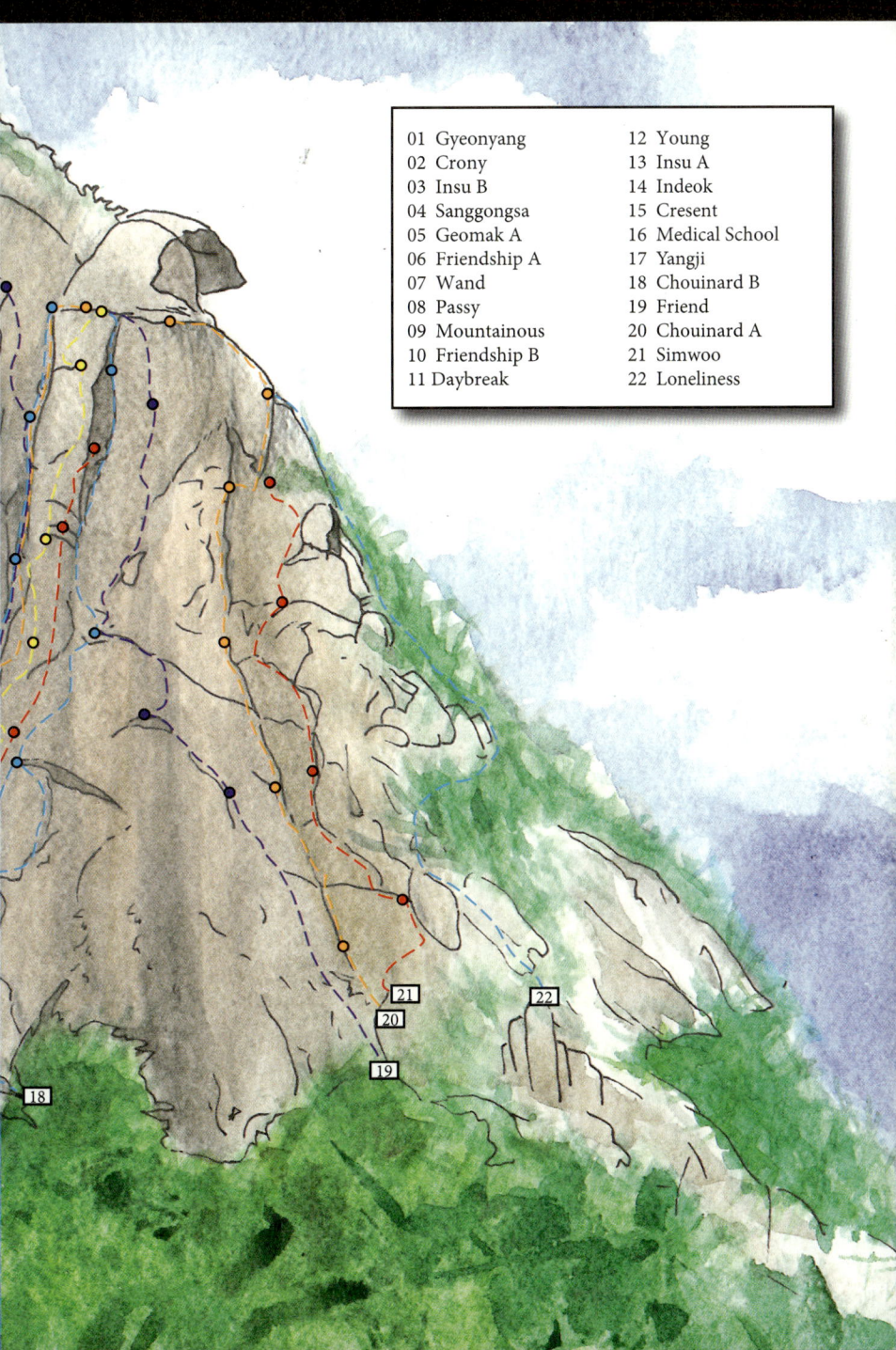

INSU-BONG 인수봉 (1 OF 3)

Route Name	Grade	Height
Our Meeting 우리들의만남	5.11a	13
Gang's Chorus 꾸러기들의합창	5.10*	10
Chilgap-san 칠갑산	5.11d	10
Jjambbong 짬뽕	5.10c	10
March For Lover 임을위한행진곡	5.12*	12
Lady 아가씨	5.12*	13
Juyeong Route 주영길	5.11c	13
Rendezvous Route 해우길	5.11b	13
Still Thinking 아직도생각중	5.11a	15
Born Again 거듭태어나기	5.11a	15
Decency Forbids 소변금지	5.10b	18
Semi-Slab 준슬랩	5.11b	20
Maninbo 만인보	5.11b	15
Friendship 우정 B	5.8	105 (4p)

1p (5.6|20m) 2p (5.8|20m) 3p (5.6|35m) 4p (5.7|30m)

Daybreak Route 여명길	5.11a/A0	119 (4p)

1p (5.8|23m) 2p (5.11a/A0|30m) 3p (5.7|36m) 4p (5.7|30m)

Young Route 영길	5.10b	40
Insu 인수 A	5.8	115 (4p)

1p (5.6|40m) 2p (5.7|20m) 3p (5.8|25m) 4p (5.7|30m)

Indeok Route 인덕길	5.11a	119 (4p)

1p (5.7|40m) 2p (5.7|19m) 3p (5.11a|40m) 4p (5.10b|20m)

Crescent Route 궁형길	5.11b	115 (4p)

1p (5.9|30m) 2p (5.7|30m) 3p (5.10a|30m) 4p (5.11b|25m)

Medical School Route 의대길	5.10b	136 (6p)

1p (5.8|27m) 2p (5.9|22m) 3p (5.10a|12m) 4p (5.8|28m) 5p (5.6|20m) 6p (5.10b|27m)

Juyoung Route 주영길	*	*
Chouinard 취나드 B	5.8	177 (5p)

1p (5.7|35m) 2p (5.8|37m) 3p (5.6|25m) 4p (5.8|40m) 5p (5.6|40m)

Friend Route 벗길	5.11a/A0	148 (5p)

1p (5.8|23m) 2p (5.11a|A0|30m) 3p (5.7|36m) 4p (5.7|30m)

Chouinard 취나드 A	5.10c	181 (6p)

1p (5.6|*m) 2p (5.7|*m) 3p (5.8|*m) 4p (5.10a|*m) 5p (5.6|*m) 6p (5.6|*m)

Simwoo Route 심우길	5.9/A0	99 (4p)

1p (5.6|25m) 2p (5.9|13m) 3p (5.7|30m) 4p (5.6/A0|31m)

INSU-BONG 인수봉 (2 OF 3)

Route Name	Grade	Height
Geomak Route 검악 A	5.9/A0	86 (4p)

1p (5.9|26m) **2p** (5.8|18m) **3p** (A0|20m) **4p** (5.6|21m)

Villa Route 빌라길	5.12a/A2	165 (6p)

1p (5.8|40m) **2p** (5.12a|28m) **3p** (5.10b|17m) **4p** (5.11c|20m) **5p** (5.9|40m) **6p** (A2|20m)

Big Dragon Route 거룡길	5.11a	176 (6p)

1p (5.10a|35m) **2p** (5.6|20m) **3p** (5.10b|28m) **4p** (5.11a|38m) **5p** (5.8|38m) **6p** (5.10a|40m)

Sky Route 하늘길	5.10c	209 (7p)

1p (5.10a|23m) **2p** (5.9|17m) **3p** (5.10a|26m) **4p** (5.8|30m) **5p** (5.10c|31m) **6p** (5.8|40m) **7p** (5.10c|20m)

Oriental Route 동양길	5.10b/A0	209 (8p)

1p (5.7|15m) **2p** (5.10a|20m) **3p** (5.10b|20m) **4p** (5.8|35m) **5p** (5.8|30m) **6p** (A0|32m) **7p** (5.10b|26m) **8p** (5.9|31m)

Cheongmac Route 청맥길	*	190 (6p)*
Journey Route 여정길	5.10c	191 (6p)

1p (5.10c|19m) **2p** (5.9|45m) **3p** (5.8|27m) **4p** (5.8|30m) **5p** (5.8|40m) **6p** (5.8|30m)

Crony Route 크로니길	5.9	237 (9p)

1p (5.7|26m) **2p** (5.7|26m) **3p** (5.7|29m) **4p** (5.8|25m) **5p** (5.10a|20m) **6p** (5.10a|21m) **7p** (5.8|26m) **8p** (5.7|24m) **9p** (5.8|50m)

*Multi-pitch info is unavailable at this time

Route Name	Grade	Height
Southeast-Side Great Chimney 동남면대침니	5.6	70 (2p)
1p (5.6|30m) **2p** (5.6|40m)		
Amidong Route 아미동길	5.10a	90 (3p)
1p (5.6|40m) **2p** (5.10a|40m) **3p** (*|10m)		
Insu 인수 B	5.9	97 (3p)
1p (5.8|37m) **2p** (5.9|30m) **3p** (5.7|30m)		
Geomak 검악 B	5.9/A0	114 (3p)
1p (5.9|37m) **2p** (A0|40m) **3p** (5.7|37m)		
Friendship 우정 A	5.9	101 (4p)
1p (5.8|23m) **2p** (5.11a/A0|30m) **3p** (5.7|36m) **4p** (5.7|30m)		
Wand Route 완트길	5.10c	162 (4p)
1p (5.9|40m) **2p** (5.10c|40m) **3p** (5.10a|40m) **4p** (5.10a|42m)		
Passy Route 패시길	5.10c	139 (5p)
1p (5.7|20m) **2p** (5.9|22m) **3p** (5.10c|35m) **4p** (5.10c|32m) **5p** (5.6|30m)		
Mountainous Route 산천지길	5.11a	119 (5p)
1p (5.8|20m) **2p** (5.10d|20m) **3p** (5.8|40m) **4p** (5.11a|13m) **5p** (5.9|26m)		
West Side Wall 서면벽 1	5.10b	78 (3p)
1p (5.9|15m) **2p** (5.10b|25m) **3p** (5.10a|38m)		
Snake Route 뱀길	5.10d	85 (3p)
1p (5.10d|35m) **2p** (5.7|30m) **3p** (5.6|20m)		
West Side Wall 서면벽 2	5.10*	90 (2p)
1p (5.10*|30m) **2p** (5.10*|20m)		
West Side Wall 서면벽 3	5.9/A0	90 (4p)
1p (5.9|35m) **2p** (5.9/A0|19m) **3p** (5.9|11m) **4p** (A0|25m)		
Dove Route 비둘기길	5.6/A1	89 (4p)
1p (5.7|35m) **2p** (5.6|17m) **3p** (A1|17m) **4p** (5.7|20m)		
West-Side Slab 서면슬랩	5.10a	72 (2p)
1p (5.9|35m) **2p** (5.10a|37m)		
South Slab 남측슬랩	5.10b	75 (3p)
1p (5.10b|15m) **2p** (5.7|20m) **3p** (5.10b|40m)		
Horizontal Route 가로길	5.11c/A0	120 (4p)
1p (5.11c/A0|35m) **2p** (5.10c|30m) **3p** (5.8|35m) **4p** (5.5|20m)		
Alpine Roses 알핀로제스	5.11c	100 (3p)
1p (5.11c|40m) **2p** (5.8|40m) **3p** (5.5|20m)		
Echo Route 에코길	5.11d/A0	106 (3p)
1p (A0|40m) **2p** (5.11d|38m) **3p** (5.8|28m)		

Dobong-san, Seonin-bong 도봉산 선인봉

Description
Seonin-bong was first climbed in 1937. It carried out a primary role as a destination for climbers in the initial stages of Korea's climbing history. With battling egos, the climbing community was split into two groups between Insu-bong and Seonin-bong. This crag offers slab, crack and an assortment of face, chimney, and overhanging climbing on protruding, granite rock in the north of Seoul. The climbs here are steeper than Insu-bong, but it has better friction. It faces southeast.

Directions
37.696496N 127.017692E
Dobong-dong, Dobong-gu, Seoul 서울 동봉구 도봉동

In Seoul, take the subway to Dobong-san Station 도봉산 and walk out from Exit 1. Cross the main road and continue towards Seonin-bong 선인봉, which can be seen from the road as you pass the many shops and vendors. Refer to the maps on your way up to the main trailhead. Take the trail that leads you to the Mountain Rescue Office 산악구조대. From the rescue office, take the trail on the right to reach the crag. The approach time will be forty minutes.

Gear
15 draws, two 60m ropes, and a full set of cams with extra small to mid-sized cams.

Safety
Rappelling can be mostly done from the anchors on the routes you climbed, so be cautious about climbers behind you. However, abseiling can also be done at the top of the crag by one rappel and walking down the backside. A helmet and extra webbing is highly recommended.

Additional Comments
Food and water can be bought at the base. For camping, a permit is required. You can get one from the ranger station. On the weekends, some of the popular routes are usually crowded.

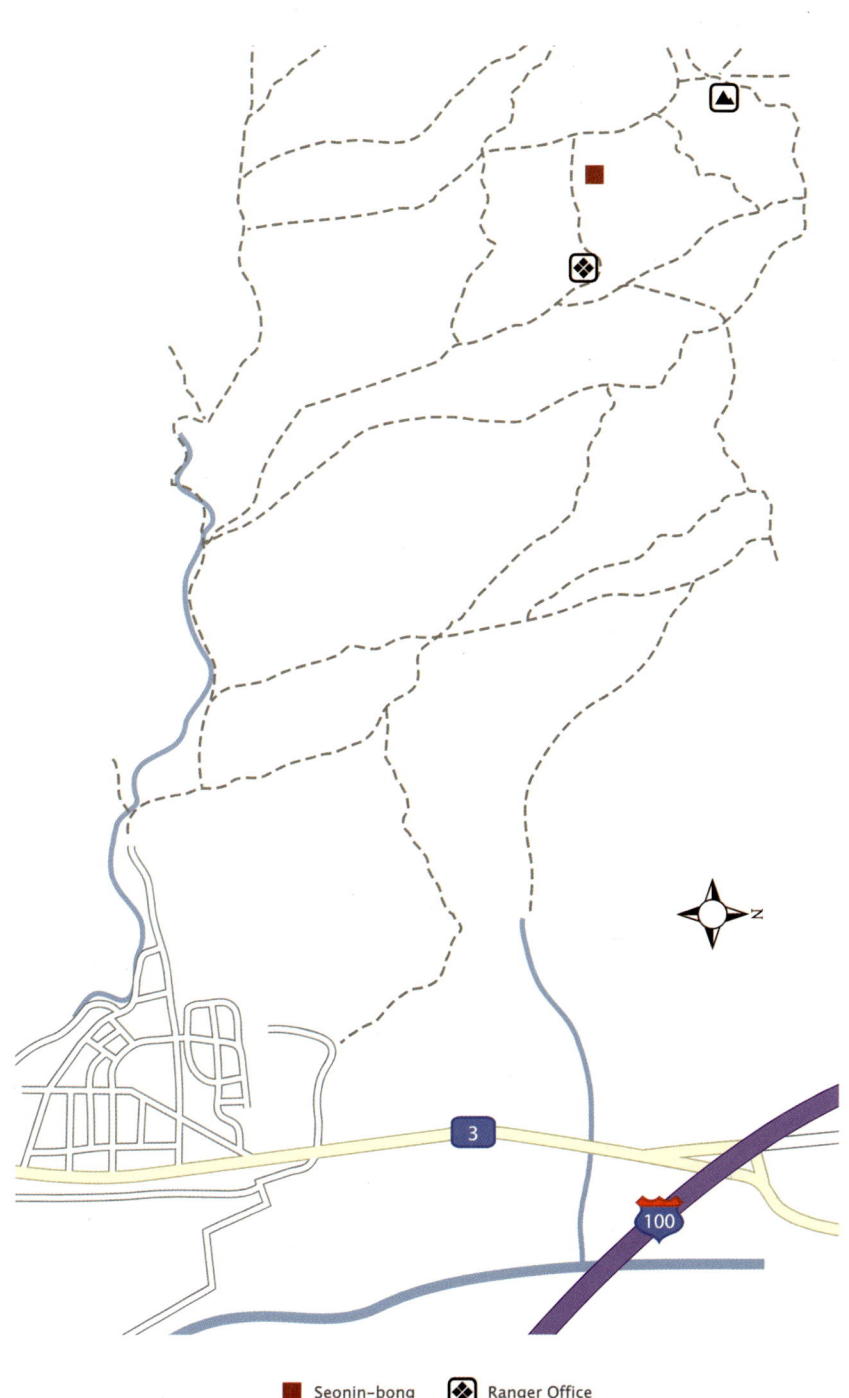

SEONIN-BONG 선인봉

Route Name	Grade	Height
Sunshine Road 양지길	5.9/A1	125 (4p)
1p (5.8|35m) 2p (5.9|25m) 3p (5.9|29m) 4p (5.7|35m)		
S Chimney 침니	5.7	35
On The South 남측	5.10a	70 (4p)
1p (5.7|25m) 2p (5.10a|15m) 3p (5.6|10m) 4p (5.6|20m)		
Overhang on The South 남측오버행	5.11c	75 (3p)
1p (5.11c|25m) 2p (5.10d|25m) 3p (5.7|25m)		
Side Route 측면길	5.8	138 (5p)
1p (5.7|26m) 2p (5.8|13m) 3p (*|50m) 4p (5.7|31m) 5p (5.8|18m)		
Waist Route 허리길	5.10a	59 (2p)
1p (5.10a|36m) 2p (5.10a|23m)		
Seal Route 물개길	5.11b	58 (2p)
1p (5.10d|25m) 2p (5.11b|33m)		
Juyoung Route 주영길	5.10c	29
Jeonghyang Route 정향길	5.11c/A0	89 (3p)
1p (A0|26m) 2p (5.11c|38m) 3p (5.10c|25m)		
Young Route 영길	5.10a/A0	97 (3p)
1p (5.9|34m) 2p (5.10a|A0|25m) 3p (5.9|38m)		
Leopard Route 표범길	5.10c	188 (6p)
1p (5.10c|30m) 2p (5.9|23m) 3p (5.9|20m) 4p (5.7|25m) 5p (5.6|40m) 6p (5.8|50m)		
Seonam Route 선암길	5.12c	188 (4p)
1p (5.12c|28m) 2p (5.10c|25m) 3p (5.11*|35m) 4p (5.9|34m)		
Bat Route 박쥐길	5.9	188 (3p)
1p (5.7|30m) 2p (5.9|35m) 3p (5.9|50m)		
Squirrel Route 다람쥐길	5.10b	128 (5p)
1p (5.10b|30m) 2p (5.9|23m) 3p (5.9|50m) 4p (5.8|25m) 5p (5.7|40m)		
Seonin 선인 A	5.8	100 (3p)
1p (5.7|25m) 2p (5.7|35m) 3p (5.8|40m)		
Sky Route 하늘길	5.11b	146 (4p)
1p (5.8|35m) 2p (5.9|35m) 3p (5.11b|38m) 4p (5.8|38m)		
Blue Route 푸른길	5.11a	139 (4p)
1p (5.9|35m) 2p (5.11a|20m) 3p (5.11a|36m) 4p (5.10a|39m)		
Hyeonam Route 현암길	5.11d/A0	149 (6p)
1p (5.9|29m) 2p (5.11c|30m) 3p (A0|21m) 4p (5.9|18m) 5p (5.11d|25m) 6p (5.9|26m)		
Seolwoo Route 설우길	5.11b	125 (4p)
1p (5.9|31m) 2p (5.10c|33m) 3p (5.11b|37m) 4p (5.11a|24m)		

Seonin-bong 선인봉

Route Name	Grade	Height
Seonin 선인 B	5.9	138 (4p)
1p (5.7|30m) 2p (5.7|30m) 3p (5.7|40m) 4p (5.9|38m)		
Hanmaeum Route 한마음길	5.10b	33
Yeodel Route 여델길	*	220 (6p)*
Yodel Buttress 요델버트레스	5.11a/A1	236 (6p)
1p (5.11a|33m) 2p (5.9|36m) 3p (5.10c|26m) 4p (5.9|20m) 5p (5.8|36m) 6p (5.8/A1|35m)		
Yodel Right Side 요델우측	*	*
Yeondae Bachelor 연대베첼러	5.9/A1	174 (5p)
1p (5.8|40m) 2p (5.9|42m) 3p (5.11a/A0|50m) 4p (5.9|27m) 5p (5.8/A1|35m)		
Summit 써미터	5.10d/A0	168 (5p)
1p (5.8/A0|27m) 2p (5.8/A0|40m) 3p (A0|32m) 4p (5.10d/A0|39m) 5p (5.7/A0|30m)		
Gyeongsong 경송 B	5.12a/A0	136 (3p)
1p (5.12a|35m) 2p (5.10c|30m) 3p (5.10b|A0|36m)		
Youngest One Route 막내길	5.11d/A0	201 (6p)
1p (5.11a|28m) 2p (5.11c|33m) 3p (5.11d|35m) 4p (5.9/A0|50m) 5p (5.9/A0|35m) 6p (5.7/A0|30m)		
(No Name) 미상	5.10c	20
Cheongam Route 청암길	5.11a/A0	190 (7p)
1p (5.8|29m) 2p (5.10a|24m) 3p (5.11a|30m) 4p (5.10c|16m) 5p (5.10b/A0|36m) 6p (5.8|35m) 7p (5.8|20m)		
Silver Route 은벽길	5.8	106 (4p)
1p (5.6|26m) 2p (5.8|20m) 3p (5.8|30m) 4p (5.7|30m)		
Gyeongsong 경송 A	5.10c/A0	145 (5p)
1p (5.10b|28m) 2p (5.9|25m) 3p (5.10c|28m) 4p (5.10a|26m) 5p (5.10b/A0|35m)		
Azalea Route 진달래길	5.11a	80 (3p)
1p (5.8|30m) 2p (5.11a|20m) 3p (5.8|30m)		
Myeongsimhana Route 명심하나길	5.10c/A0	96 (3p)
1p (5.10c|30m) 2p (5.10b|29m) 3p (A0|25m)		
Myeongsimdul Route 명심둘길	5.10d	137 (5p)
1p (5.10c|30m) 2p (5.10d|22m) 3p (5.10a|21m) 4p (5.10b|28m) 5p (5.9|36m)		
Ascent Route 어센트길	5.8	143 (4p)
1p (5.8|38m) 2p (5.6|40m) 3p (5.8|30m) 4p (5.7|35m)		
Shawshank Redemption 쇼생크탈출	5.11b	40 (2p)
1p (*|20m) 2p (5.11b|20m)		

*Multi-pitch info is unavailable at this time

SURAK-SAN, DAEJU-AMJANG 수락산 대주암장

Description
This crag offers mainly moderate slab climbs on granite rock. There are face and crack climbs. Daeju-amjang faces south. There is a diagram that describes route beta on the far right side of the wall.

Directions
37.695656N 127.077205E
Sanggyeo-dong, Nowon-gu, Seoul 서울 노원구 상계동

In Seoul, take a subway to Suraksan Station (Line #7) and take Exit 1. Walk straight for 400m. Take the first right at the end of the apartment complex. Continue on the main trail for thirty minutes until you come to an open area called "새광장" Sae Gwangjang, near a mountain spring. Past Sae Gwangjang 새광장, take the right path and scramble up to the crag. The crag is visible once you take the right at the open area. From the subway station, it takes fifty minutes to reach the crag.

Gear
15 draws and a 60m rope.

Safety
A helmet is recommended.

Additional Comments
Water can be found at the spring near the open area.

DAEJU-AMJANG 대주암장

Route Name	Grade	Height
Regret 아쉬움 1	5.10b	10
Regret 아쉬움 2	5.10b	10
Dragon Way 1st Pitch 드레곤웨이 1 피치	5.11b	20
Dragon Way 2nd Pitch 드레곤웨이 2 피치	5.13*	20
Get Up Holding A Square 네모잡고 일어나	5.10b	30
Crack Route 크랙길	5.8	30
Bbong Route 뽕길	5.10b	30
Nogada 1st Pitch 노가다 1 피치	5.11b	20
Nogada 2nd Pitch 노가다 2 피치	5.9	20
Circle 동그라미	5.10b	30
DaeJu Route 1st Pitch 대주길 1 피치	5.11b	30
Daeju Route 2nd Pitch 대주길 2 피치	5.9	30
Like The Flowing River 흐르는 강물처럼	5.11c	20

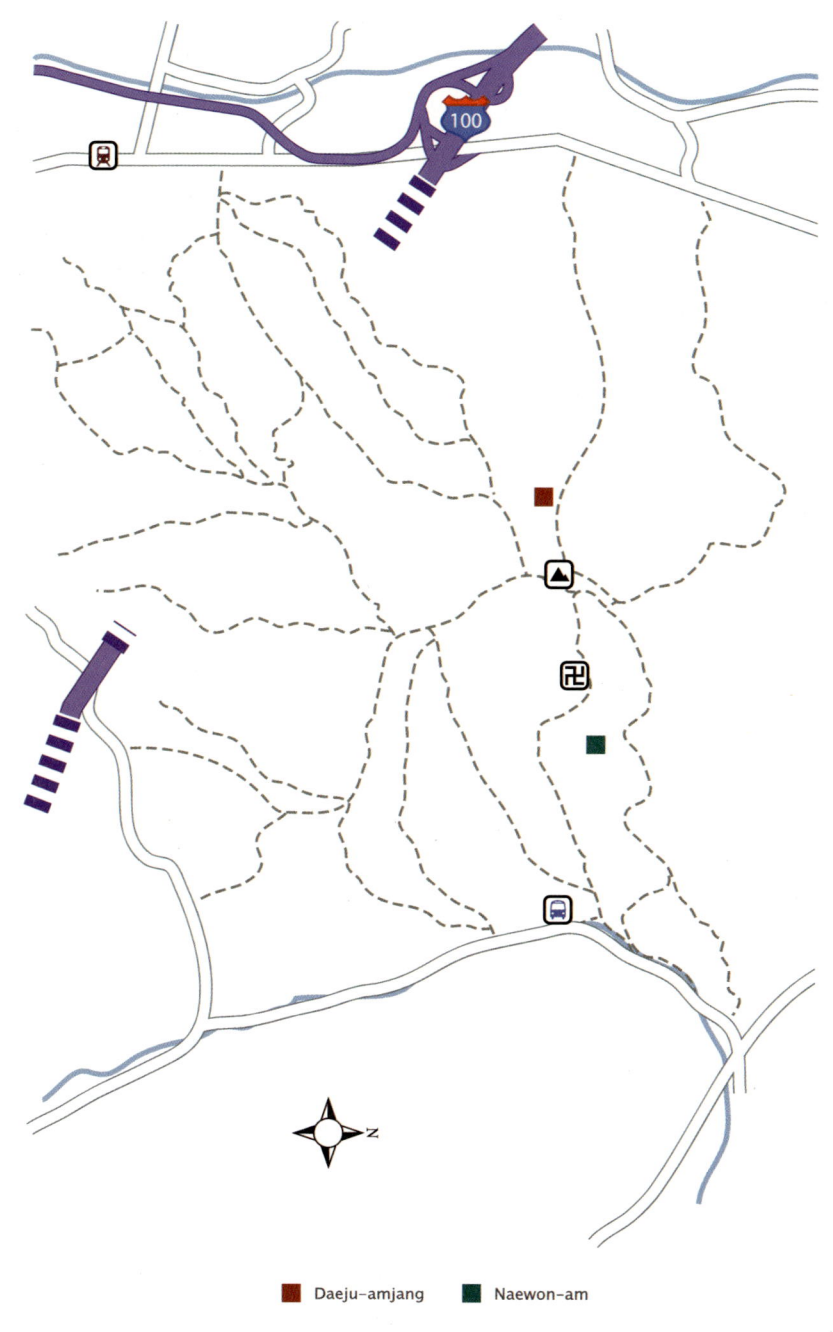

SURAK-SAN, NAEWON-AM 수락산 내원암

Description
Located in the north of Seoul, the climbs at this crag are comparable with that in Insubong 인수봉 and Seonin-bong 선인봉. However, Naewon-am will be an alternative to avoid the large crowds during the weekends. This crag offers slab, vertical face, and crack climbs on granite rock that faces east. The climbs vary from half sport and half trad climbing. On the wall, the routes start from the far right on the front wall. There is another crag called Daeju-amjang 대주암장 on the other side of this mountain. Waterfalls and picturesque scenery along the trail to the crag will give you a pleasant hike.

Directions
37.700919N 127.091925E
Cheonghak-ri, Byeolnae-myeon, Namyangju-si 남양주시 별내면 청학리

In Seoul, take a subway to Danggogae Station 당고개 (Line #4) or to Seokgyeo Station 석계역 (Line #1). Take a bus bound for Chunghak-ri 청학리 and get off at Chunghak-ri 청학리. Head towards Surak-San Amusement Park 수락산유원지 and continue on the road for ten minutes past Okryu Waterfall 옥류폭포. There are many restaurants to your right by the stream. Follow the stream and once you cross the small bridge, look for a sign to your left that says "백호암" Baekho-am. Follow the sign (don't follow the big temple sign) until you reach the small temple Baekho-am 백호암. At the temple, do not go straight forward. Instead, hike up to the immediate right with the temple to your right. The approach will be fifteen minutes from the temple.

Gear
12 draws, two 60m ropes, and a full set of cams.

Safety
A helmet is recommended even though the quality of rock is pretty good. The anchors and bolts are also in good shape.

Additional Comments
Get water at the mountain spring. As mentioned above, this crag is a good place to avoid a large crowd on weekends. There are good campsites below the crag on the left.

Naewon-am 내원암

Route Name	Grade	Height
Green 녹색	5.11a	15
Blue Fine Tree 푸른솔	5.10c	100 (2p)*
(No Name) 미상 1	5.10b	110 (3p)*
Little Prince 어린왕자	5.8	70 (2p)*
(No Name) 미상 2	5.9	70 (3p)*
(No Name) 미상 3	5.10*	90 (3p)*
(No Name) 미상 4	5.8	30
(No Name) 미상 5	5.9	90 (3p)*
Summit 써미트 A	5.10b	66 (2p)
1p (5.8|30m) **2p** (5.10b|36m)		
Summit 써미트 B	5.10a	74 (2p)
1p (5.8|38m) **2p** (5.10a|36m)		
Dongik 동익	*	*

*Multi-pitch info is unavailable at this time

MYEONGSUNG-SAN, CHAK-BAWI 명성산 책바위

Description
Chak-bawi 책바위 is granite rock that offers pleasant slab climbs. Recently, a local climbing club developed two new routes. There is a lot of potential for traditional climbs between the existing routes. It faces south.

Directions
38.073856N 127.333152E
Sanjeong-ri, Yeongbuk-myeon, Pocheon-ri 포천시 영북면 산정리

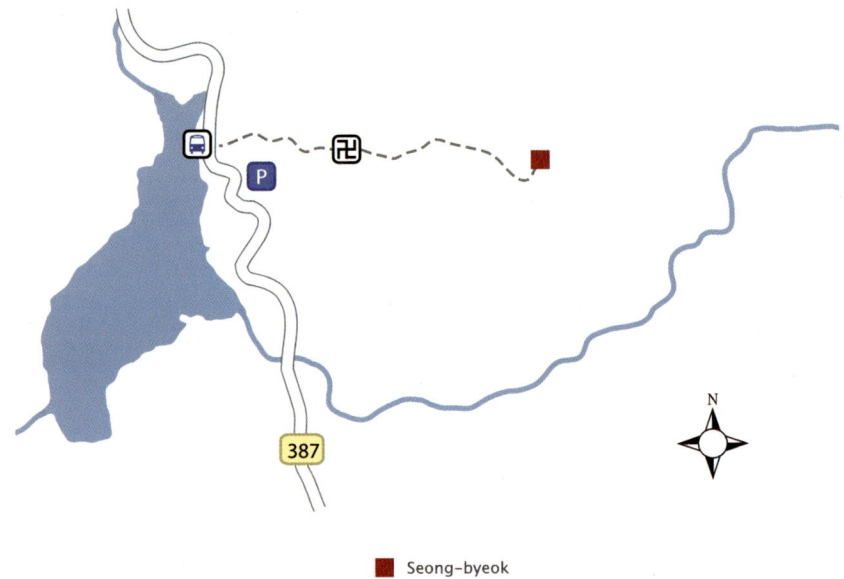

■ Seong-byeok

From either Sang-bong 상봉, Dong-Seoul 동서울, or Suyou-ri Bus Terminal 수유리, take a bus to Uncheon 운천 in Phocheon 포천 . From Uncheon, get on the bus to San Jung-Hosu 산정호수 and walk toward temple Jain-sa 자인사. Continue on the main trail for twenty minutes and then scramble to the right past Rescue Mark 3-2. Cross over the small, dry stream and then continue hiking for ten minutes.

Gear
10 draws, a 60m rope, a set of cams, and extra webbing.

Additional Comments
Unfortunately, it is hard to get accurately documented route beta. This crag is 100m high and 80m wide with low-angled slab climbing on granite rock. There are a few unknown routes that had been put up when I went in November 2011. Grades are assumed to be ranging from 5.9 to 5.11 in difficulty. There are good opportunities to develop climbs around Chak-bawi. Trees, in the middle of routes, will give you a great rest point and belay spot.

Sori-san, Samhyeongjae-bawi 소리산 삼형제 바위

Description
This crag is kind of a smaller version of Ganhyeon 간현, but it will not be as crowded as Ganhyeon, even during the peak season. It is a perfect place for a summer vacation with the family, where all can enjoy jumping into the stream. The climbing area consists of two crags. The first crag is called "Three Brothers Rock" 삼형제바위. Climbs vary from face, crack, and overhung climbing on igneous rock that faces northeast. The second crag is located 50m up from the left side of the first crag and has a cool view of the stream with its dark grey color. There are two multi-pitch climbs. The crags were developed from 1996 to 1999.

Directions
37.639451N 127.622037E
Jungdaebang-ri, Seo-myeon, Hongcheon-gun 홍천군 서면 중대방리

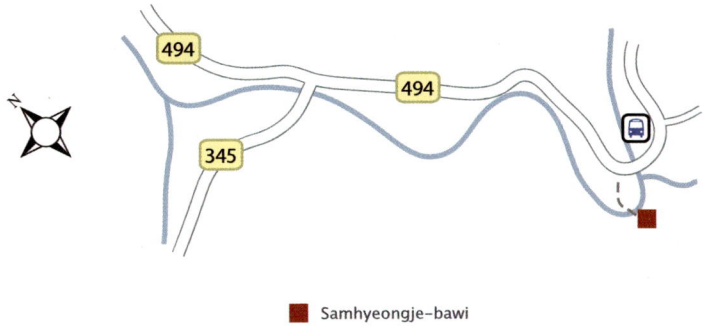

■ Samhyeongje-bawi

There are multiple transportation options to get to the crag. For those from the north, go to Cheongpyeong 청평. From there, take an intercity bus bound for Mogok 모곡 and transfer to a bus bound to Hongcheon 홍천. Get off at Seoksan Gas Station 석산. For those from the south, go to Hongcheon 홍천 and take the bus heading to Seoksan-ri 석산리 and get off at Seoksan Gas Station 석산. From the gas station, you can see the crag by the bridge. It will be hard to get to the crag by public transportation because the buses only run a couple of times a day.

Gear
12 draws, a 60m rope, and a full set of cams.

Safety
A few of the routes are crumbly and mossy so a helmet is recommended.

Additional Comments
There are good camping sites and excellent local restaurants which serve spicy fish broth. There are also minbaks 민박 and a jjimjilbang 찜질방 to stay at.

Three Brothers Rock 삼형제바위

Route Name	Grade	Height
Wedding Anniversary 결혼기념일	5.10c	22
Sohyang 소향	5.10a/b	22
Sunset 노을	5.10b	14
C & S 씨엔에스	5.11c	13
Compensation 보상	5.10c	50
Freebird 창살을벗어난새	5.10a	50
Daybreak 미명	5.11c	13
Old Pine Tree 노송	5.10a	16
Seoksan 석산	5.10c	13
Road To Husband & Wife 부부길	5.11c/d	6
Moon Hung On A Spur Of A Mountain 산모퉁이에걸린달	5.10c	18
Nut 너트	5.12b	18
Samulnori 사물놀이	5.13*	16
Nut 너트	5.11c	11
Dumundong 두문동	5.12a	14
Resentment 한	5.13 *	10
Longing 그리움	5.13*	8
Sunshine 햇살	5.12c/d	14
Sori 소리	5.11b	16
Extension 연장	5.11b	10
Brainstorm 난상	5.9	8

2nd Crag

Route Name	Grade	Height
Start 시작	5.11a	10
Whispering 속삭임	5.10b	10
Route For The Youngest 막내길	5.10*	10
1974	5.10c	15
Rapids 여울	5.10a	20
Incompletion 미완성	5.11c/d	15
Chowoo 초우	5.11*	15
One Move 한동작	5.12a	15
J Route 길	5.12c	15
Scorching Sun 땡볕	5.11a	20
Non 비	5.11b	15
Take Out The Body 몸빼	5.11b	15
Finish 마무리	5.10b	15
Practice 연습	5.9	20

*Routes start from the far right side of the wall

HANAGAE-AMJANG 하나개암장

Description
Located at Hanagae Beach 하나개 in Mueuido 무의도, the crag is divided into three areas within less than 200m of each other. Most of the routes are facing west with a unique setting. High tide usually comes around 3 p.m. and lasts about an hour, so most of the areas are climbable all day. Many of the routes can be top-roped.

Directions
37.376637N 126.409378E
Mueui-dong, Jung-gu, Incheon 인천 중구 무의동

From Seoul, take a bus or train to Incheon International Airport. Exit from Gate 6 and take a bus bound for Jangjindo 장진도 or take buses bound for the entrance of Mueuido 무의도 and walk twenty minutes to reach Jangjindo. Buses bound for Jangjin-do run every hour and will take you straight to the ferry dock. However, instead of waiting for an hour, it will be faster to take the bus bound for Mueuido Entrance 무의도입구 because the bus runs every ten minutes. Get on a ferry for Mueuido at Jangjindo dock. Hanagae Beach can be approached by either a bus or by walking through the mountain trail from the village 큰무리, where you get off the ferry. To access the crag from Hanagae Beach, take the path that is on your left as you face the sea. Continue walking along the sea for twenty minutes, past a couple of wooden fences, until you see guide ropes heading down to the crag at sea level. When the tide is low, it can be reached by walking along the seaside. The approach time from the ferry dock will be an hour.

Gear
12 draws and a 50m rope. A set of cams can be used on some of the routes.

Safety
Although the crag is a sea cliff, it is good quality stone.

Additional Comments
There are tons of amenities at the beach and great campsites around the crag.

HANAGAE-AMJANG 하나개암장 (1 OF 4)

Route Name	Grade	Height
Attention 주목	5.10b	10
New Cotton 새 솜	5.10a	10
Steal 쎄비주	5.10a	10
I Can't Stand 못살아	5.11a	10
Windy Guy 바람남자	5.10d	10
Share The Fate With Others 생공사	5.10b	10
Silver Plate 은반	5.10d	10
Courtesy 정중	5.10c	10

HANAGAE-AMJANG 하나개암장 (2 OF 4)

Route Name	Grade	Height
Guardian Angel 수호천사	5.9	10
Conehead Doctor 짱구박사	5.8	10
F4	5.10a	10
Serenada 세레나데	5.10c	10
Floor 마루	5.10a	10
Friendly 정다운	5.10b	10
Born in February 29th 2월 29일생	5.10b	10
Different World 별천지	5.10b	10

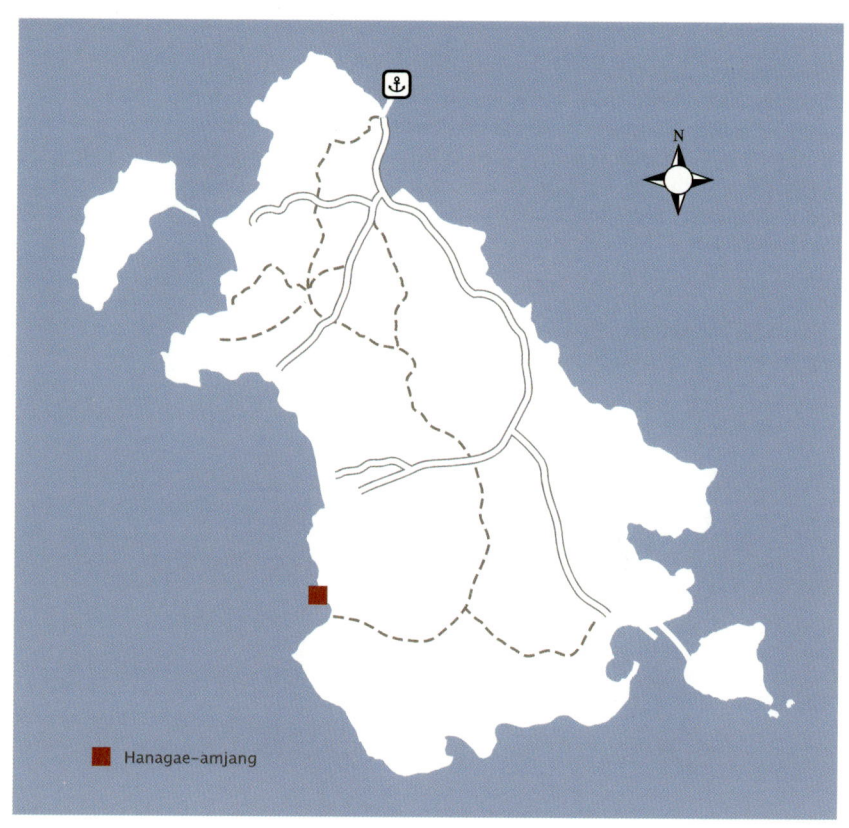

Hanagae-amjang

HANAGAE-AMJANG 하나개암장 (3 OF 4)

Route Name	Grade	Height
Number Two 큰엉아	5.8	10
Sea Squirt 멍게	5.8	10
Frog 개구리	5.9	10
Yaru 야루	5.10a	10
Shelley 쎌리	5.10c	10
Summer Angel 썸머엔젤	5.7	10
Ggi Ggi 끼끼	5.6	10
King Size Amaranth 왕좁쌀	5.10b	12
Borimudeuk 보리무득	5.10b	12
Maepsari 맵사리	5.10c	12
People 피뿔	5.10c	12

HANAGAE-AMJANG 하나개암장 (4 OF 4)

Route Name	Grade	Height
Bomal 보말	5.10c	12
Shoulder Grass 어깨풀	5.10b	12
Twister 비틀이	5.10b	12
Lily 백합	5.7	25
Gamurac 가무락	5.11c	18
Dong Juk 동죽	5.12a	16
Short-necked Clam 바지락	5.12b	15
Mindle 민들	5.10d	20
Garimat 가리맛	5.11c	20
Cockle 꼬막	5.10c	16
Garden 마당	5.10b	15
Toi 퇴	5.11b	22

HAMHEUDONGCHEON-AMJANG 함허동천암장

Description
This crag lies on the most sacred mountain in South Korea, where the legendary founding father of ancient Korea used to hold a memorial service for Heaven. It was developed in 2010 with sixteen routes. It is small, but this crag offers hard climbs on a slabby face with thin cracks in all the corners of the routes. The rock is good quality and is the perfect place for practicing cam placements. It faces east, but is shaded by the trees all day.

Directions
37.61362N 126.44819E
Sagi-ri, Hwado-myeon, Ganghwa-gun 강화군 화도면 사기리

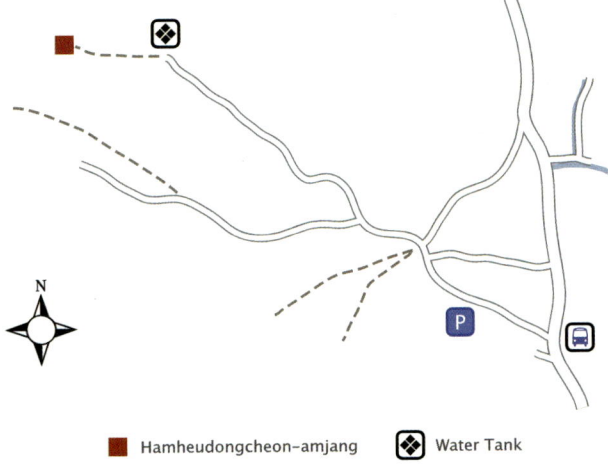

From Seoul, take a bus to Ganghwa Bus Terminal 강화 and then transfer to a bus bound for Hamheudongcheon 함허동천. Get off at Hamheudongcheon. At the bus stop, walk to Hamheudongcheon Campgrounds and stay left on the main trail, past the ticket counter. After a ten minute hike from the ticket counter, you will reach a white, rectangular water tank on your left. Go left around the tanker and if you look closely, you will see a path and a black wooden sign with a cross. Follow this path for five minutes and the crag will be on your right.

Gear
7 draws, a 50m rope, and a set of cams with extra small cams.

Additional Comments
Hamheudongcheon is one of Korea's biggest campsites with lots of facilities and good scenery.

Photo Courtesy of Lea Gang, 강레아

Hamheudongcheon-amjang 함허동천암장

Route Name	Grade	Height
Gabgocha 갑비고차	5.10a	7
Satgatchuri 삿갓추리	5.11a	8
Oduri 오두리	5.11b	10
Manmeoru 만머루	5.10b	11
Makeungol 막은골	5.9	10
Seodumari 서두마리	5.10b	12
Shade Spot 응달막	5.9	12
Muchubi 무추비	5.11c	13
Hamheudongcheon 함허동천	5.10b	13
Jingaejjagae 진개짜개	5.10d	15
Goaedari	5.11c	15
Miruji 미루지	5.10b	16
Deokdal 덕달	5.11b	13
Chilonji 칠온지	5.10b	12
Dongtulmeori 동틀머리	5.10c	10
Sunny Spot 양달말	5.10a	8

JOBI-SAN, JOBI-AM 조비산 조비암

Description
Jobi-am 조비암 has a plethora of nice roof routes above the cave, which is located in the center of the crag. It also offers both easy and hard face routes on either side of the cave. The crag is in the sun all day because it faces directly south. The hard roof routes above the cave were added recently. The crux on the roof easily disappears after a couple of hard pulls. Most of the routes have names and grades painted at the bottom. The bolts look very good and the rock quality, for the most part, is excellent. Two easy traditional climbing routes were also established on either side of the cave, where you can place a few cams if you would like to ignore the bolts on the routes.

Directions
37.117904N 127.368472E
Seokcheon-ri, Baekam-myeon, Cheoin-gu, Yongin-si 용인시 처인구 백암면 석천리

From Seoul, take a bus to Yongin Bus Terminal 용인. From Yongin, transfer to a bus bound for Baekam 백암. At Baekam Bus Stop, take a bus heading towards Jangpyeongsamgyeri 장평삼거리. From there, walk straight for five minutes on the road and hike to Jobisan Garden Restaurant 조비산가든. Continue on the unpaved road for fifteen minutes. The crag can be seen all the way from the bus stop.

Gear
10 draws and a 50m rope. Bring some trad gear if you want to practice placing pieces on the multi-pitch routes.

Safety
For the routes on the far right side, a helmet is recommended.

Additional Comments
When the weather is bad, local climbers camp out in the cave, which is large enough for two or three tents. However, there is a spacious area in front of the cave for pitching tents as well. Water and food should be bought at the bus terminal.

JOBI-AM 조비암 (1 OF 2)

Route Name	Grade	Height
Road To Eiger 아이거가는길	5.10*	14
Climbing Friend's Route 벽우길	5.10a	13
First Excursion 첫나들이	5.10a	12
Twin Dragon 쌍용	5.10c	12
Existing 기존 A	5.11c	15
Existing 기존 B	5.10d	15
Our Paradise 우리들의천국	5.10b	15
Hasty Preparation 벼락치기	5.9	15

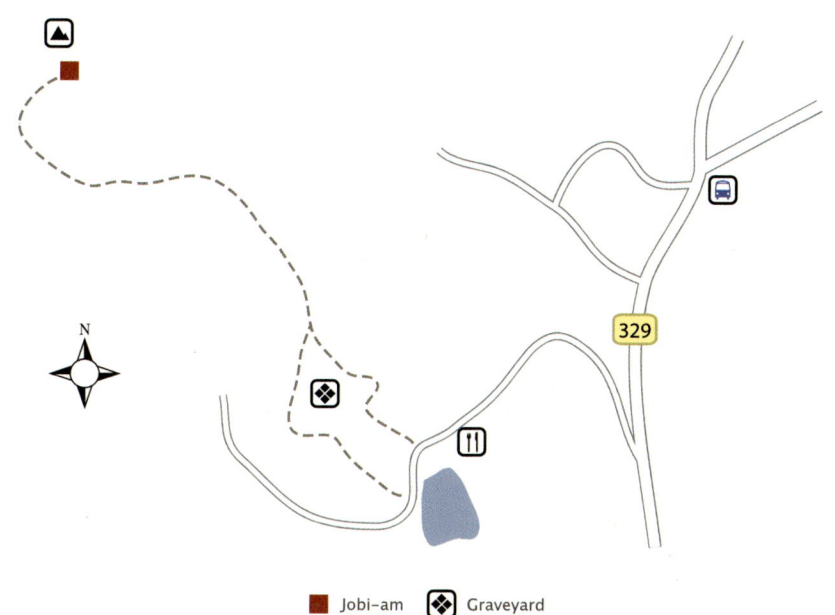

Jobi-am Graveyard

JOBI-AM 조비암 (2 OF 2)

Route Name	Grade	Height
Pheongtak Segal 평택갈매기	5.11c	14
A Piece Of Cake 칼로물베기	5.10d	12
Chorus Of Youngster 막내들의합창	5.10a	10
Connection 인연 **1p** (5.8|30m) **2p** (5.9|25m)	5.9	60 (2p)
Crazy 크레이지	5.10c	10
Odysseus 오딧세이	5.12*	10
Albatross 알바트로스	5.14*	10
My Way 마이웨이	5.14a	10
Yellow Cerepang 엘로우세르팡	5.13*	10
(No Name) 미상	5.11a	13
Azelea 진달래	5.10c/d	15
Snow Line 스노우라인	5.10b	15
Inadvertence 무심	5.11c	15
Inadvertence 무심 2	5.11d	*
Walking To The Sky 걸어서하늘끝까지 **1p** (5.8|40m) **2p** (5.8|20m)	5.9	60 (2p)
Jobi-san & Me 조비산그리고나	5.12a	15
Jobi-san Owl 조비산부엉이	5.13a	15

DWAEJIGUL-AMJANG 돼지굴 암장

Description
The crag is located on Doderum-san's 도드람산 fourth peak. Dwejigul-amjang 돼지굴암장 was developed in 2003 and has thirteen routes with one crack route in the middle that can be trad climbed. Most of the routes are angled between 80 to 120 degrees and the rock is very solid. Dodeuram 도드람 means "crying wild boar". Legend has it that one day, when a monk was collecting mushrooms at this crag by hanging from a rope, he heard a crying boar at the top of the crag. He climbed up to investigate and when he reached the top, the monk found that his rope was almost cut through by the rock. He looked for the boar that had saved him, but it was gone. Since then, people started to call this mountain Dodeuram-san 도드람산.

Directions
37.269331N 127.39082E
Mok-ri, Majang-myeon, Icheon-si 이천시 마장면 목리

From either Dong-Seoul Bus Terminal 동서울버스터미널 or Gangnam Highway Bus Terminal 강남고속버스터미널, take an intercity bus bound for Icheon 이천. Get off at Icheon 이천 and transfer to a bus bound for Yongin 용인. Get off at Pyogo Elementary School 표고 and then walk for fifteen minutes to the SK Training Center. From the SK Training Center, you can see the five peaks lined up on the mountain. There are two main trails to get to the crag. The middle trail will lead you up to the ridge, but the east trail has an easier approach. Follow the hiking map, at the trailhead, and the signs to the fourth peak. The crag is right below the peak on the east side. It will take thirty minutes to reach the crag from the trailhead.

Gear
7 draws, a 50m rope, and a set of small to mid-sized cams if you prefer placing protection.

Additional Comments
Close to this crag, there is another potential wall that will be developed sooner or later. This seldom-visited area is a pleasant thirty minute hike that offers a lot of sunshine and open space on the rocky ridge. There is also some nice bouldering if you look around the area.

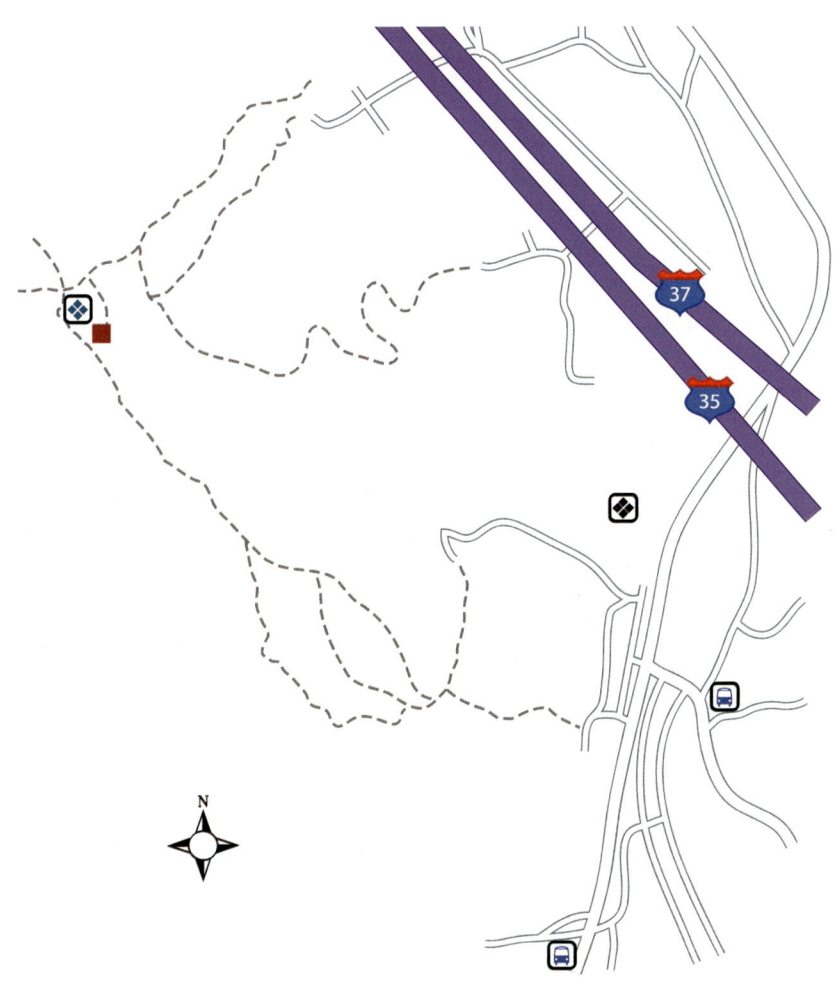

■ Dwaejigul-amjang　◆ SK Training Center　◆ Metal Staircase

DWAEJIGUL-AMJANG 돼지굴 (1 OF 2)

Route Name	Grade	Height
Rusa 루사	5.11*	15
I Believe	5.9	18
First Love 첫사랑	5.9	15
Shinchon Love 신촌사랑	5.8	22
Korak 코락	5.12*	22
Mickey Best 미키짱	5.12a	22
My Honey KANG	5.10d	18

DWAEJIGUL-AMJANG 돼지굴 (2 OF 2)

Route Name	Grade	Height
Ilmaeg 일맥	5.10c	10
Pork Route 돼지길	5.10a	18
Rock Love 바위사랑	*	*
Wishing 바라기 2002	5.10b	18
Youseong Younjeong 유성윤정	5.9	13
Deficience 미달	5.9	15

Namhansansung, Beomgul-am 남한산성 범굴암

Description
Unlike the other crags in Gyeonggi-do area, this crag has different rock textures with various edges and ledges that offer good angled, overhung climbs. All of the climbs are less than fifteen meters long and face southeast. There are also two bouldering routes on the wall.

Directions
37.45873N 127.208891E
Buldang-ri, Jungbu-myeon, Gwangju-si 광주시 중부면 불당리

In Seoul, take the subway to Sansung Station 산성역 (Line #8) and get out at Exit 2. Transfer to a village bus heading to Buldangri 불당리. The bus lines change occasionally, so be sure to ask someone in the village. Get off at Buldangri. Walk past the first bridge from the road and continue walking towards the village for 100m. Cross the bridge on your right at the mouth of the village. Pass the green fence by a restaurant and walk up the hill until the trail branches. Take the left path that goes towards the gravesite and hike up the steep trail. After a few moderate switchbacks and more gravesites, you will see the crag on your right. The approach time will be twenty minutes.

Gear
8 draws and a 50m rope.

Safety
This crag is well bolted with clamped wire anchors.

Additional Comments
Water should be bought at the village. There are good campsites around the crag.

Beomgul-am 범굴암 (1 of 2)			Beomgul-am 범굴암 (2 of 2)		
Route Name	Grade	Height	Route Name	Grade	Height
Martial Arts Hall 연무관	5.10a	25	Bandit 산적	5.11c	13
Development 개척 2002	5.8	8	Ammunition Depot 침패정	5.11a	14
Hyeon Route 현길	5.8	10	North Bound Land 북장대지	5.10d	14
Love Mountain 산사랑	5.9	12	7545	5.12b	14
Success 성공	5.11a	15	Command Post 수어장대	5.11d	13
Foundation 반석	5.10b	15	Rock Friend 석우 1997	Bouldering Route	
Free Man 자유인	5.10c	12	Jjambbong 짬뽕	5.11d	12
Habunim 하부님	5.11a	13	Tiger Cave 범굴	5.13c	10
-5.10	5.11b	13	Rock Friend 석우 4.27	Bouldering Route	

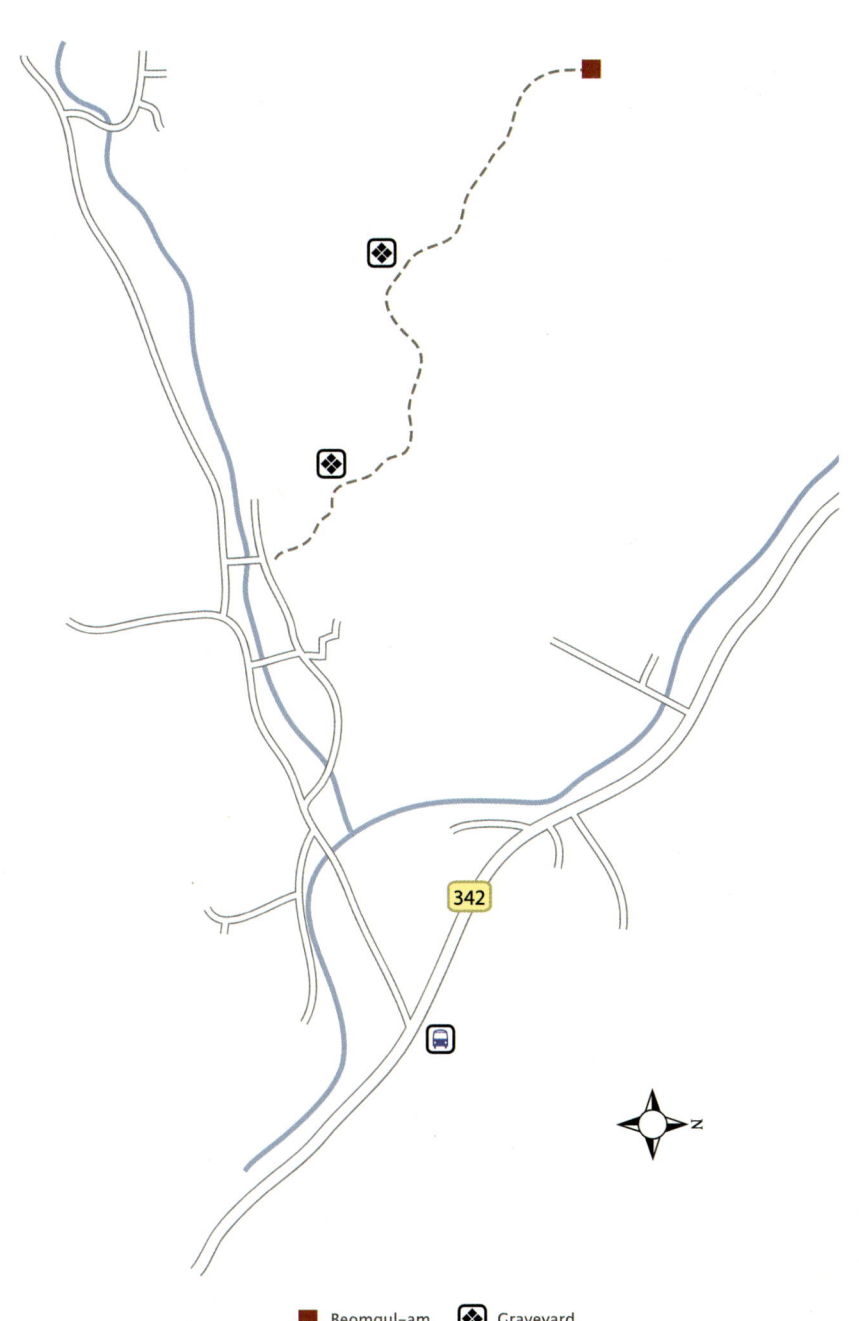

OBONG-SAN, BYEONGPUNG-AM 오봉산 병풍암

Description
This crag is small, standing at 15m high and 30m wide. It features twelve routes and offers a few moderate overhanging and face climbs. It faces north and is in the shade all day.

Directions
37.344351N 126.964509E
Gocheon-dong, Euiwang-si 의왕시 고천동

In Seoul, go to Gunpo Subway Station 군포 (Line #1) and then take a bus heading to Uiwang City Hall 의왕. There is a good trail behind city hall. Follow the trail and take the right path at the fork. Continue on for five minutes to reach the crag. The approach time will be fifteen minutes from city hall.

Gear
5 draws and a 50m rope.

Safety
The first bolts on a few of the routes are pretty run out, so be careful when leading and use a spotter if possible.

Additional Comments
You can get water and snacks from the shop at city hall.

BYEONGPUNG-AM 병풍암

Route Name	Grade	Height
Road To High Heaven 황천길	5.10a	7
Born Again 다시 태어나며	5.8	11
Beal 비알 1	5.9	7
Beal 비알 3	5.7	9
Sangick Route 상익길	5.9	12
Brother's Gesture 아우들의몸짓	5.9	15
Magpie Route 까치길	5.9	15
Beal 비알 2	5.11b	9
Existing Crack 기존크랙	5.7	9
Phoveda 포베다	5.10a	9
Toad 두꺼비	5.9	9
Motorcycle 오토바이	5.9	9

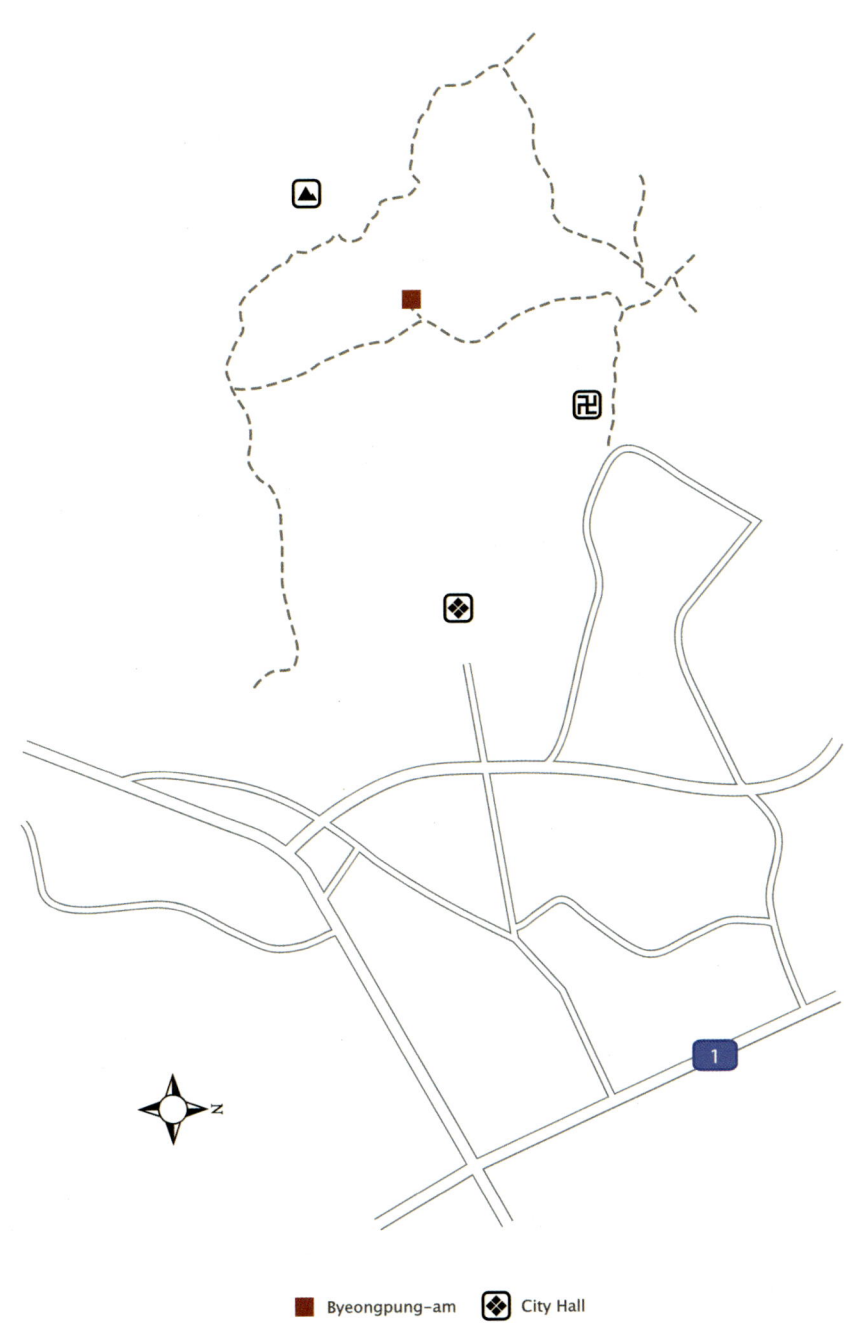

MORAK-SAN, MIRAE-AM 모락산 미래암

Description
Located in Uiwang-Si 의왕시, Mirae-am 모락산미래암 has thirty routes. It's 10m high and 100m wide. This crag was established in 1992. It has a metamorphic rock texture and angles ranging from 80 to 135 degrees, which makes it ideal for strengthening finger muscles and working on hard, technical moves. All the climbing here is intense, including the easier routes. There is a diagram on the first route with grades for each climb.

Directions
37.367804N 126.973844E
Ojeon-dong, Uiwang-si 의왕시 오전동

From Gumjung Subway Station 금정역, take a bus heading for Shinwon Rotary 신원. Get off at Uhan-Kimbery 유한양행. From Uhan-Kimbery 유한양행, walk towards Hyoseong Elementary School 효성초등학교. Continue past the elementary school, between Jindallae Apartment 진달래 and Shinwon Apartment 신원. Cross the road at the lights after these apartments. There is a spring for water by Hangwang Shine Hill Village Apartments 한광. Hike up the main trail for twenty minutes. After walking up a couple of wooden stairs, there is a Rescue Mark 1-5 near the top of the main trail. This is the top of the crag. Turn left and walk for a couple of minutes behind the sign. It will be much quicker to grab a cab to get to Hyoseong Elementary School 효성. This costs about 3,500 KRW from Geumjeong Station 금정 (Line #1) or Indeokwon Station 인덕원 (Line #4). Also, the LG Apartments Bus Stop, not available directly from the subway, is next to the trailhead.

Gear
10 draws and a 50m rope.

Safety
All the bolts are in pretty good in shape, but a few of the anchors are rusty and somewhat suspicious. Bring some slings and extra draws for lowering.

Additional Comments
This crag becomes overgrown during the summer and some of the belay stations are unstable. However, everything will still be climbable. The crag is in the shade during the morning, but from mid-afternoon it is in the sun.

MIRAE-AM 미래암 (1 OF 2)

Route Name	Grade	Height
Jinho Route 진호길	5.12a	10
Born September 5th & I Am Stupid 9월 5일생그리고나는못난이	5.11c/d	10
Do Ascending 도오름	5.11a/b	8
Two Nights, Three Days 이박삼일	5.10a/b	10
Saeromi 새롬이	5.10c/d	10
Sleepyhead 잠꾸러기	5.10c/d	11

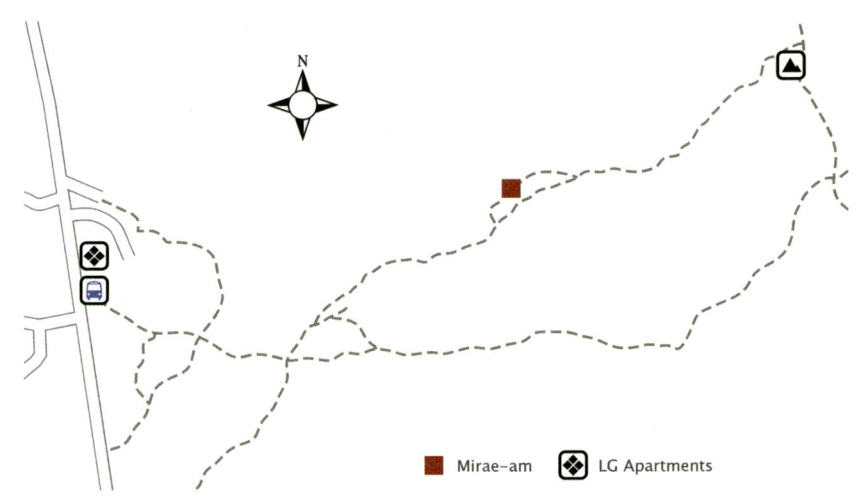

Mirae-am LG Apartments

Mirae-am 미래암 (2 OF 2)

Route Name	Grade	Height
Wolf Spider 독거미	5.11b/c	13
From Halla To Baekdo 한라에서 백두까지	5.10d	14
Fight 싸움	5.12a	15
Never Stopping Longing 오매불망	5.13a	15
Sunny Spot 양지	5.13a	15
Mom & Batman 엄마와배트맨	5.13a	15
Little Finger & Index Finger 새끼와검지	5.12a/b	15
Sunflower 해바라기	5.11b/c	15
Double Or Nothing 이판사판	5.11b/c	15
Siblings 형제	5.10a/b	12
Two Fingers 손가락 2 개	5.10c/d	8
Stone Flower 석화	5.9	12
MoMo 모모	5.10c/d	8
Something Out Of Nothing 무에서유	5.10a/b	10
Dream Of Orangutan 오랑우탄의꿈	5.12a	6
I Will Give You All 나그대에게모두드리리	5.12c/d	6
A Stupid Love Story Of A Idiot 어느얼간이의바보같은사랑이야기	5.11c/d	6
McGyver 이가이버	5.13b/c	8
I Am Going Too 나두야간다	5.10b/c	6
Untitled Subject 무제	5.9	6
Sister 누나야	5.12c/d	7
Seonyeong Route 선영길	5.12c	7
Little Rascals' Chorus 꾸러기들의합창 2	5.11c	8

SURI-SAN, MAE-BAWI 수리산 매바위

Description
Mae-bawi boasts of great high-angle face climbs with highly featured thin crack lines on granite rock. It offers something different to enjoy at every turn. The wall faces south. This crag is a hidden gem among the crags in Gyeonggi Province 경기.

Directions
37.358526N 126.905587E
Sanbon-dong, Gunpo-si 군포시 산본동

Take the subway to Geumjeong 금정 or Sanbon Station 산본 (Line #4). Take a bus heading to Gunpo Library 군포도서관 and get off there. Hike up past two mountain springs and by a big utility pole, following the sign for "슬기봉" Seulgi-bong, until you see a sign that says "임간교실" Imgangyosil. From there, you will see the crag to your right. Hike up for ten minutes. It will take thirty-five minutes to get to the crag from the library.

Gear
10 draws and a 50m rope.

Safety
This crag is well bolted with good anchors.

Additional Comments
Even though it's a bit of a small crag, I would say it is one of the best sport climbing areas in Seoul.

MAE-BAWI 매바위

Route Name	Grade	Height
No Crack, No Terrace 노크랙 노테라스	5.13*	18
Freedom 자유 2007	5.11b	15
Noddang 노땅	5.10a	12
Ouch! Hot 아! 뜨거	5.11c	12
Run To The South 남쪽으로 튀어	5.11b	12
Existing Route 기존길 1	5.11b	12
Existing Route 기존길 2	5.10c	8
Existing Route 기존길 3	5.10a	8
Existing Route 기존길 4	5.10b	8
Existing Route 기존길 5	5.10a	8
Hee Love 희사랑	5.10b	8
Little Devil 작은악마	5.10c	12
Wing 날개	5.12b	10
Hwang Punch 황펀치	5.12a	10

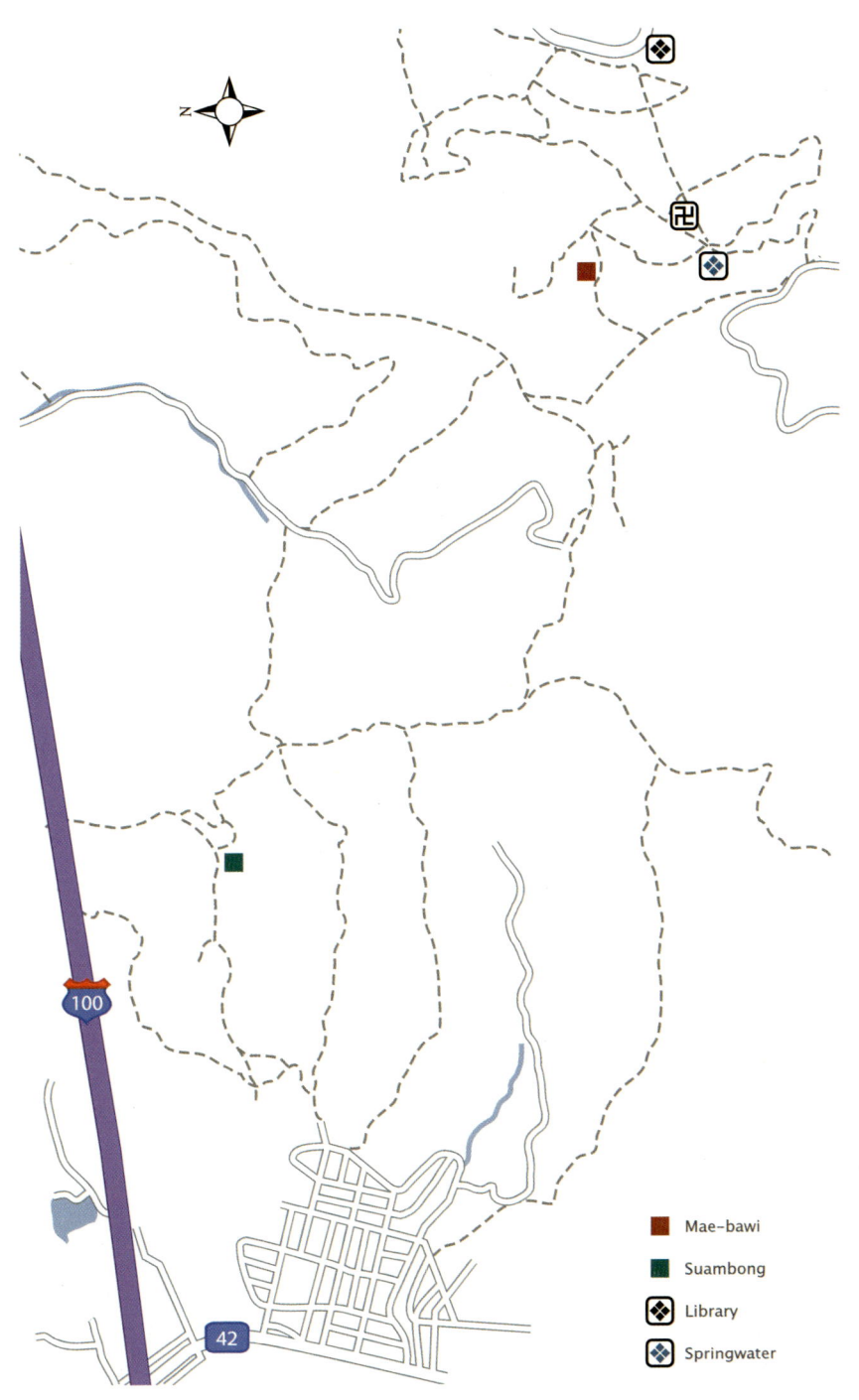

BYEONGPUNG-BAWI BAC 병풍바위 BAC

Description
About twelve separate crags are spread over the south base of Samseong-san 삼성산. Byeongpung-bawi BAC has nineteen routes that require finger strength and balance. BAC stands for the name of the club that developed this crag.

Directions
37.439361N 126.917324E
Seoksu-dong, Manan-gu, Anyang-si 안양시 만안구 석수동

From Gwanak Subway Station (Line #1), take Exit 2 and walk through the underground pass across the main road to reach the bus stop. Take Bus 6-2 or 20. Get off at either Gyeongingyodae 경인교대 or Anyanghaesol School 안양해솔학교. At the Anyanghaesol School, walk past the iron fence and to the drainage tunnel. Follow the tunnel as it winds around the highway. Once you reach the end of the tunnel, you will see a ribbon, which marks the trailhead for BAC. Follow the trail to the left for five minutes. You will reach a mountain spring. 50m north from the spring you will see BAC.

Gear
8 draws and a 50m rope.

Additional Comments
Water and snacks should be bought beforehand. According to local climbers, there are more than a dozen crags scattered on this mountain. You may possibly encounter one of the crags not described here when you walk along the trails.

BAC 매바위 (1 OF 2)

Route Name	Grade	Height
Back To The Nature 귀거래사	5.12a	15
Yearning In The West Sky 서편하늘의그리움	5.12d	15
Story Of The Swallowtail's Larva 호랑나비애벌레의사연	5.14a	13
Frozen In Time 멈추어진시간속에서	5.12b	13
B : Bawimoim 비	5.11a	11
AC : Alpine Club 약	5.10a	11
One Day In May 월어느날	5.10b	12
Get Up 일어나	5.11b	12
Wishing 바라기	5.12b	12
Serious Woman 진지여인	5.10d	12
Arirang Alone 홀로아리랑	*	7
VIP	5.12c	7
Yearning Starts When The Sun Goes Down 해가질때그리움은시작되고	5.10a	8

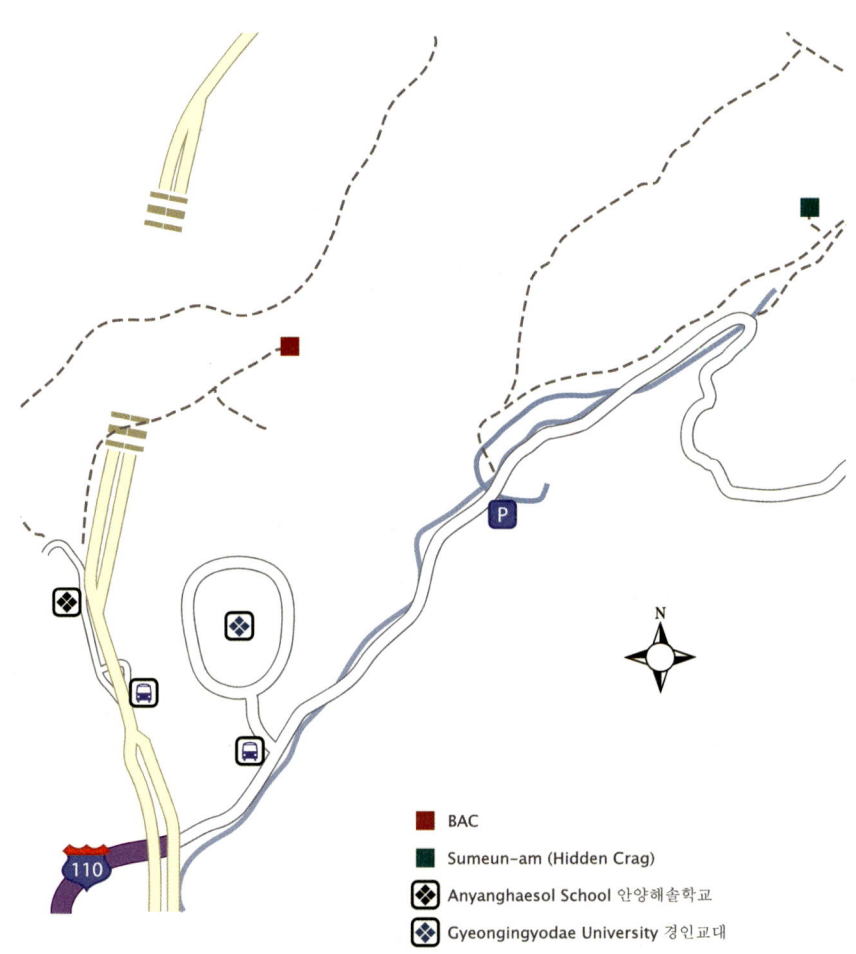

BAC 매바위 (2 OF 2)

Route Name	Grade	Height
061127 Boulder 볼더	5.12a	6
Inigyeomi 인이겸이	5.11b	11
Gouwon 규원	5.10a	11
Consideration 배려	5.8	7
Bridge Over Troubled Waters 험한세상에다리가되어	*	15
Tyrolean Bridge 티놀리안브릿지	*	*

Sumeun-am 숨은암

Description
Sumeun-am means hidden crag. As the name represents, it is hard to find on the trail because the trees hide the rock and the location hinders the view. Although this crag is relatively small with easy routes, it features various climbs on granite rock. It faces east and is good quality rock.

Directions
37.441558N 126.930531E
Seoksu-dong, Manan-gu, Anyang-si 안양시 만안구 석수동

The approach is similar to BAC. Go to Gyeonginyodae 경인교대. There is a parking lot by the bus stop. Walk 50m past the parking lot and cross the stream on your left. Continue for 20m and cross another stream. Hike right with the stream on your right (don't hike up to the top). Follow the trail along the stream for fifteen minutes and keep an eye out for a rock with a few Chinese characters written on it and a temple mark 卍 in blue by the trail on your left. About 100m past this rock, look for a path on your left. Hike up the trail for a few minutes to reach the crag. From the parking lot, it will take twenty-five minutes to get to the crag.

Gear
10 draws and a 50m rope.

Additional Comments
The crag is in the sun until late afternoon and is easily accessible by public transportation. The belay station is well established and there are also good campsites available.

Sumeun-am 숨은암 (1 of 2)

Route Name	Grade	Height
Soborang 소보랑	5.10b	25
Hug Me 안아줘	5.10a	25
Express Train 특급열차	5.12a	25
One More Time Even Though I Hate You 미워도다시한번	5.10c	25
Single Rope Walking 외줄타기	5.10d	25
Left Alone 낙동강오리알	5.10c	25
Dug Butt 오리궁뎅이	5.10b	20
My Way 마이웨이	5.10b	25

Photo Courtesy of Lea Gang, 강레아

SUMEUN-AM 숨은암 (2 OF 2)

Route Name	Grade	Height
SR Road 로드	5.9	25
Mask Dance 탈춤	5.9	15
Legend Of Yeongbo 영보의전설	5.10a	15
Hi Sky 하늘아	5.10c	13
A1	A1	15
A2	A2	15
Regret 아쉬움	5.9	15
Older Brother 형	5.10a	15
Younger Brother 아우	5.9	15

NOCLES-AMJANG 노클스암장

Description
This crag offers challenging overhanging climbs on granite rock. The grades are a little sandbagged. It faces west and gets shade all day. The rock is very solid.

Directions
37.443765N 126.958839E
Sillim-dong, Gwanak-gu, Seoul 서울 관악구 신림동

From Seoul National University Subway Station (Line #4), take Exit 3 and walk towards Gwanak-san Park 관악산공원. Continue on the main trail until the Rescue Mark K59, past the wooden bridge. Walk down and right to the valley at the end of the small wooden bridge. The crag is underneath the main trail, right before the bridge. Total approach time from the subway station will be fifty minutes.

Gear
10 draws and a 50m rope.

Additional Comments
The crag will be in the shade all day, even in the summer. The belay station offers good campsites.

NOCLES-AMJANG 노클스암장

Route Name	Grade	Height
Man Route 만길	5.10a	15
Partner 파트너	5.12a	15
OK Tension 오케이텐션	5.11b	15
Asibong 아시봉	5.12b	15
This Lady, That Lady, The Lady 이년저년그년	5.12b	15
Good Guy 좋은놈	5.9	15
Clipping Route 걸고길	5.10b	15
Assi Route 아씨길	*	15
Gyeong Route 경길	*	15
Original Intention 초심길	5.11a	15
Like First Time 처음처럼	5.11d	15
Over Route 오버길	5.12b	15
Free Route 공짜길	5.10b	15
Immorality Route 불륜길	5.10d	15
Three Odd Pair Of Shoes 신발세짝	5.10b	15
Dog Route 개길	5.10a	15

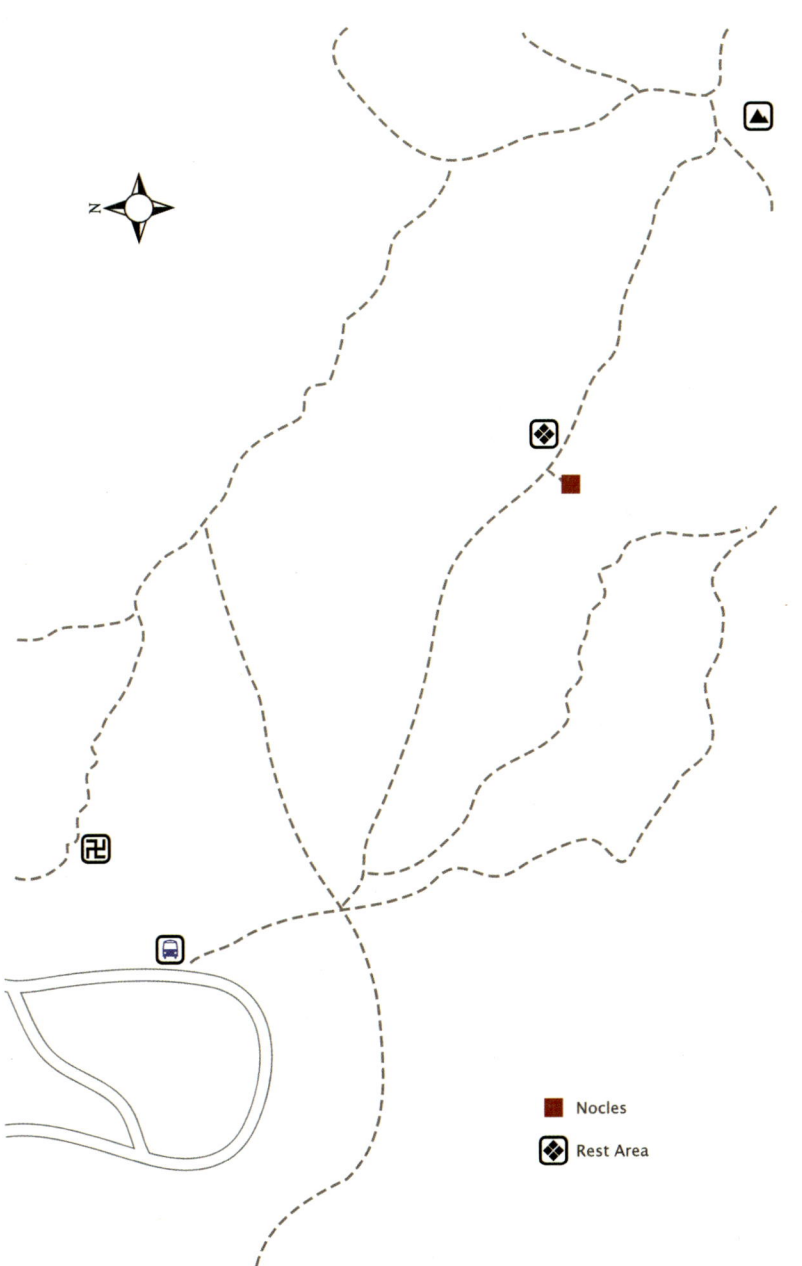

GWANACK-AMJANG 관악암장

Description
This crag was developed in 1991 and has seventeen routes. The climbs here are less than 13m and offer face, crack, and overhanging climbing on excellent granite stone. It can be reached within half an hour from the subway station and gets sun all day.

Directions
37.43747N 126.976976E
Junang-dong Gwacheon-si 과천시 중앙동

At Gwachun Subway Station 과천 (Line #4), take Exit 7. Head towards Gwachun Middle School 과천중학교. Pass the middle school and walk up to the park office. It will take fifteen minutes from the subway station. Continue to hike on the main trail for another fifteen minutes until you reach a wooden bridge. The trail will start to ascend steeply. After a few minutes of hiking, you'll see the crag to your left. Cross the valley and scramble up to the crag.

Gear
7 draws and a 50m rope.

Additional Comments
There are a few campsites around the crag. Water and snacks should be bought before getting on the main trail.

GWANACK-AMJANG 관악암장

Route Name	Grade	Height
Finger One 손가락하나	5.10 *	8
Easy Route 쉬운길	5.7	9
Empty Sky 허공	5.12 *	10
Alone 혼자서	5.9	10
Initiation 신고식	5.10b	10
Two Becomes One 둘이서하나되어	5.11a	10
In The Long Future 먼훗날	*	10
A Glass Of Wine 한잔의술	5.11b	10
To The Sky 하늘을향해	5.6	10
Attention Road 주목길	5.10 *	12
The Day With Heavy Rain 큰비내리던날	5.10a	12
Through The Leaf 나뭇잎사이로	5.10b	12
Slanderer 욕쟁이 1	5.10 *	12
Five Sound & One Tune 오성과한음	5.10b	12
Slanderer 욕쟁이 2	5.10 *	10
Pulling A Desk 책상당기기	5.11a	7
Mantling 딛고오르기	5.10c/d	11

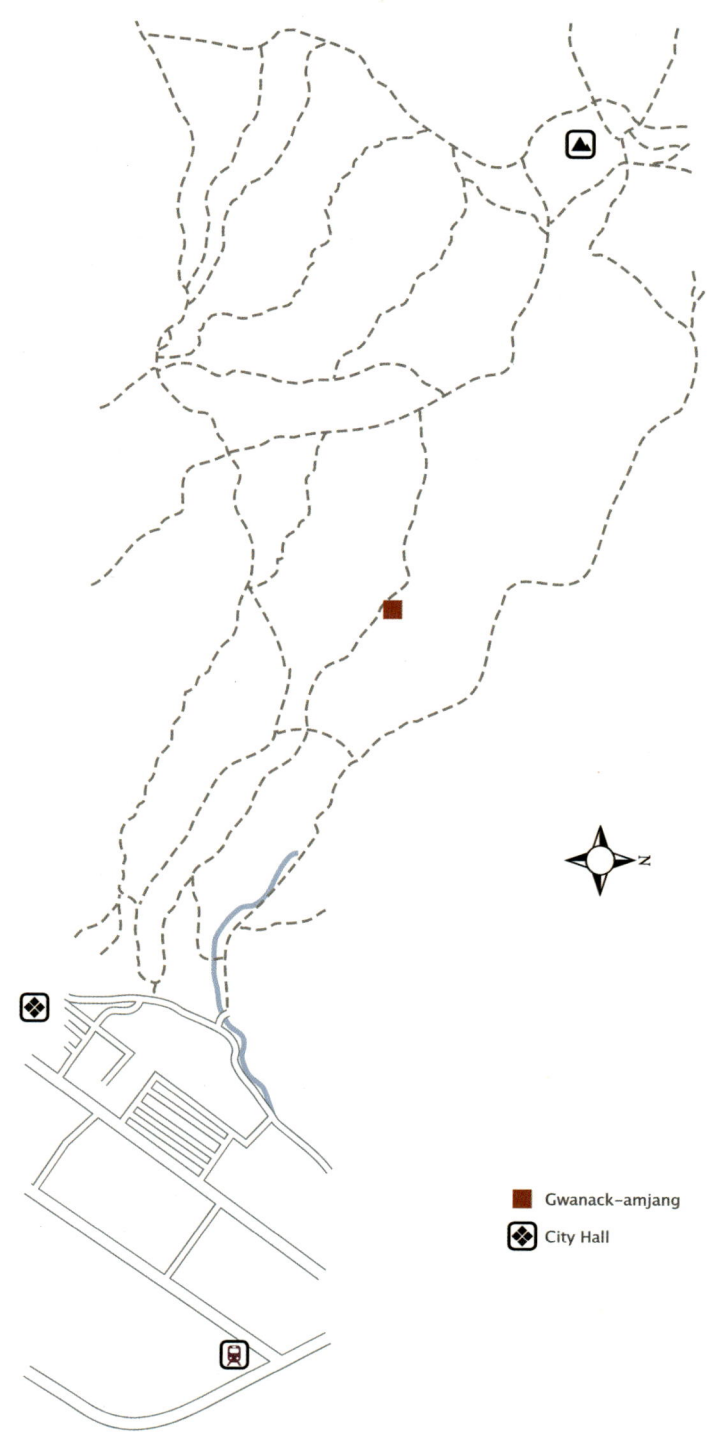

MUAKJAE ANSAN-AMJANG 무악재 안산암장

Description
Located in the middle of Seoul, this crag was developed from 1986 to 2008 by a tenacious gym owner. A couple of the routes have been used for the gym members' training on the weekends. The crag offers a variety of climbs on good quality granite rock that faces east. The routes vary between slab, crack, face, and overhanging climbing.

Directions
37.576845N 126.948116E
Hongje-dong, Seodaemun-gu, Seoul 서울 서대문구 홍제동

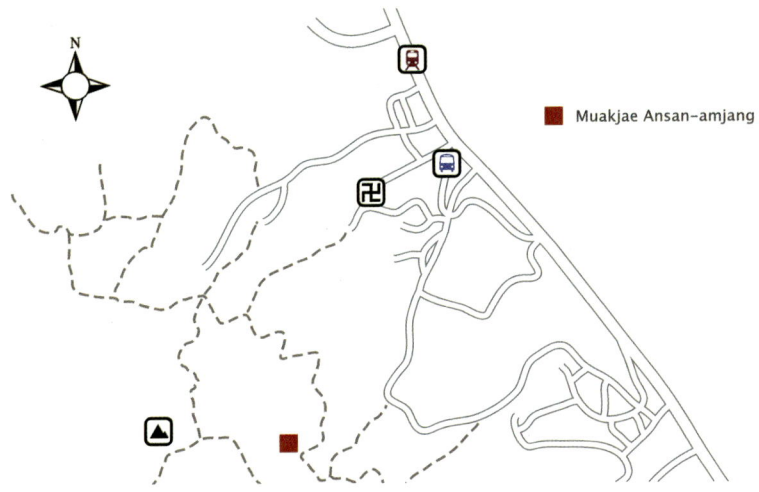

At Muakjae Subway Station 무악재 (Line #3), take Exit 3 and walk straight up the hill Muakjae 무악재 for 150m. Turn right to the small uphill road by an apartment and then continue on the road past the parking lot. Hike up the mountain trail, passing a wooden staircase, until you reach a spring with exercise facilities nearby. Past the spring, take a left on a steep trail to reach the crag. From the subway station, it will take twenty-five minutes to get to the crag. The crag can be seen from the hiking trail.

Gear
12 draws, two 60m ropes, and aid climbing equipment.

Safety
A helmet is recommended.

Additional Comments
According to the gym owner, the multi-pitch routes are mostly 60m long with most of the pitches being approximately 30m long. The belay stations, rest area, and restrooms are well established and maintained by the gym members. Be mindful of your visit to the crag. Water and snacks should be bought beforehand.

MUAKJAE ANSAN-AMJANG 관악암장 (1 OF 2)

Route Name	Grade	Height
Companion Route 동지길	5.11d	6
Waist Route 허리길	5.10*	60 (2p)
1p (5.10*|30m) 2p (5.9|30m)		
Like Beginning 처음처럼	A3	60 (2p)
1p (A3|30m) 2p (A3|30m)		
2540 Route 길	5.11c	60 (2p)
1p (5.11c|30m) 2p (5.9|30m)		
Children Route 어린아이길	5.12b	70 (2p)
1p (5.12b|35m) 2p (5.11c|35m)		
Classroom No 1 in 3rd Grade 3 학년 1 반	5.12*	60 (2p)
1p (5.12*|30m) 2p (5.10*|30m)		
Sauna Route 사우나길	5.9	80 (2p)
1p (5.9|40m) 2p (5.9|40m)		
Conflicts 갈등	5.11a	60 (2p)
1p Inhee 인희 2p Hidden Route 숨은길	5.9	60 (2p)
1p (5.9|30m) 2p (5.9|30m)		
1p Me 나 2p Only Route 하나만의 길	5.11c	60 (2p)
1p (5.11c|30m) 2p (5.11a|30m)		
18 Rain 비	5.12*	60 (2p)
1p (5.12*|30m) 2p (5.11a|30m)		
I Am For You 나는 너를	5.9	60 (2p)
1p (5.9|30m) 2p (5.8|30m)		
Great Slab 대슬랩	5.8	50 (2p)
1p (5.8|30m) 2p (5.8|30m)		
You Are For Me 너는 나를	5.9	60 (2p)
1p (5.9|30m) 2p (5.8|30m)		
Hang In There 버티고	5.9	60 (2p)
1p (5.9|30m) 2p (5.9|30m)		
Class No. 1 in 2nd Grade 2 학년 1 반	5.10b	60 (2p)
1p (5.10b|30m) 2p (5.8|30m)		

MUAKJAE ANSAN-AMJANG 관악암장 (1 OF 2)

Route Name	Grade	Height
Route For The Senior 경로 우대길	5.8	60 (2p)
1p (5.8|30m) 2p (5.7|30m)		
Chooseok Route 추석길	5.11a	60 (2p)
1p (5.11a|30m) 2p (5.9|30m)		
Remembrance 옛추억	5.8	60 (2p)
1p (5.8|30m) 2p (5.7|30m)		
Fourteen PPAK 포틴 PPAK	5.10a	60 (2p)
1p (5.10a|30m) 2p (5.10a|30m)		
Elementary School 초등학교	5.7	60 (2p)
1p (5.7|30m) 2p (5.7|30m)		
Unnamed Route 무명길	5.8	60 (2p)
1p (5.8|30m) 2p (5.7|30m)		
Concert Garden 야외 음악당	5.11d	60 (2p)
1p (5.11d|30m) 2p (5.11*|30m)		
Multilevel 다단계	A2	60 (2p)
1p (A2|30m) 2p (A2|30m)		
Sky Route 하늘길	5.11b	60 (2p)
1p (5.11b|30m) 2p (5.10a|30m)		
Wall Of Yeobyeong 여명의 벽	5.9	60 (2p)
1p (5.9|30m) 2p (5.7|30m)		
Hesitated, But Milky Way Is Viewed When Seeing Bolts 망설였는데 볼트를 보니 은하수가 보이네	5.13a	60 (2p)
1p (5.13a|30m) 2p (5.11d|30m)		
Achievement Of Goal 목표달성	5.12*	15
With An Easy Mind 편안한 마음으로	5.12*	20
Gift 선물	5.12a	20
Tyrolean Bridge 티롤라인 브리지	*	40

Gamak-san, Seolgwi-am 감악산 설귀암

Description
This crag is composed of an overhanging upper section and a vertical faced lower section on granite rock that faces south. It offers crimpy face climbing with some blunt holds. Most of the routes, including the crack climb, are sandbagged. This crag is located next to the main hiking trail, so the hikers may be distracting during the weekends, but the rock quality is good.

Directions
37.941482N 126.957407E
Seolma-ri, Jeokseong-myeon, Paju-si 파주시 적성면 설마리

From Euijungbu City Bus Terminal 의정부, take the bus bound for Jeokseong 적성 and get off at Beomryun-sa Temple 범륜사. It will take an hour. At the bus stop, walk up to the temple. Continue on the main trail for forty minutes until you see the Rescue Mark 3-3, that is located next to a spring. The crag is right by the trail, 200m after the mark.

Gear
10 draws, a 50m rope, and a full set of cams

Additional Comments
Water should be readily available at the spring. There are good campsites around the crag.

SEOLGWI-AM 설귀암

Route Name	Grade	Height
Seolgi 설귀 A	5.10*	10
New Mind 새마음	5.10*	15
New Start 새출발	5.11*	15
Outsider 아웃사이더	5.13*	18
It's Gwangchae 광채꺼	5.11*	20
Face Over 페이스오버	5.12*	20
Late Autumn 만추	5.13*	23
Wedding March 웨딩마치	5.12*	23
All Of Our Love 우리모두의사랑	5.11*	23
Only Their Love 그들만의 사랑	5.13*	20
It's Seonghun 성훈이꺼	5.11*	15
One Road 한길	5.12*	15

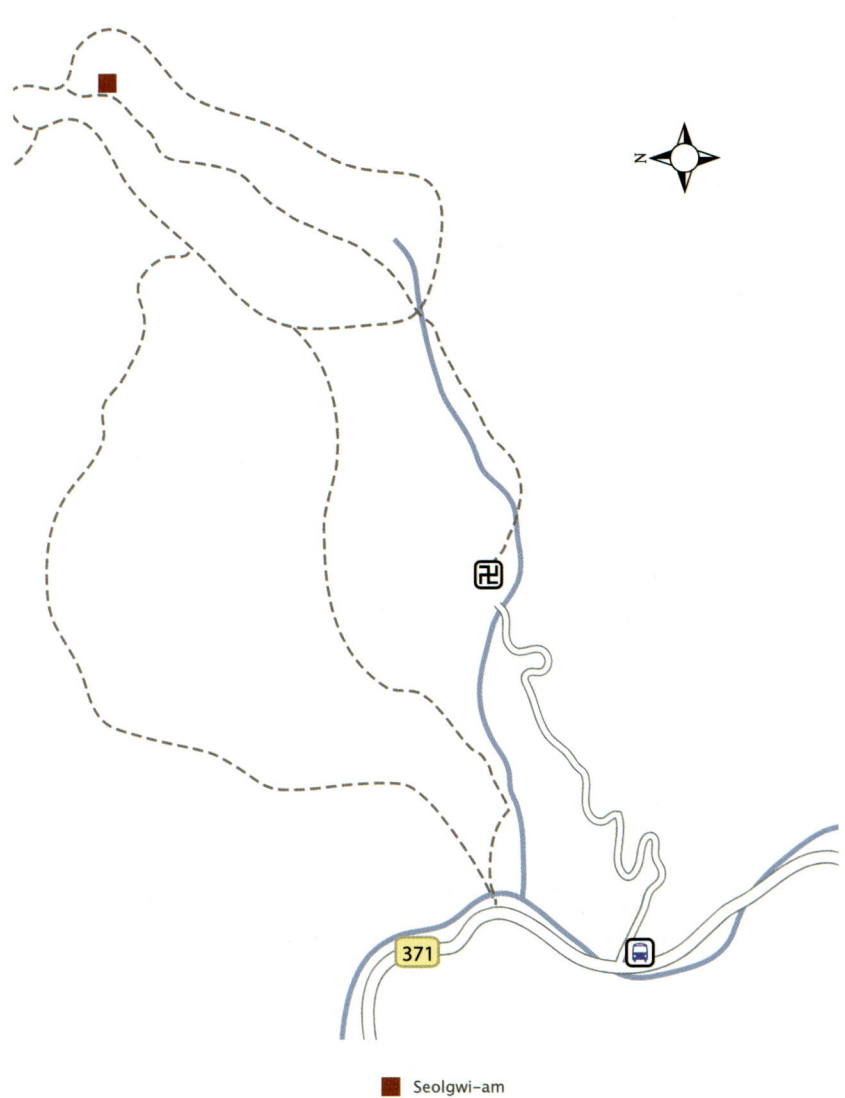
■ Seolgwi-am

JEJU-DO

제주도

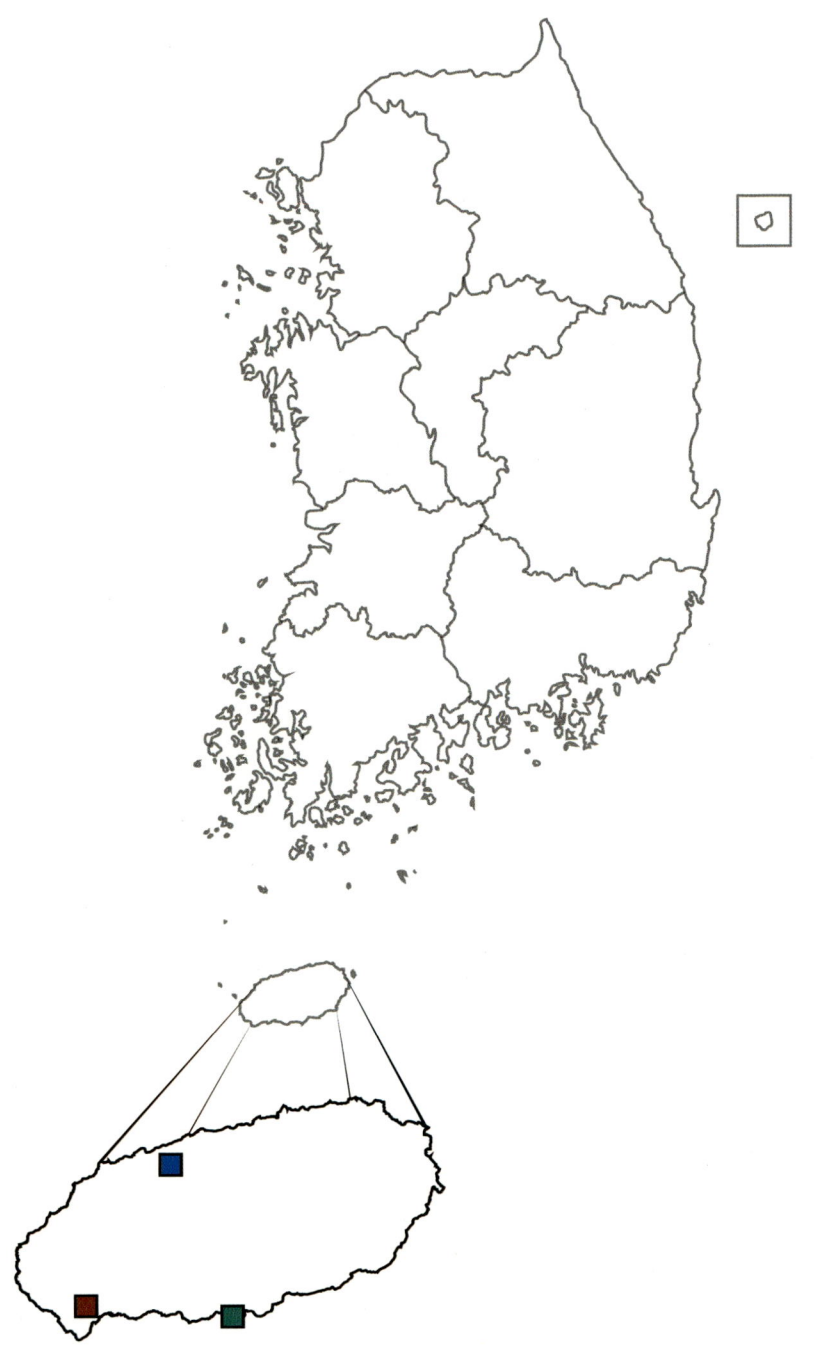

Jeju-do Province 제주도

- Musucheon Gyeogok-amjang
- Oedolgae-amjang
- Dansan-amjang

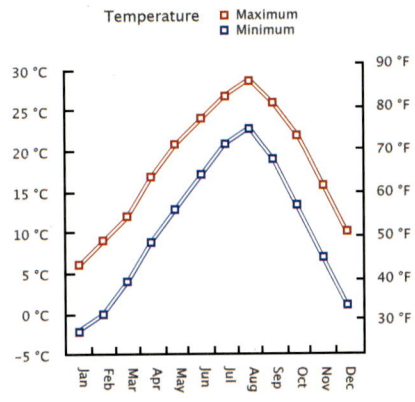

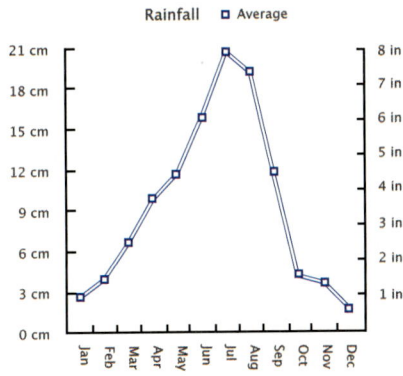

MUSUCHEON GYEOGOK-AMJANG 무수천 계곡암장

Description
This basalt rock has twenty-nine routes and was developed from 1999 to 2002. This crag is divided into two walls, one at Yaoeeumakdang Wall 야외음악당 and the other at Jisangnakwon 지상낙원, which is on the opposite side of Yaoeeumakdang 야외음악당. This crag offers powerful challenges for the grade on overhanging routes.

Directions
(*Musucheon North*) - 33.463611N 126.446414E
(*Musucheon South*) - 33.455685N 126.446521E
Gwangryeong-ri, Aewol-eup, Jeju-si 제주시 애월읍 광령리

From Jeju Airport, take the bus bound for Gwangryeong 광령, Goseong 고성, or Yangjamdanji 양잠단지. At Jungang-ro 중앙로, get off at Musucheon Rest Area 무수천휴게소. It will take twenty minutes from the airport and the buses run every fifteen minutes. From the rest area, walk along the northbound concrete road for five minutes until you reach the restaurant called Gohyang Garden 고향가든. You will see a steel door with a path behind it that leads to the stream on your right. Pass through the door and walk down the stairs to the riverbed. Walk south along the stream and you will come across the routes that are scattered in the area.

Gear
10 draws and a 50m rope.

Safety
Beware of flash floods. When the stream swells, it is very dangerous to cross over the stream.

Additional Comments
The routes are scattered along the riverbed. There are also many interesting bouldering problems around the crags with great campsites. Sunshine fades away early, so summer will be best time to climb here. There is another crag that is further south along the stream that is known as Stonebridge Crag. To access the south crag, continue following the stream to the south. It will take twenty minutes. You can also access it from the road by crossing the street from the rest area and walking towards the gas station. Look for a trail on your left 50m before the gas station and follow it with the stream on your left for ten minutes. There will be a very faint trail to your left with a guide rope. Scramble down and walk north once you reach the stream. There are two climbing groups that have been competing for this area so none of the routes have been named or graded at this time.

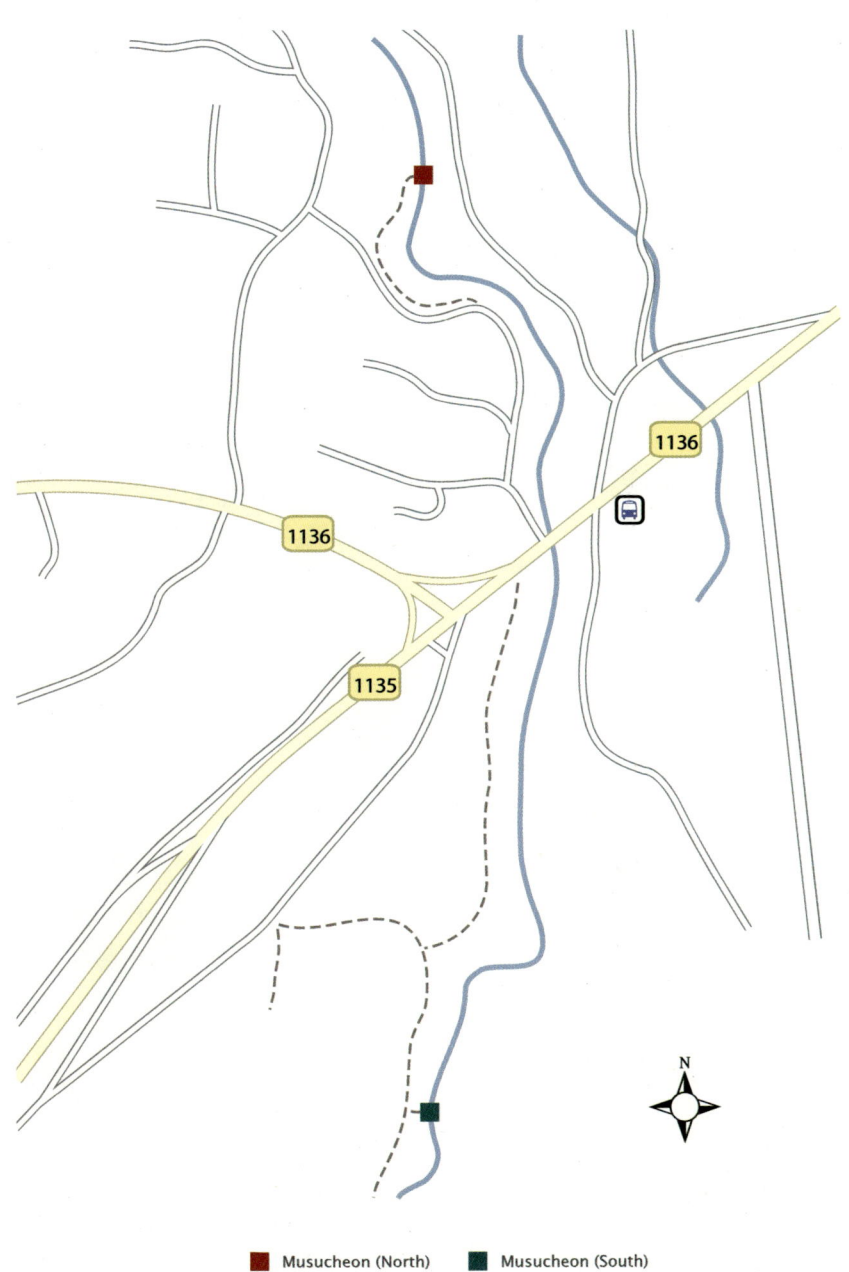

MUSUCHEON GYEOGOK-AMJANG (NORTH)
무수천 계곡암장

Route Name	Grade
Space Party 스페이스파티 3	5.12a
Space Party 스페이스파티 2	5.11c
Lonely Angel 고독한 천사	*
White Spider 하얀거미	5.11b
Revolution 혁명	5.12b
Pain & Sorrow 아픔과 슬픔	5.11d
Winter Gypsy 겨울 짚시	5.11b
Winter Gypsy 겨울 짚시 1	*
Door To Illusion 환상의 문	5.11d
Bermuda Crack 버뮤다 크랙	5.10b
Eu Route 어길	5.11d
203	5.10d
Yeongeun 연근	5.10b
First Experience 첫경험	5.10b
Rice Bug 라이스버그	5.9
Unnamed 무명	5.10a
Reunion 재회	5.11c
Day 날	5.11c
Slippery Crack 반들크랙	*
Hole 구멍	5.11b
Lazybones 뺀질이	5.11b
Bummer 봉탱이	*
*	*
*	*
Half Moon Crack 반달크랙	5.8
Gwangryeon Gentleman 광령신사	5.11c
April Direct 4 월 직등	5.11a
April 4 월	5.11c
Endless Wandering 끝없는 방랑	5.11c
Scree 돌무리 1	5.11d
Scree 돌무리 2	5.12b
New Marriage 신혼	5.11c/d
GG Twin 끄 쌍	5.11c/d
Campsite 야영장	*

NOTE: Route heights are under 20m

DANSAN-AMJANG 단산암장

Description
The routes at this crag are mostly easy slab on basalt rock. It is worth a visit because of the pleasant thirty minute approach and the amazing view of the southwest side of the island. On the hiking trail, there are a few historical spots you might enjoy, including a few interesting caves.

Directions
33.242528N 126.288636E
Sagye-ri, Andeok-myeon, Seoguipo-si 서귀포시 인덕면 사계리

From Jeju Jonghab Terminal 제주종합터미널, take a bus bound for Inseong-dong 인성동 and Moseulpo 모슬포. Get off at Sagye-ri Dongdong 사계리 동동. Walk towards Inseong-ri 인성리 for ten minutes and hike past the village. There is a map of the hiking trail near the village. Continue up to the crag on the main trail for thirty minutes. It is easy to get to the crag if you follow the map. The crag can also be easily seen behind the village.

Gear
10 draws and a 60m rope.

Safety
A helmet is recommended in case of falling rocks.

Additional Comments
There are many good campsites around the mountain. Routes start from the left with Big Mountain Slab 거산슬랩.

DANSAN-AMJANG 단산암장

Route Name	Grade	Height
Big Mountain Slab 거산슬랩	5.9	15
Dansan 단산 A	5.10*	30
Dansan 단산 B	5.9	30
Dansan 단산 C	5.10*	*
Crystal 수정	5.11b	20
Traverse 트레버스	5.8	*
Baerok 백록	5.10*	*
Robust Cicada 족재열	5.10*	*

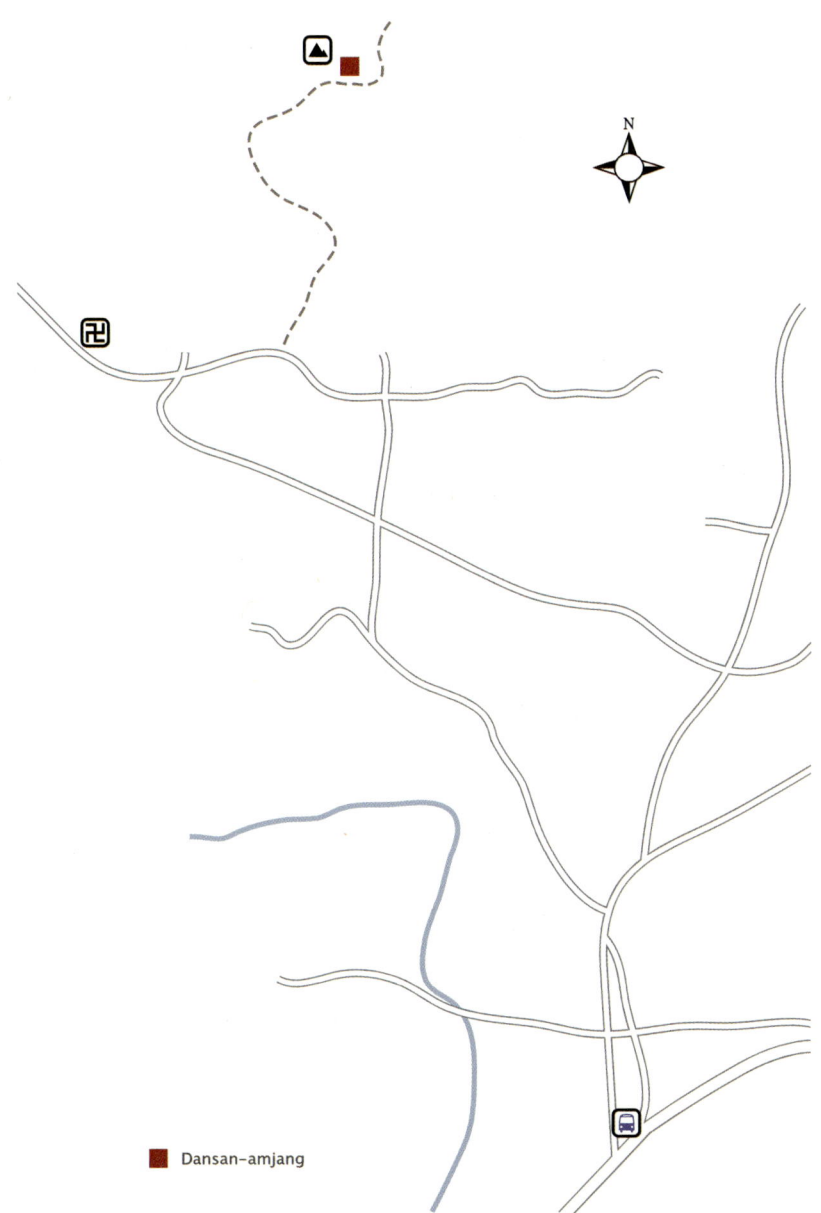

■ Dansan-amjang

OEDOLGAE-AMJANG 외돌개암장

Description
Oedolgae is a high outcropping rock that was created by a volcanic eruption 1.5 million years ago. Legend has it that during the late Goryeo Dynasty, General Choe Yeoung disguised this rock to appear like a gigantic military general to scare off the enemies lurking on Beomseom Islet. This crag is a basalt sea-cliff around Oedolgae and overlooks the beautiful ocean, which can be seen on the first page of this chapter. Although the crag is 30m high, the bottom part can not be climbed because of the waves.

Directions
33.238741N 126.54359E
Seohong-dong, Seoguipo-si 서귀포시 서홍동

From Seoguipo-si 서귀포, take a bus bound for Oedolgae 외돌개 and get off at the last stop. It takes ten minutes. The crag can be easily reached by following the tourist trail to Oedolgae from the bus stop. Continue along the fence until you reach an open area that is on the opposite side of the fence. Hop over the fence. There is a fisherman's trail that can be seen close to Oedolgae. If you walk further west along the coast, there are bolts that you can rappel from to reach the crag.

Gear
10 draws and a 50m rope. A few of the routes can be climbed traditionally so bring a set of small to mid-sized cams if you'd like to place your own protection.

Additional Comments
There are tons of tourists walking around so don't forget to pose for photos when you reach the anchors!

OEDOLGAE-AMJANG 외돌개암장

Route Name	Grade	Height
Doldoli 돌돌이	5.11c	15
Doldoli 돌돌이 1	5.11a	30
Bbong Family 뽕가족	5.11b	30
Learning 배움의	5.9	*
Jeonghwa 정화	5.10*	20
Pacific 태평양	5.8	*
Tiger 호랑이	5.10b	*
Pirate 해적	5.11a	*
Practice 연습 A	5.7	*
Practice 연습 B	5.7	*

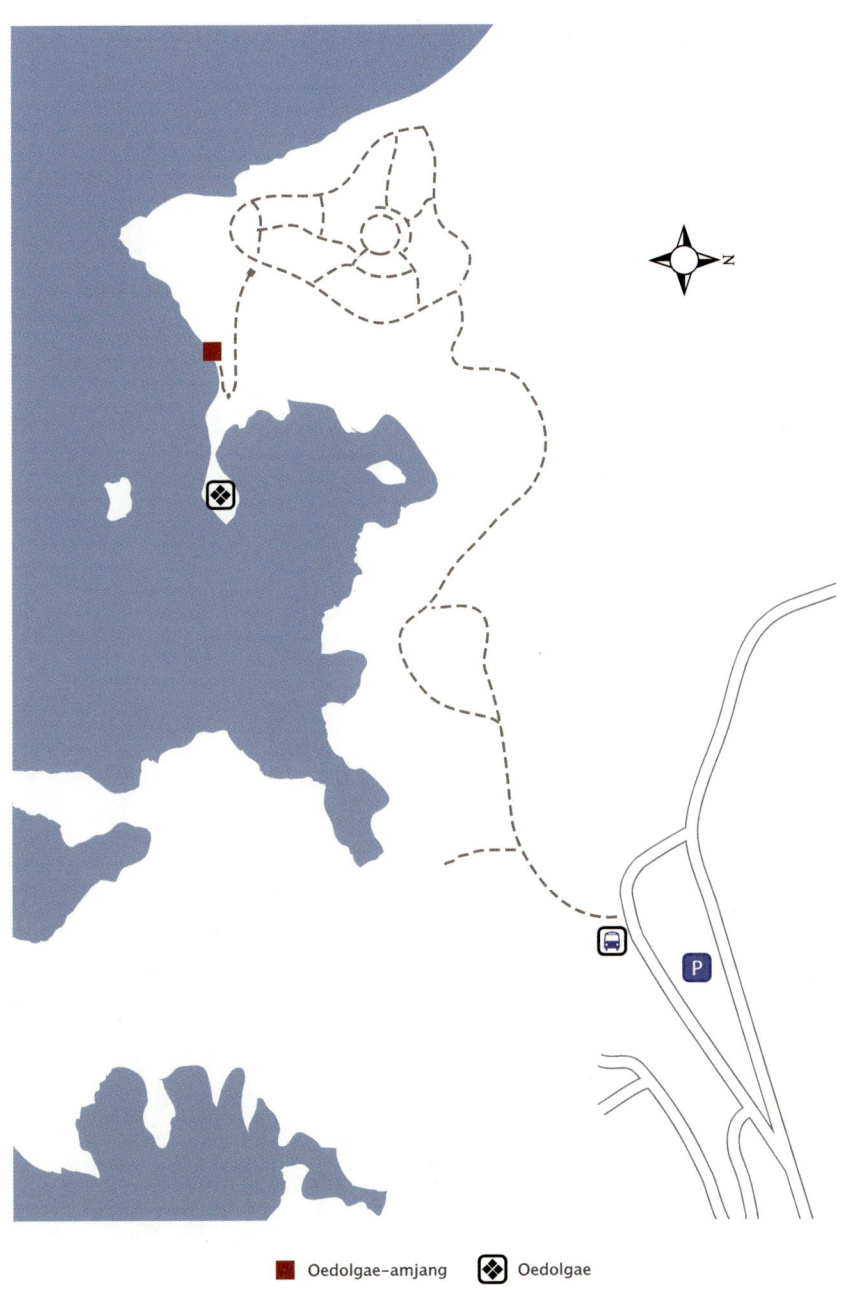

Ulleung-do

울릉도

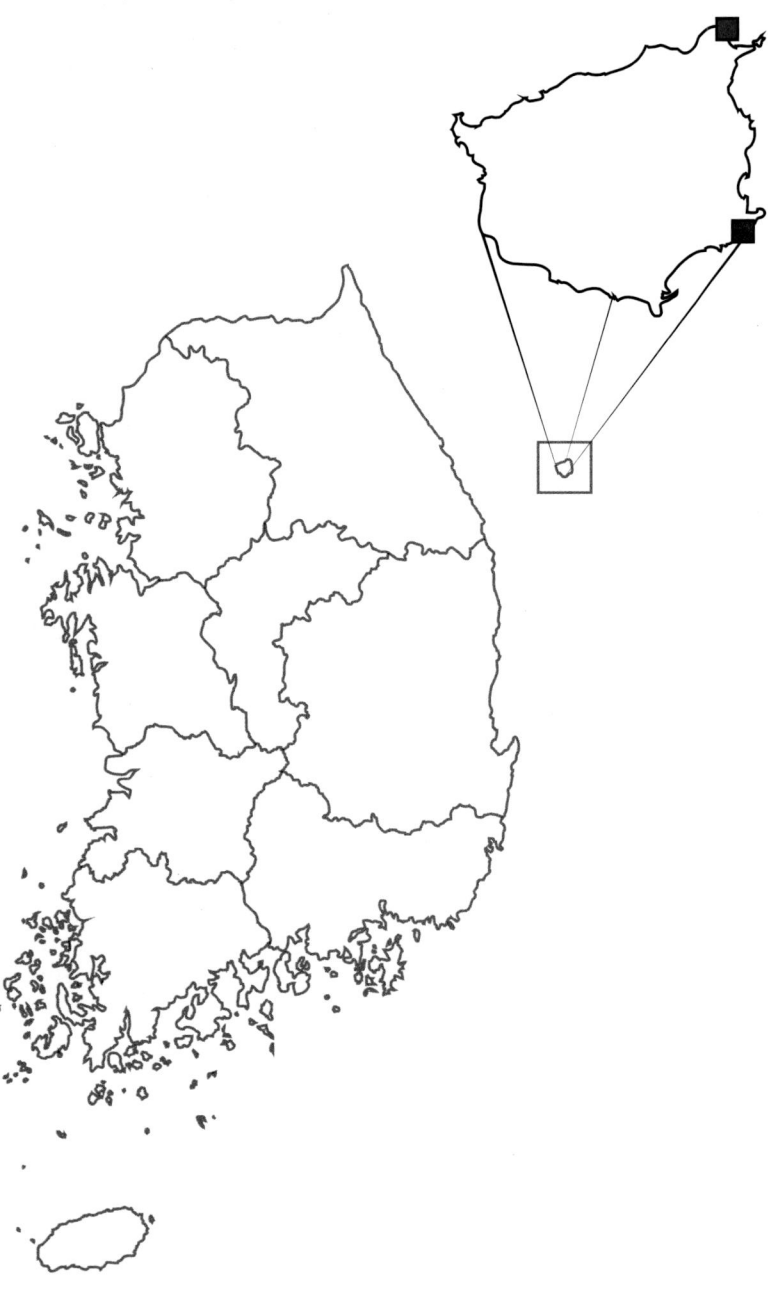

ULLEUNG-DO 울릉도

- Jowan-byeok
- Janggun-bawi
- Samseon-am

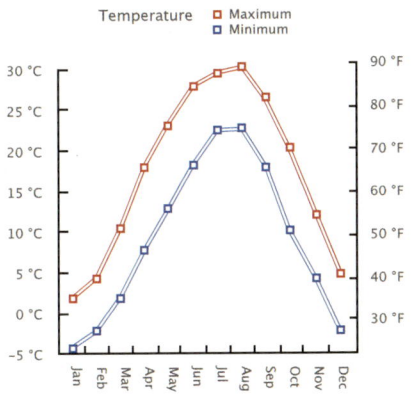

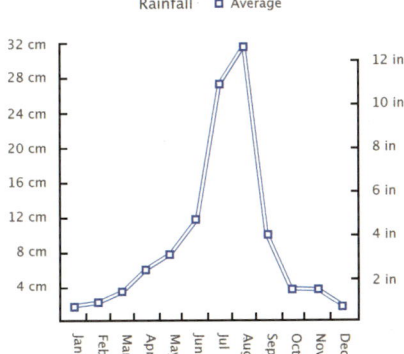

One of the furthest places you can go in Korea is the small, rocky island of Ulleung-do. To reach this island, you must take a ferry from either Donghae 동해 or Pohang 포항. For those living in the north, Donghae is closer and for those in the south, Pohang will be the best choice. The ferry from Pohang is larger and will be more stable during rough seas.

JOWAN-BYEOK 좌안벽

Description
Once you get off the ferry, you'll be eager to stretch your legs and take advantage of the small warm-up crag directly behind the ferry terminal. Jowan-byeok provides fun face climbing on volcanic rock with juggy holds. It faces southwest.

Directions
37.48161N 130.909787E

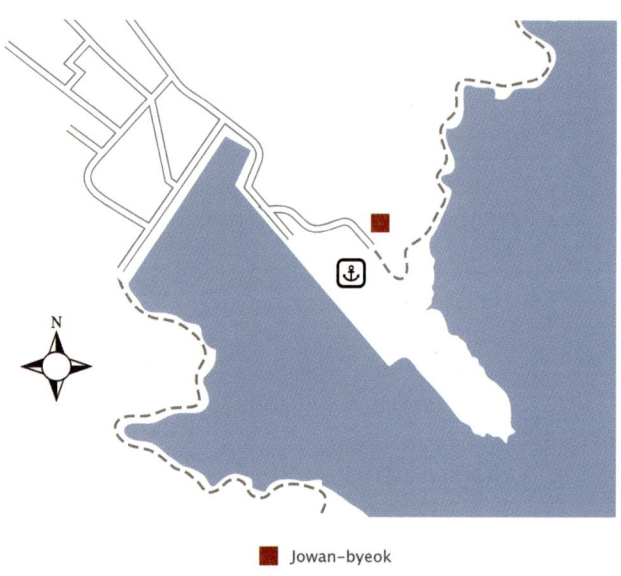

■ Jowan-byeok

Facing inland, go behind the ferry terminal to the right and you'll see bolts on the rock next to the bathrooms.

Gear
7 draws and a 50m rope.

Safety
Although it is solid volcanic rock, a helmet is recommended.

JOWAN-BYEOK 좌안벽

Route Name	Grade	Height
Terminal 터미널	5.10a	15
Ferry 여객선	5.9	13
Breakwater 방파제	5.10a	13

JANGGUN-BAWI 장군바위

Description
This crag is the most solid amongst the Ulleung-do crags. It is volcanic rock and offers face and overhanging climbing. Janggun-bawi is located by the road and faces northeast.

Directions
37.547291N 130.908054E

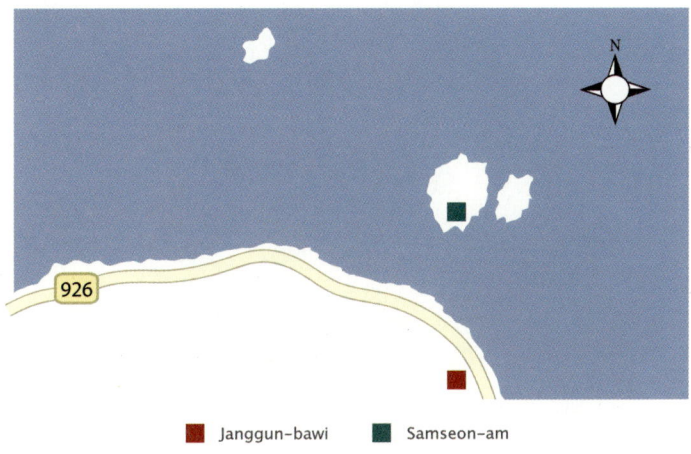

To get to the main crag, take a bus bound for Cheongbu 천부. From there, transfer to the small village bus. Here you will wind through the hills and get off at Samseon-am 삼선암. From the ferry terminal, the bus journey will take about an hour. On your right, across from the three monoliths protruding out from the ocean, is the main crag of the island. There is a small sign on the road that explains the myth of Samseon-am.

Gear
12 draws and a 60m rope.

Safety
Due to the ever-changing sea-weathered cliffs, a helmet is recommended.

JANGGUN-BAWI 장군바위 (1 OF 2)

Route Name	Grade	Height
Jetty 선창	5.10b	20
General 장군 1p (*|*m) 2p (*|*m)	5.10a	55 (2p)
Duri 두리	5.11b	25
Jeodong 저동	5.10a	25

JANGGUN-BAWI 장군바위 (2 OF 2)

Route Name	Grade	Height
Farmer's rucksack 지게	5.11a	25
Samseon 삼선	5.10c	25
High Rock 하이락 1	5.10b	25
High Rock 하이락 2	5.11a	25

Samseon-am 삼선암

Description
These three monoliths stand tall over the ocean. Among the three, the smallest has the most solid rock. The medium sized rock, on the far right, has only one four-pitch route that is graded 5.10b. According to the locals, the old natives of Ulleung-do used to scale the monoliths without climbing equipment.

Directions
37.549409N 130.90814E

The monoliths are located across the seawall from Janggun-bawi.

Gear
12 draws, a 60m rope, and a full set of cams ranging from #3 to #0.4 to climb on these colossal columns.

Safety
Due to the ever-changing sea-weathered cliffs, a helmet is recommended.

Comment
To get to the monoliths, you can either hire a sailor at the local scuba-diving shop or a fisherman around the village to take you there.

Samseon-am 삼선암

Route Name	Grade	Height
Ilsinam 일신암	*	60
Mother's Rock 어미바위	5.10b	100 (4p)
Abi-bawi 아비바위	*	80

Appendix

Korean Romanization

1. Basic Principles of Romanization
   (1) Romanization is based on standard Korean pronunciation.
   (2) Symbols other than Roman letters are avoided to the greatest extent possible.

2. Summary of the Romanization System
   (1) Vowels are transcribed as follows:

- simple vowels

ㅏ	ㅓ	ㅗ	ㅜ	ㅡ	ㅣ	ㅐ	ㅔ	ㅚ	ㅟ
a	eo	o	u	eu	i	ae	e	oe	wi

- diphthongs

ㅑ	ㅕ	ㅛ	ㅠ	ㅒ	ㅖ	ㅘ	ㅙ	ㅝ	ㅞ	ㅢ
ya	yeo	yo	yu	yae	ye	wa	wae	wo	we	ui

Note 1: ㅢ is transcribed as ui, even when pronounced as ㅣ.
Note 2: Long vowels are not reflected in Romanization.

   (2) Consonants are transcribed as follows:

- plosives (stops)

ㄱ	ㄲ	ㅋ	ㄷ	ㄸ	ㅌ	ㅂ	ㅃ	ㅍ
g, k	kk	k	d, t	tt	t	b, p	pp	p

- liquids

ㄹ
r, l

- affricates

ㅈ	ㅉ	ㅊ
j	jj	ch

- fricatives

ㅅ	ㅆ	ㅎ
s	ss	h

- nasals

ㄴ	ㅁ	ㅇ
n	m	ng

3. Special Provisions for Romanization
   (1) When Korean sound values change as in the following cases, the results of those changes are Romanized as follows:
- The case of assimilation of adjacent consonants
  e.g. 백마 / 뱅마 *Baengma*   신문로 / 신문노 *Sinmunno*
- The case of the epenthetic ㄴ and ㄹ
  e.g. 학여울 / 항녀울 *Hangnyeoul*   알약 / 알략 *Allyak*
- The case of palatalization
  e.g. 해돋이 / 해도지 *Haedoji*   같이 / 가치 *Gachi*
- The case where ㄱ, ㄷ, ㅂ, and ㅈ are adjacent to ㅎ
  e.g. 좋고 / 조코 *Joko*   놓다 / 노타 *Nota*
- However, aspirated sounds are not reflected in case of nouns where ㅎ follows ㄱ, ㄷ, and ㅂ, as in the examples below.
  e.g. 묵호 *Mukho*   집현전 *Jiphyeonjeon*

(2) When there is the possibility of confusion in pronunciation, a hyphen '-' may be used.
    e.g. 중앙 *Jung-ang*   반구대 *Ban-gudae*

(3) The first letter is capitalized in proper names.
    e.g. 부산 *Busan*   세종 *Sejong*

(4) Personal names are written by family name first, followed by a space and the given name. In principle, syllables in given names are not separated by hyphen, but the use of a hyphen between syllables is permitted.
    e.g. 민용하 *Min Yongha (Min Yong-ha)*   송나리 *Song Nari (Song Na-ri)*
    • Assimilated sound changes between syllables in given names aren't transcribed.
    e.g. 한복남 *Han Boknam (Han Bok-nam)*   홍빛나 *Hong Bitna (Hong Bit-na)*
    • Romanization of family names will be determined separately.

(5) Administrative units such as 도, 시, 군, 구, 읍, 면, 리, 동, and 가 are transcribed respectively as do, si, gun, gu, eup, myeon, ri, dong, and ga, and are preceded by a hyphen. Assimilated sound changes before and after hyphen is not reflected in Romanization.
    e.g. 충청북도 *Chungcheongbuk-do*   도봉구 *Dobong-gu*
        신창읍 *Sinchang-eup*   퇴계로 삼가 *Toegyero Sam-ga*

(6) Names of geographic features, cultural properties, and man-made structures may be written without hyphens.
    e.g. 남산 *Namsan*   연화교 *Yeonhwagyo*
        오죽헌 *Ojukheon*   다보탑 *Dabotop*

(7) Proper names such as personal names and those of companies may continue to be written as they have been previously.

(8) When it is recommended to convert Romanized Korean back to Hangeul in special cases, such as in academic articles, Romanization is done according to Hangeul spelling and not pronunciation. Each Hangeul letter is Romanized as explained in Section 2 except that ㄱ, ㄷ, ㅂ, ㄹ are always written as g, d, b, l. When ㅇ has no sound value, it is replaced by a hyphen and may also be used when it is recommended to distinguish between syllables.
    e.g. 집 *jib*   짚 *jip*
        밖 *bakk*   값 *gabs*
        독립 *doglib*   문리 *munli*

KOREAN PHRASES

English	**Korean**
Hello.	안녕하세요 (Annyeong-haseyo)
Thank you.	감사합니다 (Gamsa-hamnida)
I'm sorry.	미안합니다 (Mian-hamnida)
Could you give me some water?	물 좀 주세요 (Mul jom juseyo)
Could I have some more of this?	이거 더 주세요 (Igeo deo juseyo)
How much is it?	얼마입니까? (Eolma-imnikka)
Where is the restroom?	화장실 어디 입니까? (Hwajangsil eodi-imnikka)
Good-bye.	안녕히 계세요 (Annyeonghi-gyeseyo)
Check please.	계산서 주세요 (Gyesanse- juseyo)
Please help me.	도와주세요 (Dowa-juseyo)
Excuse me (Please come here).	여기요 (Yeogiyo)
Please take me to …	…으로 가주세요 (Euro gajuseyo)
How long does it take to get to …?	…까지 얼마나 걸립니까? (Kkaji eolmana geollimnikka?)
Do you have any vacancies?	빈방 있습니까? (Bin bang isseumnikka)
Do you mind climbing with me?	등반같이 하실래요? (Deungban Gatch-hasilraeyo?)
How long is the route?	이 루트 길이가 얼마입니까? (Irute giliga eulmaimniga)
Do you have any extra quickdraws?	여분의 퀵드로 있습니까? (Yeobuneu quickdro itsubniga?)
Please clean the route.	퀵드로 회수 해요 (Quickdro hoisuhaseoyo)
On belay.	확보완료 (Hwakbo wanyo)
Off belay.	안착 (Anchak)
Climbing.	출발 (Chulbal)
Climb on.	출발 (Chulbal)
Slack!	줄 좀 줘 (Jul-jom-jeo)
Rope up.	줄 당겨 (Jul-dang-gyeo)
Tension/Take!	추락 (Churak)
Watch me!	확보 잘 봐 (Hwakbo jalboa)
Falling!	추락 (Churak)
Ready to lower.	하강준비완료 (Hagang junbi wanyo)
Lowering.	하강 (Hagang)
Clipping.	클립 (Klib)
Rock!	낙석 (Nakseok)
Rope!	낙자 (Nakja)

Author

Dong-il Ryou
Dong-il is a certified English tour guide and train driver for Korail. He has been climbing for the past twenty-five years and has since become deeply involved with the foreign climbing community in Korea.

Photographer

Jonn Jeanneret (Jean)
Jean is a climbing photographer. He climbed in Korea during his military career. While stationed there, Jean met Dong-il Ryou and was introduced to Korean climbing.

initiatives
KOTR

KOTRI PROVIDES FOREIGN CLIMBERS WITH AN OPPORTUNITY, AS WELL AS AN OUTLET TO CONTRIBUTE AND BECOME A PART OF THE LARGER SOUTH KOREAN CLIMBING COMMUNITY BY PARTICIPATING IN CRAG MAINTENANCE, CLEANUP, ROUTE DEVELOPMENT AND OTHER SUSTAINABILITY PROJECTS HERE IN SOUTH KOREA.

KOTR Initiatives (KOTRi's) mission is to conduct cross-cultural projects that bridge borders and strive to protect the natural environment that inspires our simple, yet profound passion to climb.

If you're interested in becoming a part of KOTRi or simply learning more, please go to www.kotri.org or email Bryan Hylenski at kotrinitiatives@gmail.com.

Astroman Rock Gym

02-325-4787　　M-F 9:00-23:00　　Sat/Sun 9:00-18:00　　Closed on Holidays
1day-15,000w　　1month-90,000w　　3months-240,000w　　6months-448,000w　　1year-810,000w

Lead Climbing Communication

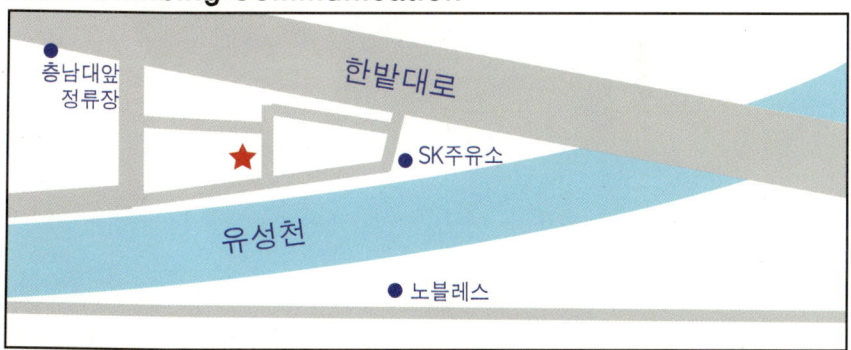

010-5369-4321　　M-F 10:00-23:00　　Sat 12:00-21:00　　Closed on Sun/Holidays
1day-10,000w　　1month-70,000w　　3months-195,000w　　1year-700,000w

Busan Climbing Center

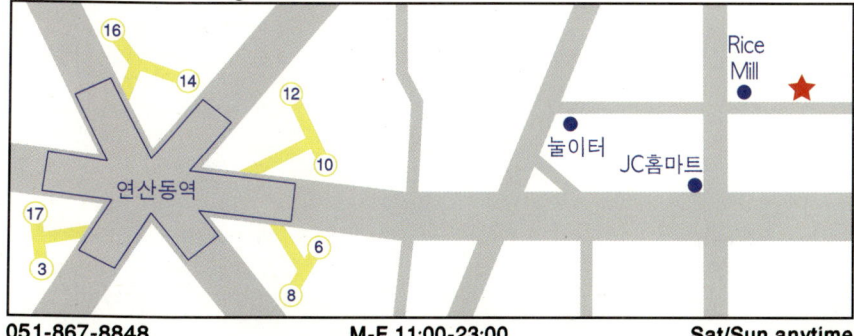

051-867-8848　　　　　　M-F 11:00-23:00　　　　　　　Sat/Sun anytime
1day- 8,000w　　3months-150,000w　　6months-270,000w　　1year-521,000w

아담 온드라 (Adam Ondra) - Montura Climbing Team
체코, 1993년생. 여섯 살 때부터 본격적으로 등반 시작. 2006년 유럽 쥬니어컵 제패.
2008년 La Rambla(9a+), Siurana, Spain. 2012년 Change(9b+), Flatanger Cave, Norway.
이 시대 클라이밍의 레벨을 한 단계 끌어올렸다는 평가를 받고있다.